T0302618

Nu Metal

a definitive guide

Matt Karpe

SONICBOND

sonicbondpublishing.com

Sonicbond Publishing Limited
www.sonicbondpublishing.co.uk
Email: info@sonicbondpublishing.co.uk

First Published in the United Kingdom 2021
First Published in the United States 2021

British Library Cataloguing in Publication Data:
A Catalogue record for this book is available from the British Library

ISBN 978-1-78952-063-7

Typeset in ITC Garamond & ITC Avant Garde
Printed and bound in England

Graphic design and typesetting: Full Moon Media

Nu Metal

a definitive guide

Matt Karpe

SONICBOND

sonicbondpublishing.com

Acknowledgements

Thank you to the following musicians for allowing me some of their valuable time to talk about their experiences of being part of the nu metal movement – Miguel 'Meegs' Rascón, Mike Sarkisyan, Kevin Jardine, Jon Wyscocki, Mikey Doling, Jarrod Montague, Shaun Glass, Robb Rivera, Tye Zamora, Fallon Bowman, Ross Robinson.

All the interviews in this book were undertaken by The Author, between 2017-2020.

Thank you to Stephen Lambe for taking on and believing in this book.

Thank you to Scott Neilson (S86 Studio) for the cover art design.

Thank you to my parents for their continued support.

Thank you to Carly for believing in and supporting my writing endeavours. I Love You.

This book is dedicated to everyone who loves nu metal and to the musicians from the original movement who are sadly no longer with us.

Contact the Author
www.facebook.com/matt.karpe1
www.instagram.com/matt_karpe

Nu Metal
a definitive guide

Contents

A Brief History of Heavy Metal

During the 1970s, Led Zeppelin, Black Sabbath and Deep Purple laid the early foundations for heavy metal, emphasising the real effect and the raw power that electric guitars were truly capable of providing. Sabbath brought the dark and gloomier side, a tad morose but technical in its delivery, inspiring others to pick up an instrument of choice, learn their craft, and then combine with friends to form their own heavy metal bands.

It wasn't long before this louder, faster and much more creative form of sound became widely acknowledged, as the 1980s were welcomed and witnessed the birth of what would quickly become known as the New Wave of British Heavy Metal (NWOBHM). The likes of Iron Maiden, Judas Priest and Saxon earned themselves and the style of music they were creating some strong mainstream focus, as did fellow Brit heroes Motörhead, whose brand of heavy metal came with oodles of punk rock energy which was drenched in whisky and Jägermeister. A once unlikely and perhaps naïve dream of conquering the world would quickly become a possibility for many of these bands, confirming the UK to be deservedly labelled the birthplace and home of heavy metal music.

Feeling a little left out and perhaps even jealous that another country was doing something bigger and better, America's attempt at putting themselves on the metal map came in the form of a handful of sub-genres, one of which would take the mainstream success of NWOBHM and raise the bar even higher. Glam rock was another popular genre of music born and bred in the UK, flying its flag high thanks to T. Rex, David Bowie, Roxy Music and Sweet, and America's answer came in the form of Lou Reed, Iggy Pop and the New York Dolls, who introduced music lovers to something called 'proto punk'. A sound that combined glam rock with an early form of what punk rock was to become, it had set the scene for the first big outbreak of the 1980s as the aesthetics of glam was about to be given the heavy metal treatment.

Men all over the country were soon putting on makeup, giving their hair more volume than the loudest of sound systems, and their lust for wearing leather and spandex provided the general look for glam metal. Also known as hair metal because of the ridiculous perms, beehives and other simply outrageous hairstyles of the scene's musicians, the likes of Mötley Crüe, Twisted Sister and W.A.S.P. helped the first wave break through and set up camp on the Sunset Strip in Los Angeles. By 1986, Bon Jovi, Poison and Cinderella were also stealing the hearts of women (and probably some men) all over the world, with stadium-sized anthems laden with pop hooks yet still driven by the raunchiness of the electric guitar. There were countless cheesy ballads, songs documenting drunken debauchery and having fun whilst not giving a fuck; but what all of them had in common was that they were effortlessly delivered with feisty guitar riffs, sumptuous solos and massive made-for-radio choruses.

With the help of music video evolution and the newly formed VH1 television network, glam metal bands reached the higher echelons of the charts while selling millions of records in the process before going on to perform in front of capacity crowds in arenas all over Europe, South America, the Far East and of course, their native homeland. It was an era of music that seemed destined to stick around for as long as it damn well liked, but at the same time, there was a large demographic of music lovers who didn't care for the whole glam thing, preferring their music to be far more aggressive and extreme.

For many, thrash metal was a very welcome alternative to the glam movement. Metallica was leading the way on the back of their ground-breaking *Ride the Lightning* (1984) and *Master of Puppets* (1986) albums, Anthrax broke out of New York with their 1985 release, *Spreading the Disease*, and Megadeth caused a state of euphoria with their sophomore album, *Peace Sells... But Who's Buying?* in 1986. Battering the senses and bludgeoning skulls, frantic tempos and shredding guitar work created relentless chaos and carnage, causing a state of dystopia which counteracted glam metal's swaggering sense of utopia.

Less publicised, to begin with, at least, evil personified was lurking in the underground as black metal attempted to jump on thrash metal's back and rear its ugly head. Through the first half of the 1980s, people in Europe were also looking for something different to emerge, and when Venom rose out of Newcastle, England, surely even the band themselves had no idea what kind of trouble they were starting. Their 1981 debut, *Welcome to Hell*, and the following *Black Metal,* which arrived just under a year later, became the catalyst for an influx of extreme metal bands, most of whom were primarily located in Scandinavia.

In 1984, Sweden's Bathory released their self-titled debut full-length, which many critics consider the first 'true' black metal record. In Oslo, Norway, Mayhem continued the genre's innovation and began an explosive and highly controversial career, while Mercyful Fate came out of Denmark and Switzerland's Hellhammer changed their name to Celtic Frost and quickly grew in stature.

Corpse paint-covered many a musician's face; the guitars were distorted to almost deafening levels, the frontmen's shrieking vocals sounded like they were attempting to summon an apocalypse, while lyrical content generally revolved around Satanism and anything anti-religion. Putting all this together – here you had the fundamental blueprint for black metal.

Glam metal was pretty much all about sex, drugs and rock and roll (with a little bit of lovey-dovey stuff in between), whereas black metal, on the other hand, would become known for all the wrong reasons – most notably murder and the burning of churches. Mayhem would be the protagonists for both, casting a dark cloud over a sub-genre of heavy metal, which was treated with great contempt and dissatisfaction by large sectors of the public from the outset. Having earned a cult following on the back of their 1987 *Deathcrush* demo, Mayhem's frontman, Per Yngve Ohlin (known as 'Dead'), shot himself in the head in 1991. Upon finding his vocalist's lifeless body, guitarist and founding member of the band, Øystein 'Euronymous' Aarseth, decided to take photographs of the grisly death-by-shotgun aftermath, as well as taking skull fragments to create necklaces for his fellow bandmates. One particular image 'Euronymous' took, which focused on what was left of Ohlin's face after the blast, was later used for the front cover of the Mayhem bootleg album, *Dawn of the Black Hearts*, which has occasionally been listed as an official Mayhem record due to the notoriety of its chosen artwork. Pressing on with a new vocalist, Mayhem continued their upward climb and gained a strong local following, but two years after Ohlin's death, 'Euronymous' would meet his own gruesome demise when he was stabbed 23 times by bandmate Varg Vikernes. At the time, there had been various church burnings around the Oslo area, and it soon transpired that as well as being capable of murder, Vikernes was also behind the sacrilegious ruination of at least four churches in Bergen, Vindafjord and Oslo. Despite claiming self-defence, Vikernes was found guilty of first-degree murder and with an unrelated arson conviction on top, he received a 21-year prison sentence. At the time of joining Mayhem, Vikernes had already completed work on a debut album through his solo project. Following up the self-titled 1992 release, the one-man band known as Burzum returned with the *Aske* EP in 1993. Ironically, of the church burnings which Vikernes was originally charged with, he was found to be not guilty of an attack on Bergen's Fantoft Stave Church – even though it was widely believed he had committed the crime and taken photographs of the aftermath. Lo and behold, an image of Fantoft Stave, post-arson, was selected as the front cover for the EP, so read into that what you will.

Back in Los Angeles, Mötley Crüe singer Vince Neil made the ill-judgement of getting behind the wheel of his car whilst drunk, taking Hanoi Rocks drummer Nicholas 'Razzle' Dingley along for a ride to a local liquor store. Having recently finished touring the band's best-selling *Shout at the Devil* album, and at a point where the whole band was over-indulging on sex, drugs and alcohol, Neil and Dingley were on their way to stock up on booze when Neil slammed into an oncoming vehicle. Leaving Dingley dead and two passengers from the other vehicle with life-changing injuries, Neil forked out nearly $3 million in restitution to his victims and served only fifteen days of a vehicular manslaughter sentence. Soon free to pick up where he left off, the Crüe continued while its members fell further into the abyss of various addictions.

There were never any church burnings on the Sunset Strip; there was more chance of people setting themselves on fire from overdoing it on the hairspray, but anyway, black metal had added itself to heavy metal's widening gene pool; and death metal wasn't too far behind. Along with Metallica, Megadeth and Anthrax, Slayer completed what many people consider the 'Big Four' of thrash metal. In many ways, Slayer played harder and faster than most of their contemporaries, as the tracks 'Angel of Death' and 'Raining Blood' firmly attest to, and understandably they are regarded as being extremely influential in death metal's development. A sub-genre built on the structures of thrash, speed and black metal, and not so much on the burning down of places of worship or the killing of fellow musicians, its pioneers largely came out of the United States. Death, Possessed and Obituary all set their stalls out early on, blazing trails for all who would come to follow, and while the guitars remained heavily distorted, schizophrenic time signatures and colossal drum sections provided extra meat and another option for music lovers of the heavier and demonic persuasion.

In hair metal city, wave after wave of longhaired wannabe sex symbols continued to join the cause, to the point where new bands were emerging weekly. Some were decent, many were not, and with something special seriously needed to inject new life into an overpopulated scene, Guns N' Roses arrived in 1987. Their debut album, *Appetite for Destruction*, sat perfectly in the middle of hard rock and heavy metal, and despite getting their big break by opening for Mötley Crüe, the quintet which featured Axl Rose and a future guitar hero by the name of Slash, did their best to avoid being lumped into the glam metal category. Currently 18x platinum, *Appetite for Destruction* indicated that glam metal was on the way out, and further up the West Coast in Seattle, another new scene was quickly brewing. Fusing elements of alternative, indie, punk rock and a little bit of heavy metal, grunge was the next musical wave to receive wide-eyed focus. Once again led by a handful of significant bands, a more serious form of music brought socially conscious issues into the public eye as lyrics of introspection and exploration were backed up by instrumentation that was often deeper, darker, slower in tempo and relayed with dissonant harmonies.

The two-month period of August and September in 1991 all but killed off glam metal and handed grunge the mantle, beginning with the introduction of Pearl Jam and the release of their now-classic debut record, *Ten*. Containing the massive anthem, 'Alive', and the hauntingly emotional song, 'Black', *Ten* put Pearl Jam firmly at the top of the grunge tree, and just over a month later, Nirvana became one of the biggest bands in the world when their sophomore album, *Nevermind*, shook the rock and metal communities to their very core. On the same day but having to play slightly second fiddle, Soundgarden released their third album, *Badmotorfinger*, and as of today, those three albums combined have exceeded a staggering 25,000,000 in record sales. As with two particular releases in 1992, the success and the legacies created prove that grunge has been able to stand the test of time, becoming a strong influence for future bands who would join the nu metal movement. A year after *Nevermind* had forged a path for others, Alice In Chains stole people's hearts with their first album, *Dirt*, and Stone Temple Pilots debuted with *Core* – both of which went multi-platinum. Chicago's elite grunge band, The Smashing Pumpkins, added their name to the honour roll with *Siamese Dream* in 1993, and two years later, when grunge's appeal was already subsiding, they dropped the incredible double-album, *Mellon Collie and the Infinite Sadness*, which would go on to sell over 10,000,000 copies in the US alone and thus earn diamond certification.

When people hear the term 'grunge', Nirvana tends to be the first band to spring to mind. Fronted by Kurt Cobain and with Dave Grohl and Krist Novoselic completing the line-up, Nirvana drew on the fast and visceral punk rock scene of the 1980s for inspiration. Fuzzy guitars with plenty of brash feedback, heavy bass lines and considerable melodies – Nirvana was different to the other grunge bands of the early 1990s who incorporated heavier aspects into their sound.

Nevermind is considered by many as one of the greatest rock albums of all time, and the pulsating lead single, 'Smells Like Teen Spirit', continues to be played on radio airwaves and music channels worldwide. With its official music video receiving over one BILLION views on YouTube, it confirms beyond any doubt that Nirvana are the undisputed kings of grunge.

Underlining the hype that surrounded the trio upon their late 1980s inception, Nirvana was soon a household name, but behind the scenes, Cobain was struggling with the pressures of newfound superstardom. Following well documented and lengthy battles with drug addiction, depression, and reoccurring health problems, and whilst still riding high on the back of Nirvana's third album, *In Utero*, Kurt Cobain stunned the world when he committed suicide in his Seattle home on 5 April 1994. Startlingly, of the five premier grunge bands, only one of their enigmatic frontmen remains with us today. Hardly a feat to be proud of, Pearl Jam's Eddie Vedder has outlived Cobain, Layne Staley of Alice in Chains, Scott Weiland of Stone Temple Pilots, and Soundgarden's Chris Cornell. Staley and Weiland both succumbed to drug overdoses in 2002 and 2015, respectively, and in what was possibly the biggest surprise of them all, Cornell hanged himself in a Detroit hotel room just a short time after playing a show in the city in 2017.

The appeal of grunge appeared to die out along with Cobain's passing, the candle burning out with its iconic leader, and although Pearl Jam and company earned further acclaim with later releases, people's attention was once again shifting onto other areas of heavy music, which were trying to get a look in.

Pantera was fast becoming the headline groove metal act upon the release of *Vulgar Display of Power* in 1992. Featuring future heavy metal classics such as 'Walk', 'Fucking Hostile' and 'This Love', the Texan mob was intent on filling the void which Metallica had apparently left, having steered away from thrash metal in favour of a more mainstream heavy metal sound on their 1991 self-titled effort. Alongside Megadeth, Pantera stepped up to the plate admirably, creating an album that would become more influential than the band could have ever imagined. *Vulgar Display of Power* continues to be included in various *Best Of* lists today, and countless musicians from the nu metal era cite Pantera and their sixth studio album as major impacts upon their own musical careers.

Industrial metal was increasing in popularity due to Ministry and, in particular, Nine Inch Nails. Another one-man band that struck gold, and then platinum, 1989 debut album, *Pretty Hate Machine*, caught people unaware upon its release. Performing most of the guitars, drum machines, keyboards and samples on the album, Trent Reznor's warped mind endeared him to many – especially with songs such as 'Head Like a Hole'. Adventurous for its time and containing themes of angst and betrayal, *Pretty Hate Machine* was one of the first independently released albums to go platinum, and it was no surprise Reznor's stock would considerably rise over the next few years with the incredible 1994 release, *The Downward Spiral*.

Suicidal Tendencies claimed the title of Godfathers of crossover thrash when they mixed their tried and tested hardcore punk with thrash metal. Most commonly known for the social conflict-themed 'Institutionalized', Suicidal Tendencies would incorporate some funk and pop hooks into their early 1990s material, the highlight being the 1992 album, *The Art of Rebellion*, which found the band at their most accessible and catchy. Jane's Addiction and the Red Hot Chili Peppers were busy mastering the art of alternative and funk rock, from which the Chilis especially became a global phenomenon. Their earlier material included heavy metal riffing, but by the time their fifth release, *Blood Sugar Sex Magik*, dropped in 1991, the Californian quartet had gone full-on alt-rock. 'Give It Away', 'Suck My Kiss' and 'Under the Bridge' put the Chilis on the main stage, and even a UK all-girl pop band attempted to cover the latter song a few years later (with laughable results). Symbolizing the alt-rock explosion taking place in America in the 1990s, the Red Hot Chili Peppers finally started to reap the rewards from their already near decade-long career, and they had plenty more up their sleeve as the decade progressed.

Genre-bending was becoming more common at the turn of the 1990s, but no one did it better than San Francisco's Faith No More. Upon the appointment of new vocalist Mike Patton, and the band's subsequent third album *The Real Thing*, Faith No More threw one curveball after another on songs that incorporated heavy metal, funk, jazz, alternative rock and so much more. Patton's diverse vocal range included rapping, growling, screaming and clean singing, as best emphasized on the fan favourite lead single 'Epic', and the simply awesome album track 'Zombie Eaters'. Epitomizing the term 'avant-garde', what Faith No More did with seemingly relative ease would be attempted by many a band throughout the decade, so if you really want to blame someone for the emergence of nu metal, then Faith No More are a worthy contender for the title of scapegoat.

Until Aerosmith collaborated with Run-D.M.C. and Anthrax teamed up with Public Enemy, it was unheard of that hip-hop and heavy music could ever come together. When the New York trio known as the Beastie Boys began mixing rock and rap, however, the floodgates suddenly opened. 'No Sleep Till Brooklyn' and 'Sabotage' perfectly encapsulate the band's formula, and with Limp Bizkit and Hed PE citing them as major influences, the Beastie Boys' legendary status cannot be denied. Cypress Hill was another early hip-hop group that would come to have a strong appeal with rock fans. Debuting in 1991 and bringing West Coast hip-hop some hefty exposure, the band's debut single, 'How I Could Just Kill a Man', was greeted with huge acclaim, before their 1993 album, *Black Sunday*, took Cypress Hill to the next level. The single, 'Insane in the Brain', whose crossover capabilities appealed to rock fans, helped the album go triple platinum in the US, thus enforcing the trio as major players in the rap game. They would later become the first Latino hip-hop group to get a star on the Hollywood Walk of Fame, which shows how highly thought of and respected Cypress Hill are by various levels of people throughout the entertainment business.

When four dudes calling themselves Rage Against the Machine exploded out of Los Angeles, revealing their revolutionary political views on a savage debut album in 1992, rap-metal was finally accepted and embraced by the heavy metal community. 'Killing in the Name' was the kick up the backside America needed, and the widely spouted line, 'Fuck you, I won't do what you tell me' has been muttered by many a renegade over the years. Raising a middle finger to authorities and establishments all around the world, just to let them know they might not be as in control as first thought, 'Killing in the Name' was written about a revolution against police brutality and institutional racism. It will forever be Rage Against the Machine's signature track, even though the majority of their material aims criticism at various policies from past and then-present US governments. In Zack de la Rocha, Rage had a spokesperson for an entire generation, not caring whom he upset or if he painted a target on his bandmates' backs. The quartet did whatever they wanted, and they became universally adored – the voices for the voiceless, you could say. A handful of bands have tried to take Rage's values and beliefs to create their own brand of revolutionary metal, but no one has come remotely close to Rage Against the Machine's ferocity and realism, and they never will.

Causing their fair share of controversy from the off, Body Count, led by hip-hop heavyweight Ice-T, brought their assault of thrash and speed metal to the party in 1992, with Ice supplying cleaner vocals as opposed to his familiar rapping talents. The band's debut album was thrown straight into the spotlight due to the scathing track, 'Cop Killer', the theme of which is rather self-explanatory. Provoking shock, horror and even negative feedback from then US President George Bush, Body Count would later re-release their self-titled album with 'Cop Killer' omitted from the tracklist; however, their intent was impossible to be censored and so Body Count's foundations had been firmly set in stone from the outset. Objective complete.

In 1993, the *Judgement Night* movie, which starred Emilio Estevez and Cuba Gooding Jr., had an accompanying soundtrack that broke down the remaining walls which had kept such collaborations at bay for so long. Fellow metal experimentalists Helmet recorded a song with House of Pain, who are responsible for that head-invading song 'Jump Around', Slayer and Ice-T squared up to each other and even Pearl Jam and Cypress Hill formed a brief but unholy alliance; setting everything in place for the next big movement to rise up and take over the mainstream.

With such a wide range of inspirations to draw from and so many styles of music to experiment with, the nu metal movement would become the most exciting era of heavy music, perhaps since the very beginning. What the NWOBHM and glam metal movements accomplished was impressive enough, but nu metal would end up blowing both of them so high out of the water that no one could have foreseen back in the early 1990s quite how bands with such names as Korn, Limp Bizkit and System of a Down could ever achieve mainstream success and worldwide reverence.

A Nu Breed of Metal

A form of alternative metal, the term 'aggro metal' was also associated with this intriguing new movement which quickly became known as 'Nu Metal'. Combining elements of heavy metal, alternative rock, funk, grunge and hip-hop to create a sonic soundscape of raw power and emotion, nu metal was primarily based on guitar riffs where down-tuned and often seven-string guitars became commonplace in an attempt to create a much heavier sound. Bass guitars emphasised funk components by occasionally adding one or two extra strings, and DJs also began to feature in band line-ups. Using their turntable skills to provide samples and scratching, they helped to create a more urbanised sound which enabled a much wider audience – some of whom may not have normally listened to rock and metal, yet with these elements incorporated, suddenly became a more attractive listen.

Vocal styles tended to include clean singing, rapping, screaming and vicious growls, while common lyrical themes dealt with subjects such as anger, emotional torture, abandonment, and personal alienation. These bands and their lyrics helped listeners of various age, race and sexuality deal with their personal, professional and social struggles, with the songs acting as remedies and self-help guides to many – especially the younger generation whose futures seemed scary and uncertain. Presented with a sound that encapsulated all their hopes and fears, nu metal music ultimately convinced many to believe that there was better to come in their lives if all they did was dare to dream.

Along with the aforementioned genres, which nu metal immersed, gothic rock, punk, new wave, industrial and jazz fusion also found themselves being tried and tested, as did heavier concoctions such as death, thrash, speed and groove metal. With such a jaw-dropping plethora of styles, nu metal was perhaps unsurprisingly cited as being the beginning of the New Wave of American Heavy Metal.

Band image and fashion was another important aspect of why the scene exploded as it did. Baggy combat trousers (pants to our American friends), shorts, t-shirts, tracksuits, sports jerseys, and baseball caps all became the norm, while hairstyles were often spiked or dreadlocked. Piercings became even more popular (especially facial piercings), and tattoos covered more and more arms, legs and torsos.

Many of the heavier nu metal bands listed the likes of Metallica, Pantera and Slayer as influences, while early bands such as Faith No More and the Red Hot Chili Peppers encouraged the next generation with their pop and funk melodies; however, it was hip-hop which gave nu metal its true groove and inspiration. Bands such as Korn, Limp Bizkit and Linkin Park have publicly stated the impacts on their sounds from game-changers such as Dr. Dre, Ice Cube, N.W.A. (which originally included Dre and Cube in the group), The Beastie Boys and Run-D.M.C., so it was hardly a surprise when rock and hip-hop collaborations became a more regular occurrence as the nu metal movement increased in popularity.

Nu metal was loved by many, loathed by others, and lamented upon its original downfall, but it was a movement that in a lot of ways broke new ground. Never could you have imagined putting the likes of Korn, Limp Bizkit, Slipknot and System of a Down in the same category, but the beauty of nu metal was – it worked. It was vast and diverse and yet everything merged into one and stood as this deafening monster intent on overpowering a dictatorship that was being overseen by manufactured artists. Nu metal was a movement where the music was angry, visceral, sinister and deafening; melodic, delicate, emotive and inspirational, and nu metal made us realise that it was fine to be different. So many people flocked to buy the latest records, propelling many of these bands to superstardom with platinum sales and number 1 chart positions, with figures that have rarely been seen since.

Putting on a CD or cassette by any of the bands from that era, when it came down to just you and the music, more often than not, you could find something you could relate to as if the song was written *for you*. From the high school horrors and tales of bullying as retold by Korn to the first time you got down and dirty with a girl as detailed by Limp Bizkit, to the moments of isolation and desperation revealed by Staind and then to the moment you finally shouted 'Fuck it!' and went crazy via the soundtrack of Slipknot; everything you ever needed as a musical backdrop was available from within the nu metal movement.

By 2004 there were only fleeting glimpses of its influence in the rock and metal music that was coming out, therefore only having a handful of years at the top after its dramatic rise in the late 1990s, but thankfully over the last few years, there has been somewhat of a revival which has put nu metal back on the map once again.

The first era of nu metal was ground-breaking, and while strong album sales and chart success are not always possible in today's climate due to the likes of illegal downloading and online streaming, it is clear that the new breed of bands coming through are intent on keeping nu metal alive with a refreshing and revitalised attention to detail, and a healthy stamp of approval from the movement's forefathers and fans alike.

The Bands Who Brought Nu Metal to the Masses

Adema

Years Active: 2000-
Location: Bakersfield, California, USA
Main era line-up: Mark Chavez (vocals), Tim Fluckey (lead guitar, backing vocals, keyboards), Mike Random (rhythm guitar), Dave DeRoo (bass, backing vocals), Kris Kohls (drums)
Albums: Adema (2001), Unstable (2003), Planets (2005), Kill the Headlights (2007)

Led by Jonathan Davis' half-brother, Mark Chavez, Adema emerged in 2000, playing some tasty alternative metal with a hard rock edge. Their self-titled debut was released in 2001 via Arista, earning significant airplay from the anthemic singles 'Giving In' and 'The Way You Like It'. *Adema* peaked at 27 on the *Billboard* 200 before going on to be certified gold through sales of over one million copies worldwide.

In 2002, the band released an EP titled *Insomniac's Dream*, containing three new songs – the most notable being 'Immortal', which was chosen as the theme song for the *Mortal Kombat: Deadly Alliance* video game. The EP also included remixes and live tracks and it acted as a nice stopgap before Adema unleashed their second full-length album, *Unstable,* less than a year later. Debuting at 43 on the *Billboard* chart and selling over 400,000 copies worldwide, *Unstable* wasn't as successful as the album prior. However, it still featured some great songs such as the title track, 'Co-Dependent', and 'Betrayed Me'.

Unfortunately, Chavez would soon leave Adema due to inner turmoil within the band, and in 2005, a third album titled *Planets* saw the debut of new vocalist Luke Caraccioli. Released via Earache Records, the mesmerising title track earned popularity through its inclusion in the horror movie *Cry Wolf,* but by the end of the year, Caraccioli himself had left the band. Former LeVeL frontman, Bobby Reeves, became Adema's third new vocalist and along with Ed Farris on guitar, the pair announced themselves on the 2007 album, *Kill the Headlights,* but once again, the line-up was short-lived as the band would go on hiatus.

After a brief reunion of the original line-up in 2009, Chavez and Mike Ransom would leave once more – paving the way for lead guitarist, Tim Fluckey, to take over vocal duties. Releasing the *Topple the Giants* EP in 2013, it unveiled Adema's first new material in almost six years, along with some re-worked versions of the band's popular hits such as 'Giving In' and 'Immortal'.

Adema were undoubtedly at their best during their first assault, where they produced emotionally charged alt-metal anthems one after another, but with the original line-up of musicians currently pressing on with ex-Orgy member Ryan Shuck enlisted as lead vocalist, the chances of more dark and melancholic *music* being released has perhaps never seemed more likely.

Killer Cuts – 'Giving In', 'The Way You Like It'

Alien Ant Farm

Years Active: 1996-
Location: Riverside, California, USA
Main era line-up: Dryden Mitchell (vocals), Terry Corso (lead guitar, backing vocals), Tye Zamora (bass, backing vocals, piano), Mike Cosgrove (drums)
Albums: Greatest Hits (1999), ANThology (2001), TruANT (2003), Up in the Attic (2006), Always and Forever (2015)

After an independently released debut album in 1999, which was boldly titled *Greatest Hits*, Alien Ant Farm exploded onto the scene when they signed to DreamWorks in 2001. Featuring Dryden Mitchell on vocals, Terry Corso on guitar, the enigmatic Tye Zamora on bass, and Mike Cosgrove behind the drum kit – the quartet released their breakthrough album, *ANThology,* not long after inking their deal. 'Movies' was released as a single before a cover of Michael Jackson's 'Smooth Criminal' quickly made Alien Ant Farm a household name. It dominated airwaves and TV channels all over the globe, later topping singles charts and bringing the band more exposure than they ever thought possible. 'Movies' then got a re-release, and its accompanying video was an at times hilarious tribute to the likes of *Ghostbusters* and *Edward Scissorhands*; before the third single, 'Attitude', also played its part in helping to send *ANThology* platinum in the US and gold in the UK.

That would prove to be the band's high point, though, as a bus crash in Spain stalled momentum in 2002, and then their next album, *TruANT,* followed in 2003 – just as DreamWorks was about to close its doors. Peaking at 42 on the *Billboard* 200, *TruANT* still contained decent songs like 'These Days', which had an accompanying video that documented Alien Ant Farm's guerrilla-style performance on a rooftop opposite the BET Awards in Los Angeles. Cameras caught the shocked responses of Snoop Dogg, Lil' Kim and others, however, the filming was soon shut down by police and the band members were arrested for their actions.

By now, the four-piece were signed to Geffen, and although another album was ready to be released, Geffen denied the quartet the rights to put it out. Bootleg copies were later made and given out at live shows under the unofficial title, *3rd Draft*, but in 2006 the officially titled *Up in the Attic* was finally released via Universal Music Enterprises. It would be a commercial flop though due to very little support for the album, underlined by the track 'Forgive & Forget'- which was released as a promo to radio stations but received minimal airplay.

Various line-up changes ensued over the next few years before Alien Ant Farm put out a crowdfunded EP titled *Phone Home* in 2014, and a third full-length, *Always and Forever,* a year later. 'Let 'Em Know' and 'Homage' were both chosen as singles; in fact all four mastered tracks from the EP were to be included on the record and with their fans at least, the release was considered a success.

Still making music and with a dedicated following behind them, Alien Ant Farm will always be remembered for 'Smooth Criminal'- a song which wasn't

their own, but a song which gave them their big moment in the spotlight and underlined the power that the nu metal movement had behind it at the turn of the new millennium.

Killer Cuts – 'Smooth Criminal', 'Movies'.

Tye Zamora speaks:

The only way I'd say Alien Ant Farm fitted into the nu metal movement was that we had the same fans. I guess we were heavy enough to fit in with a lot of these bands, but I don't think a lot of those bands were necessarily nu metal. I considered a nu metal band to include rapping at some point in their songs – some kind of hip-hop element – but with us, I saw us as a hard rock band that was kind of all over the map. We would play ballad-type stuff, we would do reggae-type stuff, and Latin stuff, but we didn't do that on *ANThology*. I would consider us a rock band, like a hard prog rock band. We didn't get too crazy into concepts, but we tried to push the plain envelope a little more than I think most bands did.

'At first, we wanted to be more of a Mr. Bungle-type band. We wanted to create music that was a little more avant-garde and we wanted to do the mask thing – that was a big influence for us. As we got together and started playing music, we started doing more songwriter-type stuff, like a traditional prog rock band at the time, so we wanted to do something very spacey ... thinking *Masters of the Universe*; not that we would ever be able to use that. The way our band name came about was, I think Terry (Corso) was hanging out at his workplace and he was watching *The X-Files*, and he just came up with the name. He called us saying, 'Hey, I've got a name for the band – it's called Alien Ant Farm. It basically means the planet earth, and that we were all put here by aliens and they're kind of watching us all from afar – doing what we do, developing, and becoming civilized'. I think it just fit into what we were doing at the time. I think we were Alien Ant Farm before we even rehearsed.

'As the band progressed, we showcased for every major label but everyone passed on us. There was this magazine called *Hits* and it kept all the industry people up to date of what was happening and what was current, what local bands were going to get signed or who they thought was going to get signed. It keeps all the industry folk hip on who is the next band they should be signing and making a load of money off of. We had made a pact with Papa Roach because they were from Northern California and we were from Southern California, and we would switch gigs with each other. We got along so well and believed in each other's work ethic that we both thought we were going to make it out of all the bands we played with at the time. We really thought our two bands had the best shine out of all of them, and we made a pact that whoever got signed first would help the other band get signed.

Papa Roach got signed a year before we did by DreamWorks, and they blew up. When they sold a million records and DreamWorks were listening to what they had to say, those guys basically told them, 'Hey, you guys need to go and sign this band.' We were doing showcases and people were interested, but no one wanted to pick us up, and I kind of blame myself for that. I think our management blamed me too because I was a little bit overweight, and it wasn't a typical formula because I was a showman, where the singer is supposed to be the showman and everyone else is supposed to just stand behind him. We didn't have the coolest image and I definitely had no image, so I think I stalled us from getting signed.

We got turned down by everyone except for DreamWorks, and then we said, 'Screw it, we're gonna release the record on our own and get investors involved'. We did a showcase for a bunch of people like that, and our A&R from DreamWorks happened to show up at that showcase and when he showed up, everyone knew we were going to get signed. I'm glad DreamWorks took a gamble on us and they actually won pretty big when we released 'Smooth Criminal'.

'Movies' came out as a single first and it was doing pretty well but then 'Smooth Criminal' hit and it killed the momentum of 'Movies' immediately. That is why we went back and did another video for 'Movies' later on, because we didn't feel enough people heard it. 'Movies' on its own probably sold (in the US) at least a quarter of a million records for us so it was definitely a successful single, but 'Smooth Criminal' was doing that in a couple of weeks. I was one of those kids who would come home every day and watch *Moonwalker* since I was probably in the 7th Grade. I always loved 'Smooth Criminal' and I wanted to play it, so when I came to practise with the guys, I started jamming it. We used to take a long time between songs and I just started playing it and people went nuts, and we sat there and thought if people go nuts just hearing the bass line, and then the drummer came in and started to play – when we did that the response, we got was unbelievable. So, I don't think we knew it was going to be a freakin' monster and be one of the biggest songs in the world at the time, but I think we all felt if we covered 'Smooth Criminal', it was going to connect us with a lot of people.

We went over to the Czech Republic in 1999 and did a little tour around Europe for about six or seven weeks, and we always saved 'Smooth Criminal' for last. Everywhere we played we broke through and became a band that everyone wanted to know. We put it on *Greatest Hits* because we wanted people to hear our version, but the amount of exposure it got, I don't think anyone could have anticipated that. Michael Jackson actually wanted us to reshoot the scene with the kid in the video. Everything else he was cool with, except for the surgical mask prop. So, we had to re-shoot the scene without the mask and then he watched it and thought the version with the surgical mask was better, and it actually ended up costing the band $30,000 for the time and effort in re-shooting the video.

When we would do any event or music awards, we would run into someone like his personal photographer, for example, and they would always come over and let us know what they thought about the track. We did a tribute show for him in Cardiff and his photographer was there and came and sat down with us for a long time. He gave us the story behind it because Quincy Jones hated 'Smooth Criminal' and never thought it should have been a single. Michael went to Quincy after we had made it go to number one and he was like, 'See dude, I told you.' His close friends would tell us about that stuff.

Some people saw Alien Ant Farm as being a novelty band and I think we were in some ways, and it's unfortunate because there are a lot of people who got *ANThology* and really got the band who were probably not a fan of 'Smooth Criminal'. You get those guys who liked 'Sticks and Stones' as their favourite or 'Flesh and Bone', and those people were not listening to 'Smooth Criminal'. We covered a song that happened to be maybe a little too big, and too good of a song to overshadow. It would have taken a monster of a song to bounce back from that and I feel like we had songs that were good enough to bring the band respect and seriousness and had real potential to climb the charts, but 'Smooth Criminal' really killed everything for us. I don't regret covering that song because it was an amazing ride, but it is what it is.

With things going well with *ANThology*, we then got in a bus wreck which really messed us up and it really stalled the band. We were on our third single at the time ('Attitude') and we believed in it, and the label thought it would carry us into the next record, which we had started writing. We thought we were going to be able to put something out quick, and had we not got in that bus wreck I think we would have been able to have the record out three or four months after that point, and I think the heat would have still been on the band.

We had a song which we felt would have been a huge hit, and it was a huge hit at the one place they promoted it. So, by the time we got to trying to promote the *TruANT* record, DreamWorks was selling, and they were out. They only put the record out so they could make their catalogue more valuable. When they sold and we were given over to Geffen, they had no interest whatsoever working the album we had just put out. There was a guy in New Zealand who worked for Universal, and he pushed us with 'Glow' and it went to number 1 for eight weeks, so we knew it was going to do that kind of business everywhere in the world; but DreamWorks wasn't having it because they were selling so they weren't spending any money, and then Geffen wasn't having it because they didn't help us put out the record; so we really got screwed on that.

I don't think we ever thought we would get lost in the shuffle because a lot of the bands around at the time didn't experience the same kind of success that we did. They didn't make probably $30 million for their company like Alien Ant Farm did. We definitely were not a band that had to worry about getting lost in the shuffle because we were respected.

We were given a bunch of money and they immediately wanted us to go back into the studio and record another record, and here we are going, 'Dude, we just did!' We had been spending the last year or so not only writing music but healing from the bus accident, plus, we lost our guitar player and had to get a new guy in. We met with the president of Geffen and we were handled very well, and had we delivered and maybe written another 'Smooth Criminal' or another 'Movies', they would have been right behind us and would have dumped $2 million into pushing that record; but we didn't deliver one of those songs. I wouldn't say we were tapped out because I still think we wrote a really good record, there just wasn't a really good song we could put out as a single. From there the band kind of got in a weird spot and it became self-destructive, and it was just one of those things that's like, 'We had a good run, it's a good band, there is good chemistry, we can always continue writing cool stuff and being a good band, but it's never gonna be what it was'.

We ended up releasing bootleg copies of the *Up in the Attic* album, which I didn't think that was cool at all. We were under contract and the label gave us a bunch of money to do another record, and we gave them a cool record but not a record they could sell, and so they gave us the option to go back into the studio and pretty much keep writing at their expense. At that time, I don't think any of us were hurting for money, we had all the time in the world and all the resources to go back into the studio and spend four or five months if we wanted to – writing hit songs or trying to write at least one hit song. My attitude was, 'Let's go back in the studio and do that, let's try to get them to release this record', but it was Mike and Dryden who thought we should go out and do the guerrilla-style and buy a van, take the album and duplicate it, and sell it this way; and I wasn't into that at all. I didn't want to go out in the world without label support because I know it doesn't work. We already had a hard time with the second record not doing anything in the States and Europe because we had no one working it, only doing well in New Zealand because just one person in the whole Universal spectrum worked on it, so I saw the repercussions of not having the label there. In no way did I want to work without a label because I knew we needed them and I knew that was the way the world turned, and it took us five years to get out the trenches and then these guys wanted to climb back in. I always wanted our career to go up and up and up and up, not end up in the gutter again. It was just a bad decision and I was outvoted, so we hit the road in a van and I hated it, and it ultimately ended up with me leaving the band because of it.

In 2008, I was still in school. I was asked to come back to the band. It was sold to me as a 'Hey, do you wanna make some extra money because there's this booking agent that we're working with now who says we can get a minimum of this amount of money every show we play, and we'll be flown in and we don't really have to hang out with each other. All we have to do is play the music…' and I was like 'Sure, but only if they could get Terry to do it again.' I only said I would do it because I really didn't think Terry would come back, but when Terry actually said yes, I was like 'Oh man, here we go'. We had conversations and hung out together and we had a good time. We put our past in the past and I never really had a problem with the guys in the band, I just had disagreements, but everything was squashable.

As we started playing more shows, we started to realise there was a crowd still there and it felt bigger than when I left the band. It felt like people really wanted us. We toured, we started writing music we really liked, and it was going down well live; and then we ended up signing with a label which kind of killed us. They wanted us to be like a pop band and basically just wanted to use our name and the sound, and it turned it into a real poppy kind of thing which really bothered me, so I had to get out of there again and quit the band.

'My best memories of being part of Alien Ant Farm was meeting people that I have always looked up to as a kid – like meeting Brian May from Queen. Getting nominated for Grammys and all those music awards was nice, and hitting gold and platinum – having those plaques, that is the stuff that stays with you. There were personal dreams that I actually fulfilled which blew my mind. When I was in High School, 311 was probably one of my absolute most favourite bands at the time, and I always wanted to play the Hollywood Palladium, which was where I saw some of my first shows. I was in 8th Grade and saw Primus play before the Pixies, who both opened for Jane's Addiction on their *Ritual de lo Habitual* tour, which to me was a dream gig. So, I've always wanted to play that venue because of stuff like that, and then the main singer for 311, Nick Hexum, called me when they were playing a show that night which I was planning on attending and he called me up and said, 'Hey, do you wanna play 'Homebrew' with us at the Palladium tonight, on stage?' So, I not only got to play with 311 which was a dream come true, but I got to do that on the stage of the Palladium too, and that is one of those moments where I'm like, 'I made it!

Amen

Years Active: 1994-2009
Location: Los Angeles, California, USA
Main era line-up: Casey Chaos (vocals), Sonny Mayo (guitar), Paul Fig (guitar), John Fahnestock (bass), Shannon Larkin (drums)
Albums: Amen (1999), We Have Come for Your Parents (2000), Death Before Musick (2004)

Amen broke through after the band's brainchild, Casey Chaos, was introduced to producer extraordinaire Ross Robinson; who helped secure the band a record deal with Roadrunner Records at the end of the 1990s.

Amen **was released on 21 September 1999 and introduced the world to Chaos' fiery vocals, while Sonny Mayo and John 'Tumor' Fahnestock were enlisted after the untimely end of their previous band, Snot. Another album produced by the in-demand Robinson,** ***Amen*** **consisted of some chaotic hardcore punk blended with alternative metal. The single 'Coma America' provided the highlight; however, Amen's relationship with Roadrunner would prove short-lived and by 2000, they had signed to Virgin Records. Dropping their storming second record** ***We Have Come for Your Parents,*** **the album seemed destined to send Amen into the major leagues. Once again overseen by Robinson and featuring politically and socially charged lyrics, the singles 'The Price of Reality', 'Hard to**

Be Free' and 'The Waiting 18' advertised more aggressive metallic hardcore that conspired to include fist-pumping choruses. Reaching 77 in the UK album chart, it was to be, as promised, Amen's breakout album.

After leaving Virgin, Amen released a B-sides album titled *Join, or Die* via Chaos' new label, Refuse, in 2003, and after the departures of much of the band's original line-up, April 2004 saw the release of *Death Before Musick*, which included guitarist's Matt Montgomery and Rich Jones, as well as Scott Sorry on bass. It included the popular single, 'California's Bleeding'; however, *Death Before Musick* was to be the last Amen record to date.

Chaos did put out the wonderfully titled, *Pisstory: A Catalogue of Accidents, a Lifetime of Mistakes,* in 2005 through Refuse Music, and the compilation included a large number of unreleased Amen tracks, while a live album was also released in 2005 – recorded at a 2003 show in Manchester, England, and titled *Gun of a Preacher Man*. Since 2014, Amen has played a few live shows, but no new material has emerged in that time.

Killer Cuts – 'Coma America', 'The Price of Reality'

American Head Charge

Years Active: 1997-2009, 2011-

Location: Minneapolis, Minnesota, USA

Main era line-up: Cameron Heacock (vocals), Dave Rogers (guitar), Wayne Kile (guitar), Chad Hanks (bass), Chris Emery (drums), Aaron Zilch (samples, electronics)

Albums: Trepanation (1999), The War of Art (2001), The Feeding (2005), Tango Umbrella (2016)

You can thank Minneapolis, Minnesota, for bringing our attention to post-apocalyptic metallers, American Head Charge. After a self-released debut titled *Trepanation*, Head Charge signed with Rick Rubin's American Recordings, which at the time was under Columbia Records. System of a Down's Shavo Odadjian had reportedly told Rubin to check out the band, and within six months they were given a record deal.

The War of Art came out on 28 August 2001 and the album went on to sell over 250,000 copies. Containing monstrous industrial and bruising alternative metal, the lead single, 'Just So You Know', received strong airplay and exposure, while lead singer Cameron Heacock quickly became one of the most iconic frontmen of the nu metal era. *The War of Art* earned the band a cult following, and American Head Charge quickly became one of the most popular underground acts in all of heavy metal, but unfortunately, addictions had begun to take over within the band and soon after, the band asked to be let out of their Columbia contract.

Guitarist's Bryan Ottoson and Karma Singh Cheema replaced David Rogers and Wayne Kile in time for the 2005 sophomore album, *The Feeding*, which was released via DRT Entertainment. Receiving positive reviews, the record sold over 100,000 copies and featured the hard-rocking single 'Loyalty', as well as the hellraising 'Cowards', which was included on an *Ultimate Fighting Championship* music compilation to further boost the release.

Sadly, turmoil seemed to follow American Head Charge around at every turn, with line-up changes occurring all too frequently. After the release of a DVD in 2007- *Can't Stop the Machine,* which also included a CD of live and unreleased material, the Minnesotan monsters announced their split in 2009 and it looked as though they were well and truly finished for good. Two years later, though, social media pages began motoring again and it was soon announced that American Head Charge was back. With a couple of new members as well as much of the original line-up, the band began to tour around the US and Europe before they released a brand-new EP in 2013 titled *Shoot*. It was then followed by a third full-length album, *Tango Umbrella* in 2016, which was released via Napalm Records. Songs such as 'Let All the World Believe', 'Drowning Under Everything' and 'Perfectionist' proved that American Head Charge still had the knack of writing robust yet accessible melodic metal; in fact, the record sounded like the band hadn't ever been away.

Another period of relative inactivity followed, and then in November 2017, the band's founding member, Chad Hanks, tragically passed away. The incredible support shown from the metal community underlined just how popular a person and musician he really was, and while various members of the band came together to honour their fallen brother, no new music has ever followed and it appears that American Head Charge's third album may have been nothing more than a final swansong.

Killer Cuts – 'Just So You Know', 'Loyalty'.

Anyone

Years Active: 1995-2006, 2019-
Location: Laguna Beach, California, USA
Main era line-up: Riz Story (vocals, guitar), 'Static' (bass), Dave 'Nipples' Murray (drums)
Albums: Live Acid (1999), Anyone (2001), On the Ending Earth… (2020)

The brainchild of Riz Story, Anyone originally began under the name Sylvia in 1995 – playing a mix of heavy metal and psychedelic rock which would later be described as 'Maximum Acid'. After band member Taylor Hawkins went to play in Alanis Morissette's band (and later in a little band called the Foo Fighters), Sylvia changed their name to Anyone and pressed on as a trio.

A demo album was recorded in 1996 but never received an official release, and it would pave the way for the band's first official output to be a live album in 1999, titled *Live Acid*. From there, Roadrunner Records came calling and a self-titled debut album emerged in 2001. 'Don't Wake Me' created a stir for the band (especially in Europe) but it wouldn't be long before Roadrunner dropped Anyone and pulled the album from circulation – which ultimately led to line-up changes within the band and a period of uncertainty.

2006 saw some promising signs when a DVD was released (*The Story of Maximum Acid*), as well as an EP (*A Little Sip*), but Story would then pull the plug on Anyone altogether. While he was getting into film production, Story then teamed up with ex-Korn drummer, David Silveria, to form the band Infinika, releasing the album *Echoes and Traces* in 2014. The record would get a re-release under the Anyone name in 2016, and five of the songs would be included in the movie and on the soundtrack to Story's film *A Winter Rose*, which starred Taryn Manning, Billy Zane and Edward Furlong.

Think Jane's Addiction-meets-Radiohead-meets-Tool and you might be somewhere close to Anyone's sound, and out of nowhere in 2020, Story returned under the Anyone moniker to release the album, *On the Ending Earth…*, as well as putting out a 20th-anniversary deluxe edition of *Live Acid*; much to the delight of many a fan who may have given up on this obscure and talented band.

Killer Cuts – 'Don't Wake Me', 'She'

Apartment 26

Years Active: 1999-2004
Location: Leamington Spa, Warwickshire, England
Main era line-up: Terence 'Biff' Butler (vocals), Jon Greasley (guitar), Louis Cruden (bass), Kevin Temple (drums), Andy Huckvale (keyboards)
Albums: Hallucinating (2000), Music for the Massive (2004)

Apartment 26 took their name from David Lynch's *Eraserhead* movie, where the main character lived in, drum roll please… Apartment 26. Combining exciting and energetic metal with industrial, electronica and drum 'n' bass, the band – whose lead singer Terence 'Biff' Butler is the son of a certain Black Sabbath legend, Geezer Butler – played the second stage of Ozzfest in 1999 with the likes of American superstars-in-waiting Slipknot, Static-X and Fear Factory.

An EP titled *Within* was released in the same year, and a number of the tracks would be remastered and added to the band's debut album, *Hallucinating*, which came out in 2000 via Hollywood Records. A fantastically heavy yet sumptuously appealing record that had a strong Americanised sound, the lead single 'Basic Breakdown' reached 33 on the US Mainstream Rock Chart. Further enhancing the band's credentials, 'Backwards' was included on the *Mission: Impossible II* movie soundtrack and 'Doing It Anyway' was used in *High Fidelity*, as the Brits appeared to be adopted by their American counterparts.

Apartment 26 then scrapped two years of production for their second album before self-financing *Music for the Massive*, which was sold to Atlantic Records in 2004. Produced at Peter Gabriel's recording studio in Wiltshire (UK), the album captured a live sound and incorporated elements of jazz and swing into the band's tried and tested industrial metal. Lead single 'Give Me More' found its way to 39 on the US Mainstream Rock Chart, but any further success was made impossible after Atlantic dropped Apartment 26 amongst a big roster clear out upon their merging with Elektra Records. This prompted the Leamington quintet to call it a day, however both *Hallucinating* and *Music for the Massive* remain some of the best British nu metal albums ever to be released.

Killer Cuts – 'Basic Breakdown', 'Give Me More'

The Apex Theory

Years Active: 1999-2008
Location: Los Angeles, California, USA
Main era line-up: Ontronik 'Andy' Khachaturian (vocals), Art Karamian (guitar), Dave Hakopyan (bass), Sammy J. Watson (drums)
Albums: Topsy-Turvy (2002), Faces (2008)

While there were certainly a lot of bands who sounded alike in the late 1990s and early Noughties, there were also some excellent bands who developed their own style and brought something different – enter The Apex Theory. Featuring System of a Down's original drummer, Ontronik 'Andy' Khachaturian, in their line-up, this Armenian/American band incorporated Mediterranean and middle eastern music into their distinctive progressive metal template; and within two years of getting started, The Apex Theory signed to DreamWorks Records in 2001. A self-titled EP arrived in the same year, as did slots on the Warped and *MTV2* tours, before the band's debut album, *Topsy Turvy*, dropped in April 2002.

Produced by Don Gilmore, who was very much in demand having helped Linkin Park become global superstars back in 2000, *Topsy Turvy* reached number 6 on the *Billboard* Heatseekers chart, as well as 157 on the 200. Helped by the singles, 'Shh ... (Hope Diggy)' and 'Apossibly', similarities were made to System of a Down other than just the Amenian/American link, in particular the music's frantic time signatures and multi-layered textures. As The Apex Theory looked to be going from strength to strength, Khachaturian then decided to leave the band and Art Karamian took over on vocals. Kicking on as a three-piece and after releasing their 2004 EP, *inthatskyissomethingwatching*, The Apex Theory changed their name to Mt. Helium and released the album, *Faces*, in 2008.

Killer Cuts – 'Shh ... (Hope Diggy)', 'Apossibly'.

The Blank Theory

Years Active: 1998-2005
Location: Chicago, Illinois, USA
Main era line-up: Nathan Leone (vocals), Michael Foderaro (guitar), Matthew Leone (bass), James Knight (drums), Shawn Currie (synthesizers)
Albums: Beyond the Calm of the Corridor (2002)

After a couple of early self-released EPs (*Blinding Process* and *Catalyst*), which saw The Blank Theory performing alternative rock, the Chicago five-piece moved into alternative metal territory in a bid to join the nu metal movement. Signing to the independent label, New Line Records, the band's debut album was co-produced by Smashing Pumpkins guitarist James Iha, who would guest on the track 'Killing Me', which featured on *Beyond the Calm of the Corridor*. Released on 24 September 2002, the album was led by the strong single 'Middle of Nowhere', which was included on the *Freddy vs. Jason* movie soundtrack, as well as actually being included in the *Final Destination 2* flick. A cover of Portishead's 'Sour Times' was chosen as a second single and it was used in the trailer for the *Wicker Park* movie, but with The Blank Theory seemingly hitting their stride, some of their integral members quit the band, which in turn caused an overall disbandment.

The album track 'Addicted' showed how capable The Blank Theory was of crafting strong and catchy anthems, but sadly a longer stint in the limelight wasn't to be; however, Nathan and Matthew Leone would return a short time later with their new band Madina Lake, who would earn significant success with their brand of emo and post-hardcore musings.

Killer Cuts – 'Middle of Nowhere', 'Addicted'

Blindspott

Years Active: 1997-2007, 2018-
Location: Waitakere, Auckland, New Zealand
Main era line-up: Damian Alexander (vocals), Marcus Powell (guitar, backing vocals), Gareth Fleming (bass), Shelton Woolright (drums), Karl Vilisini (turntables, keyboards)
Albums: Blindspott (2003), End the Silence (2006)

One of New Zealand's finest musical exports, Blindspott started making strong moves with their very first single in 2001, titled 'Nil By Mouth', which gained major airplay in the quintet's homeland. 'Room to Breathe' and 'Phlex' were put out next, and all three tracks were included on Blindspott's self-titled debut album when it came out in 2002. Licensed for release by EMI, *Blindspott* contained a tracklist full of rap metal, alt metal and hard rock delights, going straight to number 1 in New Zealand's album chart. Within a week of release, the album had also gone platinum, and as of today, that figure has risen to 3x platinum.

A couple of line-up changes occurred ahead of the band's second album, *End the Silence,* in 2006, but it didn't stop Blindspott going straight to number one again upon its release. Ditching the rap metal elements for a darker metal sound, 'Drown' and 'Yours Truly' were considered ideal singles to express the record's direction, and to promote things further, the band went over to Tokyo to play a festival alongside the mighty Deftones, Linkin Park, Tool and Metallica.

A few months later, Blindspott announced they were disbanding before reuniting for a one-off show at the Vodafone Homegrown Music Festival in Wellington in 2009. A year later, they confirmed they were back full-time, but in 2011 they changed their name to Blacklistt due to legal issues with former member Shelton Woolright. A self-titled album was released in 2013 as the band returned to their original nu metal sound.

Killer Cuts – 'Nil By Mouth', 'Phlex'

Boiler Room

Years Active: 1996-2001
Location: New York City, New York, USA
Main era line-up: Chris Lino (vocals), Rob Caggiano (guitar), James Meselsohn (bass), Mike Meselsohn (drums)
Albums: Boiler Room (1996), Can't Breathe (2000)

Building up a name for themselves around New York from their early inception, Boiler Room opened for metal royalty such as Type O Negative, Life of Agony and Korn before their big break came in 1999 after a successful show alongside Orgy.

Boasting guitarist Rob Caggiano amongst their ranks, who would later go on to play in thrash metal legends Anthrax and Danish rockers Volbeat, Boiler Room had already self-released an album by the time Roadrunner Records came knocking at their door. Signing to the label and recording their second album, *Can't Breathe*, trouble then began as the release was repeatedly delayed with no real reasons as to why. Choosing to leave Roadrunner and join Tommy Boy Records on a short-term contract, *Can't Breathe* was finally knocked out in November 2000. Featuring some powerful alt metal bringing Rage Against the Machine and the then up-and-coming Disturbed to mind, tracks such as 'Do It Again', 'Hopeless' and 'Superficial' earned the quartet a healthy fan base. Once their contract with Tommy Boy expired Boiler Room was dropped, and they chose to disband in 2001; however, their one big release remains popular and well thought of to this very day.

Killer Cuts – 'Do It Again', 'Superficial'

Breed 77

Years Active: 1996-2018
Location: Gibraltar/London, England
Main era line-up: Paul Isola (vocals), Danny Felice (guitar, backing vocals), Pedro Caparros Lopez (guitar), Stuart Cavilla (bass), Peter Chichone (drums)
Albums: Breed 77 (2000), Cultura (2004), In My Blood (En Mi Sangre) (2006), Insects (2009), The Evil Inside (2013)

Gibraltar's Breed 77 may have been based in the UK, but their distinctively original brand of metal endeared them to a lot of people around the world, courtesy of some additional flourishes of flamenco. Having already been together almost five years, Breed 77 signed a five-album deal with Albert Productions in 2001, who was the renowned publisher for rock legends AC/DC. A self-titled album emerged in the same year, and the band continued to lay their foundations and plot their big break – which would come with their second album, *Cultura*. Released in May 2004 and led by the huge singles 'La Ultima Hora', 'The River' and 'World's On Fire', Breed 77's time had truly come. Paul Isola's diverse vocal range was highly impressive, as was the excellent guitar work of Danny Felice, and to those living in the UK at the time, Breed 77 featured in every magazine, rock-orientated TV channel and gig venue in the country for a sustained period of time.

As the nu metal movement took a back seat from the mainstream, Breed 77 also struggled to get the exposure they had received prior to this. However, they still put out more strong releases in the form of 2006 effort, *In My Blood* and *Insects* in 2009. A successful ten-year anniversary tour for *Cultura* brought Breed 77 back into the spotlight for a short period in 2014, before the band finally called it a day at the end of 2018.

Killer Cuts – 'La Ultima Hora', 'The River'

Chevelle

Years Active: 1995-
Location: Grayslake, Illinois, USA
Main era line-up: Pete Loeffler (vocals, guitar), Joe Loeffler (bass, backing vocals), Sam Loeffler (drums)
Albums: Point #1 (1999), Wonder What's Next (2002), This Type of Thinking (Could Do Us In) (2004), Vena Sera (2007), Sci-Fi Crimes (2009), Hats Off to the Bull (2011), La Gàrgola (2014), The North Corridor (2016), Niratias (2021)

Chevelle was born in a suburb of Chicago where Pete, Sam and Joe Loeffler (yes, all brothers) named the band after their love of fast cars; and for their debut album, they were able to obtain Steve Albini for production duties. A guy who had previously worked with a couple of small bands by the name of Nirvana and Pixies, Albini put his stamp on *Point #1,* which was released in 1999 and earned moderate success. To continue getting their name out to the masses, Chevelle toured with Sevendust, Machine Head and Powerman 5000, and with nu metal pretty much at its peak, Chevelle signed with Epic Records and released *Wonder What's Next* in 2002. The phenomenal lead single 'The Red' took over *Kerrang!* and *MTV2* for weeks on end, and it helped the accompanying record sell over one million copies in America. 2004 effort, *This Type of Thinking (Could Do Us In),* peaked at 8 on the *Billboard* 200 and went gold within six weeks, as Chevelle continued with their alternative metal, which included some intriguing progressive elements- as shown on the standout tracks 'Vitamin R (Leading Us Along)' and 'The Clincher'.

Joe would then leave the band and he was replaced by brother-in-law Dean Bernardini, who debuted on Chevelle's fourth album, *Vena Sera,* in April 2007.

60,000 copies were sold in the first week and three killer singles were released ('Well Enough Alone', 'I Get It' and 'The Fad') before the trio toured the US with Evanescence and Finger Eleven. The slightly more standard hard rock stomp of *Sci-Fi Crimes* came out in 2009 which also had increased melody, as proven by the singles 'Jars', 'Letter from a Thief' and 'Shameful Metaphors', but still the record reached number 6 on the *Billboard* 200.

Continuing to remain busy with their output, the band released a live album/ DVD at the start of 2011 (*Any Last Words*) and another record at the end of it (*Hats Off to the Bull*), and as Christmas 2012 approached, they compiled *Stray Arrows: A Collection of Favorites*, which contained previous singles as well as the unreleased track 'Fizgig'. Chevelle then scored their highest *Billboard* position in 2014 with *La Gàrgola-* peaking at number 3, and as well as the scintillating album track 'Choking Game', 'Take Out the Gunman' and 'An Island' were popular additions.

The heavier and more aggressive *The North Corridor* marked Chevelle's return in 2016, and another lengthy spell away led to the band's latest release, *Niratias*, which was unveiled in March 2021. The powerful tracks of 'Self Destructor' and 'Mars Simula' showed the Loeffler's haven't lost their knack of creating stirring alternative metal music, and they should be commended for being able to remain relevant and consistent after over two decades at the top of the rock and metal tree.

Killer Cuts – 'The Red', 'I Get It'

Chimaira

Years Active: 1998-2014, 2017
Location: Cleveland, Ohio, USA
Main era line-up: Mark Hunter (vocals), Rob Arnold (lead guitar), Jason Hager/Matt DeVries (rhythm guitar), Jim LaMarca (bass), Andols Herrick (drums), Chris Spicuzza (keyboards, synth)
Albums: Pass Out of Existence (2001), The Impossibility of Reason (2003), Chimaira (2005), Resurrection (2007), The Infection (2009), The Age of Hell (2011), Crown of Phantoms (2013)

One of the heavier acts to come out of the nu metal movement, Chimaira – their name derived from a monstrous creature in Greek mythology ('Chimera') – spent much of their early existence honing their live performances around the Ohio area. When their second demo began to get some good airplay on college radio stations around Ohio, it led to Chimaira performing their promising track 'Dead Inside' on USA Network's *Farmclub.com*. A performance that clearly went down well with all who watched it, Roadrunner Records soon came calling and signed Chimaira to a lucrative contract. Releasing their storming debut album, *Pass Out of Existence*, on 2 October 2001, a crunching combination of groove metal and metalcore was given a nu metal edge due to the heavy usage of electronics.

It was also the only Chimaira album to include drop-A tuning and the use of seven-string guitars; the highlight tracks proving to be 'Dead Inside', 'Sp Lit', and 'Rizzo' – which featured Deftones guitarist Stephen Carpenter. Selling over 50,000 copies in the US, Chimaira toured the country and earned legions of fans all over before they returned to the studio to work on their next album.

Moving away from nu metal on their best-selling release *The Impossibility of Reason,* which emerged in May 2003, the melodic and mainstream-esque 'Down Again' saw Chimaira's stock rise farther. Reaching 117 on the *Billboard* 200 and selling over 200,000 copies, the album was backed up by 'Army of Me', which was included on the *Freddy vs. Jason* soundtrack, and 'Power Trip', which became one of the band's signature songs. A stint on Ozzfest in 2003 also continued Chimaira's upward surge.

Going full-on metal for later albums, Chimaira remained prominent until their split in 2014, by which time Mark Hunter was the only original member left in the band. A reunion show at the back end of 2017 went down a storm, and another reunion is planned for sometime in the near future; however, the band's first two records remain their most successful and popular with heavy music lovers and deserving of their spots in nu metal's illustrious history.

Killer Cuts – 'Dead Inside', 'Down Again'

Clawfinger

Years Active: 1989-2013, 2017-
Location: Stockholm, Sweden
Main era line-up: Zak Tell (vocals), Erlend Ottem (lead guitar), Bard Torstensen (rhythm guitar, lead guitar), Andre Skaug (bass), Henka Johansson (drums)
Albums: Deaf Dumb Blind (1993), Use Your Brain (1995), Clawfinger (1997), A Whole Lot of Nothing (2001), Zeros & Heroes (2003), Hate Yourself with Style (2005), Life Will Kill You (2007)

Considered by some as underappreciated for helping bring rap metal into the mainstream, Sweden's Clawfinger started out at the back end of the 1980s and included some industrial-tinged instrumentation to accompany songs that contained socio-political subject matter.

The quintet set pulses raising with their very first demo, especially through their anti-racism track, 'Nigger', which understandably caused a stir yet brought Clawfinger significant exposure and success. MVG Records promptly signed the band, and released their *Deaf Dumb Blind* album in April 1993. Along with 'Nigger', 'The Truth', 'Rosegrove' and 'Warfair' were popular additions, all helping the album sell over 600,000 worldwide and thus allowing Clawfinger to travel throughout Europe and share stages with the likes of Anthrax and Alice in Chains.

Vital experience was earned ahead of returning to the studio to work on their next album, which Clawfinger titled *Use Your Brain*, and it continued to promote their pounding and unapologetic form of rap metal in 1995. 'Pin Me Down' and 'Do What I Say' were strong singles, and a self-titled effort followed suit two years later. *A Whole Lot of Nothing* saw Clawfinger adding some synth for the first time in 2001 before more complex and melodic guitar rhythms entered the fray on later albums such as *Zeros & Heroes* (2003) and *Hate Yourself with Style* (2005).

After one final studio album in 2007 (*Life Will Kill You*), Clawfinger announced their separation in 2013; however, reunion shows have frequently taken place in the years since and two new songs, 'Save Our Souls' and 'Tear You Down', have emerged in the last couple of years. It remains to be seen if Clawfinger will return with another full-length album, but these shit-kicking Swedes certainly deserve credit for putting Europe on notice, as rap metal slowly but surely became one of the most popular new additions to the heavy metal genre.

Killer Cuts – 'Nigger', 'The Truth'

Coal Chamber

Years Active: 1993-2003, 2011-2016
Location: Los Angeles, California, USA
Main era line-up: Dez Fafara (vocals), Miguel 'Meegs' Rascón, Rayna Foss/Nadja Peulen (bass), Mike Cox (drums)
Albums: Coal Chamber (1997), Chamber Music (1999), Dark Days (2002), Rivals (2015)

It has been said that Coal Chamber could, in fact, have been the very first band to be labelled as nu metal after a live review of the LA quartet back in the mid-nineties. With an image more in common with gothic subculture, scary-looking things Dez Fafara, Miguel Rascón, Rayna Foss and Mike Cox burst onto the scene with their eponymous self-titled debut album in February 1997 – put out by the renowned Roadrunner Records. Spawning the song 'Loco', which would become a nu metal highlight, *Coal Chamber* – engineered and produced by Orgy's Amir Derakh and Jay Gordon, earned gold certification for 500,000 copies sold in the US alone, thanks also to now-classic Coal Chamber numbers such as 'Sway', 'Big Truck' and 'Oddity'.

Unlike any other band of that time, Coal Chamber's nightmarish gothic metal brought about a new sound, and Fafara's growl rapping mixed with deafening screams appeared to hit the right spot with all kinds of metal fans. The sophomore album, *Chamber Music,* followed in September 1999, and it was a much more melodic record compared to its predecessor, featuring primarily cleaner vocals displays from Fafara. Included was a cover of Peter Gabriel's 'Shock the Monkey', which featured Black Sabbath and overall heavy metal legend Ozzy Osbourne. Selling over 270,000 copies, it didn't match the success of the band's debut album, but it was nonetheless an intriguing change of direction which earned Coal Chamber a new following from those who liked their metal with a little more approachability; and songs like 'El Cu Cuy' and 'Tragedy' are still popular today.

Often considered to be the band's most aggressive record, *Dark Days* emerged in 2002 and led by the bruising single 'Fiend', it was clear that Coal Chamber had indeed turned the heavy dial up a few notches. By this time, though, Coal Chamber were having internal issues, which led to the band calling it a day in 2003 after putting out a compilation album (*Giving the Devil His Due*) of demos and unreleased songs. Fafara went on to form the massively popular groove metal band DevilDriver, while the other members of Coal Chamber largely stayed out of the limelight, but in 2011, Coal Chamber announced their reformation with the line-up of Fafara, Rascón, Cox and Nadja Peulen – who had originally been brought in years before to replace Foss when she left the band to focus on motherhood. After various live shows and festival spots, the band confirmed they were working on a new album, and in May 2015, *Rivals* was released via Napalm Records. It included elements of the band's classic nu metal sound, but in reality, this was a bludgeoning assault of groove metal with standout moments coming in the form of 'I.O.U. Nothing', 'Another Nail in the Coffin' and 'Suffer in Silence' – which featured Ministry's Al Jourgensen.

Coal Chamber are once again done due to Fafara's involvement with DevilDriver, and at the end of 2017, Rascón joined popular alternative metal band Gemini Syndrome; but at their peak, these ghoulish oddities exemplified what nu metal was all about and 'Loco' will forever remain synonymous with everything that was great about that era.

Killer Cuts – 'Loco', 'El Cu Cuy'

Miguel 'Meegs' Rascón speaks:

> Nu metal wasn't a phrase we knew back then; we were just trying to do something heavy and groovy. Bands were more unique and distinct in that era and we knew we were doing something different, and audiences perceived that. I remember having a gut feeling that something was happening, but I was a young kid – how would I have known anything before that?
>
> That era of going to clubs seemed so big and you would kind of push your chest out because you were a part of what was happening, even if you didn't know what the fuck it was. I actually felt like I was part of a family. Everybody would go to these shows and clubs like the Whisky and The Roxy and they were getting super-packed. Everybody would go crazy in the pit and you would be like, 'Is this really happening?' I remember being at one of Korn's shows and there was maybe twenty or thirty people there in the very beginning, but I could tell they were going to do something because they were badass. We were friends with them because we were at their shows and when they got signed, we would go to Indigo Ranch and hang out in the studio with them while they were recording their first album.
>
> I was part of the club scene and I would go to every show, so I would see System of a Down, Static-X, Korn – I would see every band. We were in that era where we

handed out flyers, which was weird, but it worked big time. It was a 1980s thing and it carried over into the next decade, and then it fizzled out after everyone got signed. Record companies were all over the place in LA. Everybody wanted to sign everybody. When you first heard the songs, you couldn't really hear radio hits, but labels saw the attraction. Coal Chamber and the other bands were selling out everywhere in LA, so I guess the labels saw potential to make money off of us, and because of Korn, Coal Chamber was getting a lot of attention. An A&R guy at Geffen tried to sign us and we had meetings, but I don't think he was powerful enough of an A&R guy to make it happen, but he really tried. Roadrunner Records had a bunch of bands on their roster that I loved, like Type O Negative, Machine Head and Sepultura, and it was a cool label who had a lot of push because they were starting to get big. They wanted us really bad, and Monte Connor was coming from New York to LA all the time and taking us out to dinner. In the end, we got a lawyer and we got signed. We didn't have management because we were so new that we didn't know shit, and so the lawyer got us the deal with Roadrunner.

With our first album, I was influenced by the likes of White Zombie and Helmet, so I wanted to make unrelenting music that was kind of like a truck hitting you. Dez (Fafara) had this rhythmic, growly voice, and the heavy music fit his voice perfectly. We would try anything, like tuning down, and I would do a lot of whacky shit to my guitars and amps. Our look was so weird, but we didn't care – we were young, and we wanted to do something really different. Even if it looked goofy, we would do it.

On 'Loco', with its intro and that groove, I feel like I really tapped into something with that type of riff. The word 'Loco' is obviously Spanish, and LA has a big Latino community, but just the song title alone was different, and then when you put the sound to it... It wasn't a hit, but it broke us through. We weren't trying to do radio rock, but radio stations played it and it was a really cool thing. I know our debut record is over twenty years old now, but people still send me links and videos of covers, especially of 'Loco'. Kids are playing these songs and it is cool that nobody has forgotten about Coal Chamber or the music. It is nice to see people are still into it.

After the first record, we didn't want to do a part two. I wanted to get away from that style and do some more experimental stuff like using synth and electronics. We thought we were going to piss off everybody, and we kind of did, but I am very proud of *Chamber Music*. We also wanted to do a cover song on the album, and we thought we could do 'Shock the Monkey' differently and make it heavy. We were on Ozzfest with Sharon Osbourne and we said we should have Ozzy on that song, and Sharon said she could get it done. It was fucking awesome to see Ozzy in the studio, we went to his house, and it was all like a dream. I think we made that song our own.

Dark Days is definitely our heaviest record. We got *Chamber Music* out of our system and we weren't going to do that again, so our headspace was 'Let's go heavier'. The riffing, the vocals and the grooves were relentless, and I think that might be my favourite Coal Chamber album. It was very hard, but I put a lot of work into *Dark Days*. That was when Dez and I were not getting along and it was difficult. We knew the band was done because we just could not see eye-to-eye, and it sucks because our fans didn't want us to break up, but sometimes you have to do what you have to do.

We played Ozzfest in 1996, 1997 and 1998, and it was a dream playing in front of a lot of my idols. We played the second stage both of the first two years and it was fucking huge. Of course, it wasn't the main stage, but the stage we played on was awesome and there was a ton of people watching us. Ozzfest was a new thing at the time and it was really exciting. I think it was in 1997 and Coal Chamber was getting pretty big, and I remember we were on the side stage and I kept hearing through the grapevine that Sharon Osbourne was saying we needed to be on the main stage. We were getting such a big crowd and people were telling us we were the best part of the side stage. Bands and kids kept saying, 'There's no doubt you have to be on the main stage next year', and then it happened. For me, it was an exciting time because we had that feeling we were doing something people really liked. One time I remember I was playing, and I saw Vinnie Paul and Dimebag at the side of the stage, just rocking out. These were my idols as a snotty-nosed kid, going to their signings and taking pictures with them, and now they were side-stage rocking out and headbanging while I was playing 'Big Truck'. It was fucking crazy. Dimebag is a legend on the guitar, and I was playing simple shit – and he was rocking out to my music. I knew he could kill me at any moment because he was like Godzilla and I was just a little mouse. The Pantera guys would party all day and every night, so I would go in and they would grab me, get me all fucked up, and then I would go back to my bus completely wrecked. Me and Dimebag actually shared the same birthday, and we had a couple of birthdays on those tours, and that would be crazy. I really don't remember much of those at all.

I was literally on stage in 1998 watching Lynn Strait from Snot getting blown in front of everyone while Limp Bizkit was playing their set. Everything was happening so fast, but where I was on the stage, I thought he was faking it. Later, I found out it was a real thing, but I remember security rushing the stage and Lynn flying right past me. That was the talk of the day. All the shows were great on Ozzfest and every band was on their A-game every night.

Looking back, I don't know if that era of music and those feelings will ever be repeated in my lifetime. That was like the cosmos and the universe colliding into a special little segment of years, like five or six years. It was a speckle of a timeline I do not think will ever be re-created. The response, and all these different bands who became successful in their own right, all in a little speckle of time. I am really proud of being part of that little collision in the universe, and a lot of us were at the end of where you could make money off of record sales, which doesn't happen anymore. It is difficult for bands now and they are never going to experience what we did. I was at the cusp, I had a gold record, and so I feel really good that I was right at the end of that period and I happened to experience it.

We were all young and trying to do something which wasn't your typical rock and roll. The memories of playing something which made people's heads turn, to have a scene so strong – I wish someone had created a time machine to go back and see it all because the whole world was looking at it, and at one point, all eyes were on us. And we knew it.

Cold

Years Active: 1986-2006, 2009-
Location: Jacksonville, Florida, USA
Main era line-up: Scooter Ward (vocals, rhythm guitar, keyboards), Kelly Hayes (lead guitar), Terry Balsamo (guitar), Jeremy Marshall (bass), Sam McCandless (drums)
Albums: Cold (1998), 13 Ways to Bleed on Stage (2000), Year of the Spider (2003), A Different Kind of Pain (2005), Superfiction (2011), The Things We Can't Stop (2019)

Coming out of Jacksonville, Florida, Grundig changed their name to Cold and consisted of Scooter Ward (vocals, guitar), Kelly Hayes (guitar), Sam McCandless (drums) and Jeremy Marshall (bass). Their self-titled debut album was produced by Ross Robinson and released through Flip/A&M at Polygram- gaining minor success. Fusing alternative metal with post-grunge, tracks such as 'Go Away' and 'Give' (which featured Korn's Jonathan Davis and Limp Bizkit's Fred Durst in the official promo video) showed the band's ability to write moody but infectious hard rock songs. Fellow Jacksonville native Durst would also provide additional vocals on 'Go Away' and 'Blame'.

Terry Balsamo joined the band on guitar to make Cold a quintet ahead of the release of their second and breakthrough album, *13 Ways to Bleed on Stage*, hitting record stores in September 2000. Nu metal super track 'Just Got Wicked' was the lead single, followed by the grunge-influenced 'No One', 'End of the World' and 'Bleed'. Themes on the record explored drug addiction, relationship troubles and social indifference, and although *13 Ways to Bleed* only peaked at 98 on the *Billboard* 200, it still went on to reach gold status in America.

A third album titled *Year of the Spider* was released via Geffen in 2003, predominantly sticking to the now-familiar post-grunge sound whilst steering away from the darkness encapsulating the band's earlier efforts; and it became Cold's most commercially successful record when it debuted at number 3 on the *Billboard* chart and sold over 101,000 copies in its very first week. The pulsating singles 'Stupid Girl' and 'Suffocate' were two of the strongest tracks in Cold's discography, with crisp verses leading into arena-sized choruses and sung passionately by Ward with his instantly recognisable vocal tones.

Continuing with their foray into softer alternative rock territory, Cold returned in 2005 with *A Different Kind of Pain*. Clearly moving away from the aggressive sound of their earlier years, tracks such as 'Happens All the Time' and the album title track showed a more sensitive side to Scooter, who was dealing with personal issues at the time. Nonetheless, it was an album that was raw and relatable, and it would go on to sell over 160,000 copies in the US. Towards the end of 2006, Cold announced that they were calling it a day, but in 2008 the band thankfully announced a reunion and a new line-up. However, there would be more comings and goings in the band ahead of their fifth album *Superfiction*, which was released in 2011 via Eleven Seven Music.

Clearly a band that still had a large fan base, the record peaked at 37 in the US and spawned modern Cold classics such as 'Wicked World', 'The Break' and 'Welcome2MyWorld', and in 2019, the current version of Cold released the softer and ballad-driven album, *The Things We Can't Stop*, through Napalm Records.

Killer Cuts – 'Just Got Wicked', 'End of the World'

Crazy Town

Years Active: 1995-2003, 2007-
Location: Los Angeles, California, USA
Main era line-up: Seth 'Shifty' Binzer (vocals), Bret 'Epic' Mazur (vocals, keyboards), Anthony Valli (guitar), Rust Epique (guitar), Doug Miller (bass), James Bradley Jr. (drums), DJ AM (turntables)
Albums: The Gift of Game (1999), Darkhorse (2002), The Brimstone Sluggers (2015)

Crazy Town invaded nu metal in 1999 with their debut album *The Gift of Game*; however, it was their first single, 'Butterfly' which gave the septet worldwide exposure. Dominated by the distinctive sample of the Red Hot Chili Peppers' album track 'Pretty Little Ditty', 'Butterfly' stormed to number 1 on the *Billboard* Hot 100, number 3 in the UK singles chart, and dominated lists all around the globe. The dreamy promo video placed itself on countless TV channels and refused to budge, and featured in various music magazines, showing that Crazy Town were a boyband-looking rap-rock group who everyone appeared to take a shine to. The band's follow-up single, 'Revolving Door', sampled a Siouxsie and the Banshees track, although it didn't have the mainstream power of its predecessor, but regardless, *The Gift of Game* would still go on to sell 2.5 million copies worldwide – underlining the influence that one song can have on ultimately making or breaking a band.

The often labelled 'tricky second album' proved to be, as for so many other artists over the years, the one which stalled Crazy Town's momentum. *Darkhorse* was released in 2002 and focused on a more straightforward hard rock sound, as proven by the first single, 'Drowning'. With only a handful of songs that could be considered potential radio hits, the album only reached 120 on the *Billboard* 200 and Crazy Town would announce their split not long after. Partly blaming record label pressure to make another song as strong as 'Butterfly', which was always going to be unachievable, alcohol and drug addiction had also hit various band members who either struggled with the pressures of fame or endorsed it a little too much.

Seth 'Shifty Shellshock' Binzer and Bret 'Epic' Mazur would return under the Crazy Town name in 2007 as the vocal duo released their third album, *The*

Brimstone Sluggers, in 2015 through Membran Records. Primarily delving into hip-hop territory, the record received mixed reviews, but there were still some great highlights such as 'Born to Raise Hell', 'A Little More Time' and 'Come Inside'. Mazur announced his departure in early 2017, leaving Binzer as the sole original member who is still carrying on the Crazy Town name today.

Killer Cuts – 'Butterfly', 'Drowning'

Creed

Years Active: 1994-2004, 2009-2012
Location: Tallahassee, Florida, USA
Main era line-up: Scott Stapp (vocals), Mark Tremonti (lead guitar, backing vocals), Brian Marshall (bass), Scott Phillips (drums)
Albums: My Own Prison (1997), Human Clay (1999), Weathered (2001), Full Circle (2009)

One of the most successful American artists in music history, Creed began their journey in 1993 when vocalist Scott Stapp and future guitar wizard Mark Tremonti met in high school. Becoming a four-piece in 1995 with the additions of Brian Marshall (bass) and Scott Phillips (drums), the Tallahassee natives earned local success playing shows in the area, before the owner of one such establishment had been so impressed with Creed's performance that he funded $6,000 for the band's debut album, *My Own Prison*. Self-released on Creed's own Blue Collar Recordings label, the album sold well in Florida State, leading to Wind-Up Records signing the band in 1997. *My Own Prison* was remixed and re-released, and it would go on to sell over six million copies after catching people's attention with lyrical themes of questioning faith and spirituality, on top of heavy post-grunge and hard rock power. Singles released from the record were the popular album title track, 'Torn', 'What's This Life For' and 'One', before Creed's eagerly anticipated sophomore album, *Human Clay,* emerged in September 1999.

Powering its way to the top spot of the *Billboard* 200 by shifting 315,000 copies in its first week, huge singles included 'Higher' and 'With Arms Wide Open', the latter of which topped *Billboard*'s Hot 100 chart and also won a Grammy Award for Best Rock Song in 2001. Darker themes enveloped Creed's second release, as focus was shone on sex abuse and hostility, as well as lighter muses of personal dreams and fatherhood; and *Human Clay* would later be certified an astounding 11x platinum, with worldwide sales of over 20 million.

By now, Creed were one of the biggest bands in the world and naturally, fame came with its pitfalls. In 2000, Marshall left the band due to his battle with alcoholism, and his bass work would be covered by Tremonti for Creed's third album, *Weathered*, which again debuted at number 1 in America upon its release in November 2001. Selling 880,000 copies in its first week, *Weathered* dominated the *Billboard* 200 top spot for eight consecutive weeks, and it was helped by the stunning lead single, 'My Sacrifice', which took over TV and radio. The album's second single, 'Bullets', might just be the heaviest track

Creed has ever written, and along with four other singles, *Weathered* ended up going 6x platinum.

Stapp would later be involved in a car accident, leading to him suffering damage to his vertebrae. On top of already existing alcohol struggles, Stapp would then become addicted to painkillers, and after a poor live performance in Rosemont, Illinois (where he was reportedly under the influence), it led to four concert-goers filing a lawsuit against the band (although the case would later be dismissed). After that, Creed remained inactive until 2004, when they officially announced their breakup.

Stapp went on to launch a solo career while Tremonti and Phillips reunited with Brian Marshall to form the hard rock band, Alter Bridge, with Myles Kennedy on vocals; but in April 2009, Creed announced through their website that they had reunited and confirmed plans to tour and record a new album. *Full Circle* emerged later in the same year, debuting at number 2 in the US thanks to the classic Creed-sounding single, 'Overcome'. 'Rain' and 'A Thousand Faces' were later singles and to tour the record, Creed went out with Hoobastank, Staind and Saliva, who acted as direct supports. Further touring ensued through 2011 and 2012, and at some shows, *My Own Prison* and *Human Clay* were played in their entirety, but as talk of a new record continued in the media, it was soon announced that Stapp and Tremonti's relationship had appeared to break down; ultimately leading to Creed calling it a day once more.

With relatable, soul-baring lyrics and crushing hard rock anthems aplenty, Creed's record sales are to be admired, as they became one of the best-selling artists in American history and a worthy addition to the nu metal movement.

Killer Cuts – 'Higher', 'My Sacrifice'

Crossbreed

Years Active: 1996-2010

Location: Clearwater, Florida, USA

Main era line-up: James Rietz (vocals), Chris Nemzek (guitar), Charlie Parker (bass), Travis Simpkins (drums), Dan Izzo (turntables, electronics)

Albums: .01 (1998), Synthetic Division (2001), KE 101 (2009)

Another band to bring some feisty industrial metal to the table was Crossbreed, who started out in 1996 and gained some local recognition on the back of their 1998 EP, *2Twenty2*, and their *.01* album which followed in the same year. In 1999, the six-piece caught the eye of a handful of record labels due to their visually appealing live shows, and after performing at the 98Rock Radio Festival in Tampa in April 2000, a meeting with the girls in Kittie led to a copy of Crossbreed's latest demo, *Baby Doll,* falling into the hands of an A&R rep at Artemis Records. A deal was quickly made between the band and label, and Crossbreed's first major release arrived in 2001, courtesy of the album *Synthetic Division*. Led by the rollicking singles 'Underlined', 'Seasons' and 'Breathe', the album would go on to sell over 100,000 copies worldwide, while the music video for 'Underlined' earned a *Billboard* Music Award nomination. Tours with Rammstein and Static-X followed, though Artemis would then drop Crossbreed, which in turn caused a mass exodus of bands members.

Leaving vocalist James Rietz and guitarist, Chris Nemzek, holding the fort, the duo decided to press on and find some new bandmates, and after taking on former KISS manager, Bill Aucoin, to fight their corner, the new version of Crossbreed dropped a new and self-produced EP in the summer of 2005, titled *New Slave Nation*. Some decent tours with Mushroomhead, Dope, and Nothingface helped Crossbreed build up a new fanbase, and then they would sign to Driven Music Group, which was owned by Korn guitarist, Brian 'Head' Welch. In late 2009, a new album dropped (*KE 101*), of which the tracks 'Kill Everything' and 'Saints of Grey' were highlights. However, all momentum was soon lost and Crossbreed would officially disband in 2010. As this book goes to press, a reunion has been announced and it will be interesting to see what happens with the band next.

Killer Cuts – 'Underlined', 'Seasons'

Crossfade

Years Active: 1993-
Location: Columbia, South Carolina, USA
Main era line-up: Ed Sloan (vocals, guitars), Mitch James (bass, backing vocals), Brian Geiger (drums), Tony Byroads (turntables, samples)
Albums: Crossfade (2004), Falling Away (2006), We All Bleed (2011)

Originally called The Nothing and then Sugardaddy Superstar (thankfully, they didn't stick with that name), Crossfade was born in 2002. After signing to a division of Columbia Records called FG Records/Earshot, the band struck gold with their self-titled debut in 2004. The highly successful single 'Cold' broke Crossfade into the mainstream as the song reached number 3 on *Billboard*'s Mainstream Rock Tracks chart and also got into the Top 100, and the later singles 'So Far Away' and 'Colors' also helped to send *Crossfade* platinum in 2005.

After the departures of Tony Byroads and Brian Geiger, Crossfade continued as a trio (Ed Sloan on vocals and guitar, Mitchell James on bass and James Branham on drums) and a second album followed in 2006. Perhaps unsurprisingly, *Falling Away* failed to match the success of its predecessor, although 200,000 copies sold wasn't to be sniffed at, and there was still some strong material within the ranks, such as the singles 'Invincible' and 'Drown You Out'.

Crossfade then split from Columbia and penned a deal with the flourishing Eleven Seven Music, although their next album wouldn't follow until 2011 when *We All Bleed* came some seven months after its planned release date. 'Killing Me Inside' was the standout moment on a darker-sounding record, and the drums were performed by Will Hunt, who would later join Evanescence. *We All Bleed* still managed to creep inside the top half of the *Billboard* 200, which proved that Crossfade still had somewhat of a dedicated fan base out there. Sloan has since released some solo material while Crossfade remains on the backburner; however 'Cold' remains a true gem of nu metal's final flourish.

Killer Cuts – 'Cold', 'So Far Away'

Cyclefly

Years Active: 1995-2003
Location: Cork, Ireland
Main era line-up: Declan O'Shea (vocals), Ciaran O'Shea (guitar), NoNo Presta (guitar), Christian Montagne (bass), Jean-Michel Cavallo (drums)

Although based in Ireland, Cyclefly was indeed a multi-European outfit – consisting of two Irishmen, an Italian and two Frenchmen. Declan O'Shea was known for his energetic live performances and diverse vocal tones, and Cyclefly released their debut record in 1999, titled *Generation Sap*. Playing a blend of alternative rock with a hardened edge, the band's high point came with the release of *Crave* in 2002 via Radioactive/MCA Records. Standout track 'No Stress' was included on an official *Kerrang!* Compilation CD, while 'Karma Killer' saw Linkin Park's Chester Bennington provide guest vocals on a stirring chorus. During their short career, Cyclefly toured with the likes of Bush, Linkin Park, Metallica and Muse, but they ultimately split up in 2003 without ever really getting the credit they perhaps deserved.

Killer Cuts – 'No Stress', 'Karma Killer'

Darwin's Waiting Room

Years Active: 1995-2004
Location: Miami, Florida, USA
Main era line-up: Jabe (vocals), Michael 'Grimm' Falk (rap vocals), Eddie Rendini (lead guitar), Alex Cando (bass), Joe Perrone (drums)
Albums: Orphan (2001), Apology Accepted (online) (2003)

Starting up in the mid-nineties in Miami, Darwin's Waiting Room struck gold in 2001 when the rap rock quintet inked a deal with MCA. By the summer, they had dropped their debut full-length, *Orphan,* which appeared to have more than a few Limp Bizkit influences to it, minus the potty-mouthed lyrical content, of course. The single, 'Feel So Stupid (Table 9)', had an accompanying video which received decent airtime on *MTV*, while the most outrageous addition to the album's tracklist saw Shaggy – known for the terrible song 'Boombastic' – feature on the eyebrow-raising 'Innosense'.

With the vocal combination of emcee Michael 'Grimm' Falk and Jabe's clean deliveries, Darwin's Waiting Room had a strong duo upfront, as the band earned exposure through sharing stages with nu metal heavyweights such as Godsmack,

Deftones and Nonpoint. A second album was due to follow in 2003 (*Apology Accepted*). However, it never got an official release, and the band themselves would call it quits not long after.

Killer Cuts – 'Feel So Stupid (Table 9)', 'Live for the Moment'

The Deadlights

Years Active: 1998-2000
Location: Long Beach, California, USA
Main era line-up: Wilfred 'Duke' Collins (vocals), Billy Roan (guitar), Jerry Montano (bass), Jimmy Falcone (drums)
Albums: The Deadlights (2000)

A very short career for a very promising band – The Deadlights rose out of Long Beach in 1998 and worked their way to a pretty impressive elevation by the start of the new millennium. A self-titled debut emerged in February 2000 through Elektra, where four powerhouse promotional singles were released – 'Bitter', 'Amplifier', 'Nothing' and 'Sweet Oblivion'; while a video was also made for 'Junk'.

Combining alt metal, hard rock and post-grunge, The Deadlights' first record became somewhat of a cult classic amongst nu metal fans and, making a good year even better, the band joined the likes of Primer 55, Reveille, Taproot, Disturbed and Kittie on the second stage of Ozzfest.

The Deadlights then abruptly announced they had called it a day, with bassist Jerry Montano most notably going on to play in Nothingface and then the supergroup, Hellyeah – alongside Mudvayne vocalist Chad Gray. Wilfred 'Duke' Collins, whose captivating vocal range made The Deadlights stand out that little bit more, sadly passed away in 2015.

Killer Cuts – 'Bitter', 'Sweet Oblivion'

Deadsy

Years Active: 1995-2007, 2017-
Location: Los Angeles, California, USA
Main era line-up: Elijah Blue Allman (vocals, guitar), Carlton Bost (guitar), Craig Riker (bass), Alec Puro (drums), Renn Hawkey (keyboards)
Albums: Deadsy (1996), Commencement (2002), Phantasmagore (2006)

Formed by Elijah Blue Allman – the son of Cher and Greg Allman, Deadsy signed to Sire Records to release their first album in 1996. With a largely darkwave sound, *Deadsy* featured Orgy's Jay Gordon on bass duties, while the standout track, 'Sleepy Hollow', included a guest spot from Korn's Jonathan Davis.

Following up with the sophomore release *Commencement,* via DreamWorks and under Korn's Elementree sub-label in 2002, the popular single 'The Key to Gramercy Park' again saw Jonathan Davis provide guest vocals, as well as

Jay Gordon on the album track 'Seagulls' (his bass work was also included on three other songs). The mixture of synth rock, shrill melodies and heavy guitar distortion saw Deadsy following their influences of the new wave scene of the 1980s, and along with touring beside the likes of Static-X, Staind, Linkin Park and Stone Temple Pilots, Deadsy gained mainstream notoriety through their associations with both Davis and Limp Bizkit's Fred Durst.

Rather surprisingly, both albums ultimately failed to sell as many copies as the band's popularity suggested they might, and when *Phantasmagore* was released in 2006 through Immortal, like nu metal at that time, Deadsy had been left behind.

Killer Cuts – 'Sleepy Hollow', 'The Key to Gramercy Park'

Defenestration

Years Active: 1999-2004
Location: Kettering, Northamptonshire, England
Main era line-up: Gen Tasker (vocals), Jamie Thompson (guitar), Robert Reeves (guitar), Scott Warner (bass), Stacey Maher (drums)
Albums: One Inch God (2001), Ray Zero (2003), For Us It Ends When We Drown (2004)

Defenestration was another band that demonstrated their power through female fury. Gen Tasker's mix of scream and clean vocals gave the band their edge, releasing the albums *One Inch God* in 2001 and *Ray Zero* in 2003. Their most popular tracks were 'Stitch' and 'Away or Dead' – which earned small exposure on *Kerrang!* and *MTV2*, while their last release was a mini-album titled *For Us It Ends When We Drown*.

Defenestration's career was surprisingly short-lived, especially when you consider they earned the right to share stages with metal heavyweights such as Napalm Death, Slayer and Megadeth, at various stages of their career.

Killer Cuts – 'Stitch', 'Away or Dead'

Deftones

Years Active: 1988-
Location: Sacramento, California, USA
Main era line-up: Chino Moreno (vocals, rhythm guitar), Stephen Carpenter (lead guitar), Chi Cheng (bass), Abe Cunningham (drums), Frank Delgado (keyboards, turntables, samples)
Albums: Adrenaline (1995), Around the Fur (1997), White Pony (2000), Deftones (2003), Saturday Night Wrist (2006), Diamond Eyes (2010), Koi No Yokan (2012), Gore (2016), Ohms (2020)

Forming in Sacramento, California, in 1988, Stephen Carpenter, Abe Cunningham and Chino Moreno were friends from childhood. After regularly playing jam sessions together, Chi Cheng joined on bass in 1990, and the band played the local scene until breaking out further towards LA and San Francisco. It was whilst playing with Korn that their live performances caught the attention of a Maverick Records representative, and Deftones would later go on to sign for the record label.

Carpenter reportedly created the band name by combining the hip-hop slang of 'Def' with the suffix 'Tones', which was popular with bands from the 1950s. The name was intentionally planned to appear vague, so the band couldn't be associated with just one style of music, and trying to put the band into a specific genre would prove to be impossible as their sound ever evolved as time progressed.

Produced by Terry Date (Pantera, Soundgarden), Deftones released their debut album in October 1995. *Adrenaline* was initially unsuccessful, although the band continued to create a dedicated fan base through extensive touring, word of mouth, and promotion via the increasing popularity of the internet. The predominant rap metal style spawned fan favourites such as 'Bored' and 'Engine No. 9', while the non-album track, 'Teething', featured on the movie soundtrack for *The Crow: City of Angels*. Deftones can in fact be seen performing the song during the movie, playing to a rapturous crowd while the protagonist fights his archenemy towards the end of the film.

With a buzz surrounding it, *Around the Fur* followed in October 1997, again produced by Terry Date. 'My Own Summer (Shove It)' and the massive anthem 'Be Quiet and Drive (Far Away)' received strong radio airplay, in part due to the more accessible sound compared to the rough-around-the-edges rap metal on *Adrenaline*. Here, melodic grooves and Moreno's sharper vocal structures gave Deftones a much bigger platform, and *Around the Fur* peaked at a respectable 29 on the *Billboard* 200 before reaching platinum status in 2011, three years after *Adrenaline* had done the same. After some part-time playing in the band, Frank Delgado (keyboards, turntables) became a full-time member of Deftones in time for the release of *White Pony* in June 2000, which would well and truly cement the Sacramento crew as one of the leaders of the nu metal movement. A stunning cacophony of heavy and hard metal mixed with ambient mood swings and diverse experimentation, *White Pony* threw yet another curveball into nu metal's aesthetics. With tracks such as 'Passenger' (featuring Tool's Maynard James Keenan), 'RX Queen' (featuring Scott Weiland from Stone Temple Pilots), plus the haunting genius of 'Change (In the House of Flies)', this bonafide magnum opus debuted at number 3 on the *Billboard* 200 and 13 in the UK, going platinum within a year of its release through sales of 1.3 million copies in the US alone. Success continued to follow when Deftones won a Grammy in the Best Metal Performance category for the album track, 'Elite', which was by far the most visceral moment heard on *White Pony*.

Sometimes they say it is a band's second album that is the tricky one, but in Deftones' case, it was their fourth. Following up an album so critically acclaimed as *White Pony*, the self-titled fourth release continued the success when it entered the album chart in the US at 2 and sold 167,000 copies in its first week in May

2003. 'Minerva' and 'Hexagram' continued with an experimental metal sound which Deftones were becoming known for, although 'Minerva' especially had the sound of a band attempting to endear themselves further to the mainstream. Reviews for *Deftones* were generally positive, but there appeared to be a general consensus by fans, especially that it was a far less rewarding record than its predecessor, which in a lot of aspects seemed to be a justified statement.

Although as captivating a band as ever, Deftones were to stumble across some internal conflict and personal tragedy over the next few years. Their fifth album, *Saturday Night Wrist* (released in 2005), found Chino coming to terms with addiction, and hostility within the group was reaching boiling point. To those on the outside, however, the new record was typically engrossing. A body of work that only a band like Deftones could produce, highlights included the gloriously melodic and atmospheric 'Hole in the Earth', 'Kimdracula', and 'Mein', which featured System of a Down's Serj Tankian on backing vocals. The alternative metal spectacle peaked at a creditable number 10 on the *Billboard* 200.

In 2008, Chi Cheng was involved in a serious road accident which left him in a semi-conscious state for the next four years. An incident that naturally rocked the whole band as well as the whole rock and metal community, it was later confirmed that Deftones had been working on a new album, with a working title of *Eros*. However, it was shelved due to Chi's worrying situation. Instead, Quicksand bassist Sergio Vega was hired and Deftones returned in 2010 with their sensational sixth studio album, *Diamond Eyes*. Rave reviews followed and, although it was a record that focused on a more straightforward metal sound, it included some of the best material from the band since *White Pony*. Infectious tracks such as 'Rocket Skates', 'Prince', and the sinister 'You've Seen the Butcher' were instant classics, and the album debuted at 6 in the US.

Teaming up with grunge icons Alice in Chains and sludge rockers Mastodon, both of whom had also recently released new records, Deftones toured their latest release across the US before returning to the studio in 2011 to work on a covers album released on vinyl in support of Record Store Day. Popular renditions included The Cure's 'If Only Tonight We Could Sleep', Sade's 'No Ordinary Love' and a brilliant version of Lynyrd Skynyrd's 'Simple Man', which featured a stunning vocal performance from Chino.

In November 2012, *Koi No Yokan* would see Deftones experiment with progressive metal and shoegaze elements, and it was another record to earn critical acclaim. The track 'Rosemary' showed what kind of headspace the band were in, while the groove-laden 'Leathers' and 'Swerve City' confirmed that Deftones were possibly on the best form of their whole career. After initially making a partial recovery from his accident a few years prior, Chi Cheng sadly passed away in April 2013 after falling into cardiac arrest in a Sacramento hospital. The metal world came together and showed how well-loved and respected Chi was by fans, friends, fellow musicians and everyone else in the music industry, and it is perhaps fitting in a way that *Eros*, which features the final recordings of Chi's work, has still never seen the light of day.

After taking some time out and then returning to touring, Deftones announced in 2015 that they had begun work on their next album, and *Gore* followed in the first quarter of 2016 – debuting at number 2 in the US and, maybe more surprisingly, number 5 in the UK. Again, containing an experimental sound that included some space rock elements, lead single 'Prayers/Triangles' represented *Gore* perfectly, before the dreamy stomp of 'Phantom Bride' revealed itself as a spine-tingling rocker equal in both heaviness and melodicism.
In 2020, *Ohms* found Deftones to be on top form once again, such stomps as 'Urantia', 'The Spell of Mathematics' and 'The Link is Dead' proving the band are still way ahead of everyone else; and to celebrate the twentieth anniversary of *White Pony*, the album was re-released under the title *Black Stallion* – comprising remixes from the likes of Linkin Park's Mike Shinoda and The Cure's Robert Smith.

Always evolving, Deftones have now been around for over three decades and there is something magical in every record the band puts out, confirming them to be one of the most intelligent and consistent metal bands there has ever been.

Killer Cuts – 'My Own Summer (Shove It)', 'Change (In the House of Flies)'

Disturbed

Years Active: 1994-2011, 2015-
Location: Chicago, Illinois, USA
Main era line-up: David Draiman (vocals), Dan Donegan (guitar), Steve Kmak/John Moyer (bass), Mike Wengren (drums)
Albums: The Sickness (2000), Believe (2002), Ten Thousand Fists (2005), Indestructible (2008), Asylum (2010), Immortalized (2015), Evolution (2018)

Disturbed may have been born in the mid-1990s, but it wasn't until the year 2000 when they signed with Giant Records and started to put the metal word on notice. Releasing the game-changing debut record, *The Sickness,* which peaked at 29 on the *Billboard* 200, it was an album that spent 103 weeks on the chart. Helped in part by the massive nu metal classics, 'Down with the Sickness' and 'Stupify', as well as 'Voices' and 'The Game', people were introduced to David Draiman's venomous lyrics of abuse, depression and isolation, and *The Sickness* quickly spread to listeners worldwide, as even today, the album remains Disturbed's best selling – currently certified as 4x platinum.

The sophomore album, *Believe,* followed in 2002 and it cruised straight in at number 1 in America, and later it went double platinum. Featuring a greater emphasis on melodic dynamics compared to its predecessor, the singles 'Prayer', 'Remember', and the frantic 'Liberate' showed a step up in songwriting ability, although the rawness of the band's debut was slightly missed by hardcore fans. Disturbed headlined the Music as a Weapon II Tour in 2003 with Chevelle, Taproot and Ünloco also on the bill, before bassist Steve Kmak was fired and replaced by John Moyer.

Ten Thousand Fists came out in 2005, again going straight in at number 1 in the US after selling over 238,000 copies in its very first week. It featured more of the same crushing alt metal with anthemic choruses, and highlights came in the form of 'Stricken', 'Just Stop', and a cover of Genesis' classic, 'Land of Confusion'. With another platinum-selling record under their belt, the band headlined Music as a Weapon III, this time taking along Flyleaf, Corey Taylor's Stone Sour, and Nonpoint, as well as topping the bill for Ozzfest 2006; and after relentless touring, the band headed back into the studio to write and record their next opus; which arrived in June 2008. *Indestructible* made it Disturbed's third album in a row to debut at the top of the *Billboard* 200. 'Inside the Fire' and 'Perfect Insanity' were early singles – in fact, the latter of the two was originally written before *The Sickness* all the way back in the late 1990s. The album's title track and 'The Night' were also released as promos, and by April 2009, *Indestructible* had received platinum certification.

In March of the following year, *The Sickness* was remastered and re-released, with additional B-sides 'God of the Mind' and 'A Welcome Burden' joining the original tracklisting, and later in 2010, *Asylum* became Disturbed's fourth record in a row to hit number 1. 'Another Way to Die' and 'The Animal' were two of four strong singles put out and Disturbed later co-headlined Music as a Weapon V with nu metal heroes Korn, in 2011. Then in July of the same year, the band surprised everyone by announcing an impending hiatus, which would take place after finishing up their US tour, which was running through to October. What seemed like a swansong at the time, a B-sides compilation album was released under the title of *The Lost Children,* which included excellent covers of Faith No More's 'Midlife Crisis' and Judas Priest's 'Living After Midnight', although the record only peaked at 13 in the US.

It would be almost four years before Disturbed would return, when in June 2015 and quite frankly out of nowhere the quartet announced they had already written and recorded a brand-new album. First came the release of the video for the lead single, 'The Vengeful One', and the accompanying sixth studio album *Immortalized* bolted out the gate in August. Unsurprisingly, the album went straight to number 1 in the US (8 in the UK wasn't bad either) and it featured an extraordinary cover of Simon & Garfunkel's 'The Sound of Silence', which would, around its time of release as a single, be played on radio stations that never would have considered playing Disturbed ever before. On Spotify alone, the cover has amassed over 475,000,000 streams since its release.

Led by the hugely popular Draiman, whose distorted vocal style and diverse baritone range set him apart from his contemporaries, Disturbed wasn't just one of the biggest bands of the nu metal era – they became one of the biggest bands in all of heavy metal. Their latest album, however, 2018 release, *Evolution*, saw Disturbed take a softer turn with radio friendly active rock anthems which still went down well with the majority of the band's humungous fan base.

Killer Cuts – 'Down with the Sickness', 'Stupify'

Dope

Years Active: 1997-

Location: New York City, New York, USA

Main era line-up: Edsel Dope (vocals), 'Virus' (lead guitar), Acey Slade (rhythm guitar), Sloane Jentry (bass), Racci Shay/Preston Nash (drums), Simon Dope (keyboards)

Albums: Felons and Revolutionaries (1999), Life (2001), Group Therapy (2003), American Apathy (2005), No Regrets (2009), Blood Money, Part 1 (2016)

Dope hit the ground running when they were signed to Flip Records by Jordan Schur and released their debut album *Felons and Revolutionaries* in 1999. Distributed via Flip/Epic, it remains the band's best-selling album to this day by moving over 236,000 copies, and it introduced the metal world to a dreadlocked, almost gothic-looking frontman in Edsel Dope, who became idolised by the band's cult following. The industrial metal album included a hard rock cover of the N.W.A. hip-hop classic, 'Fuck Tha Police', and a later re-release saw Dope cover Dead Or Alive's 'You Spin Me Right Round (Like A Record)', which was also featured on the *American Psycho* movie soundtrack. As well as the covers, original track, 'Debonaire', earned the band equal exposure with its inclusion on the *Scream 3* soundtrack and latterly on the first instalment of *The Fast and Furious* movie franchise. Before the release of their second album, Dope toured with the likes of shock rock extraordinaire Alice Cooper and nu metal heavyweight Kid Rock, and then in 2001, *Life* announced itself by focusing on a more accessible hard rock sound. Rap metal verses and infectious choruses galore, singles such as 'Now or Never' and 'Slipping Away' saw Dope attempting to break into the mainstream, and although the band had gone through some line-up changes, the latest incarnation sounded extremely cohesive and bang on form.

2003 album, *Group Therapy,* featured was more of the same, released via Artemis Records after the band had parted ways with Epic. The infectious 'Bitch' and fan favourite 'I Am' were strong singles, and Edsel and his group of ghoulish rockers showcased a softer side on tracks such as 'Sing' and 'Easier', as they appeared to be heading further into an alternative rock direction. That preconception was shown to be mistaken however when their 2005 effort, *American Apathy,* hit the shelves. Containing the aggressiveness of *Felons and Revolutionaries* with the industrial metal formula apparently returning, 'Always' was a great choice of lead single, while a cover of Depeche Mode's 'People Are People' was also a nice inclusion. *American Apathy w*ould go on to sell over 100,000 copies in the US before Dope's fifth album, *No Regrets,* launched in 2008. Debuting at 88 on the *Billboard* 200 – which made it the band's highest-ever charting record – *No Regrets a*gain featured heavy influences, and raging numbers such as 'Violence' and '6-6-Sick' showed the band's intention of creating some violent rock. A decent rendition of the well-covered 'Rebel Yell' went down a treat, and for a long time it seemed that *No Regrets* might be the last we would hear from Dope; but that was until 2013, when a teaser for a brand-new song was released ('Drug Music'), and it was followed by a new single the following year titled 'Selfish'.

Edsel then confirmed that *Blood Money Part 1* would be the name of Dope's upcoming sixth studio record, but before that, a reunion tour with the classic line-up of Edsel, Acey Slade, Virus and Racci Shay took place in 2015 and it led to them releasing their first live album in 2016 – recorded in Moscow, Russia.

Dope released their already promised sixth album, *Blood Money Part 1,* in October 2016 via eOne Entertainment. Containing elements of Dope's various sounds from the last twenty years, 'Hold On' and 'Razorblade Butterfly' harked back to their *Life* record, while the rest of the album included the industrial metal edge of *American Apathy* and *No Regrets*; serving as a friendly reminder of just how good Dope has been throughout the nu metal movement and beyond.

Killer Cuts – 'Debonaire', 'Bitch'

Downer

Years Active: 1993-2001
Location: Orange County, California, USA
Main era line-up: John Scott (vocals), Aaron Silberman (guitar), Jed Hathaway (bass), Tracy Sledge (drums)
Albums: Wrestling with Jesus (1997), Downer (2001)

Downer fused hardcore with metal and catered for more than just a nu metal audience upon their mid-1990s inception. A 1995 EP, *Pinman*, and a 1997 album, *Wrestling with Jesus*, provided Downer with some solid material to tour with, engaging crowds as they shared stages with a mixture of heavy artists from Ignite and Earth Crisis, to Korn and Deftones. A record deal with Roadrunner Records followed, and Downer released their Bob Marlette-produced major label debut in 2001. 'Weed Eater', 'Flex' and 'Mud Bath' underlined Downer's meaty prowess. However, the self-titled affair received generally underwhelming reviews and sold poorly. For one reason or another, Downer called it quits not long after the album's release, becoming another band who was finished before they ever really had a chance to get started.

Killer Cuts – 'Weed Eater', 'Flex'

Downset

Years Active: 1989-2009, 2013-
Location: Los Angeles, California, USA
Main era line-up: Rey Oropeza (vocals), Brian Schwager (guitar), Rogelio Lozano (guitar), James Morris (bass), Christopher Lee/Chris Hamilton (drums)
Albums: Downset. (1994), Do We Speak a Dead Language? (1996), Check Your People (2000), Universal (2004), One Blood (2014)

A band that formed in the late 1980s under the name Social Justice, Downset arose in 1992 and moved away from their hardcore punk origins in favour of some tasty rap and funk metal. Praised for their social awareness lyrical content, a self-titled album emerged later in 1992 through Mercury Records, before the commercially successful sophomore, *Do We Speak a Dead Language?* came out in 1996. 'Empower' and 'Pocket Full of Fatcaps' were singles from the record, and then Downset released the albums *Check Your People* (featuring the powerful opening track, 'Fallen Off') via Epitaph in 2000, and *Universal* on the indie label Hawino Records, in 2004. The LA crew headlined the second stage of Ozzfest in 1997 and over the years, they also toured with Korn, Linkin Park, Pantera and Slayer, before returning in 2014 with their fifth record, *One Blood*.

Killer Cuts – 'Anger', 'Empower'

Downthesun

Years Active: 1994-2003
Location: Kansas City, Missouri/Des Moines, Iowa, USA
Main era line-up: Anthony Stevens (vocals), Aaron Peltz (vocals), Bruce Swink (guitar), Lance Collier (bass), Danny Spain (drums), Nathan Church (keyboards, samples)
Albums: Downthesun (2002)

Downthesun arose in 1999 and, through their friendships with various members of Slipknot, the alternative metal maniacs signed to Maggot Recordings in 2001. Line-up changes would soon take their toll before the updated version of the band briefly signed with London-Sire. However, the label would soon fold and pave the way for Roadrunner Records to come calling in 2002. Downthesun put out their self-titled debut later in the same year, with the song 'Medicated' chosen as the lead single. The rest of the tracklist (like 'Medicated', and the album highlight, 'We All Die') had death metal elements incorporated into the band's brash sound, but as Downthesun appeared to be on an upward trajectory, a mass exodus of members led to the band officially calling it quits by the end of 2003.

Killer Cuts – 'Medicated', 'We All Die'

Dreadlock Pussy

Years Active: 1997-2006
Location: Roermond, the Netherlands
Main era line-up: Patrick Smeets (vocals), Ferry Duijsens (guitar, vocals), Bart Gooren (guitar), Jaap Melman (bass), Twan Bakker (drums)
Albums: Sharp Instead v1 (1999), Sharp Instead v2- Next Attack (2000), Tsumi (2002), Palm Bridge Rd. (2005)

A popular band nationally, Dreadlock Pussy came out of the Netherlands in 1997 with some groovy rapcore which showed that Europe was cottoning on to what America was doing. During their time, the band supported Machine Head, Hed PE, Disturbed and Rammstein, and released the albums *Sharp Instead, Tsumi,* and *Palm Bridge Rd*. The strong singles 'Leaves of Grass', 'T Minus' and 'Jacob's Ladder' all had accompanying music videos, and without ever really venturing outside of their homeland, Dreadlock Pussy disbanded after one final show in Eindhoven, in 2006.

Killer Cuts – 'Leaves of Grass', 'T Minus'

Drowning Pool

Years Active: 1996-
Location: Dallas, Texas, USA
Main era line-up: Dave Williams (vocals), C.J. Pierce (guitar), Stevie Benton (bass), Mike Luce (drums)
Albums: Sinner (2001), Desensitized (2004), Full Circle (2007), Drowning Pool (2010), Resilience (2013), Hellelujah (2016)

Drowning Pool may have powered into the mainstream in 2001 but it was actually in 1999 when vocalist Dave Williams joined the then-instrumental trio. Getting their first break by touring with Hed PE and Kittie, the band also earned enough radio play from demo tracks to catch the eye of Wind-Up Records. Alternative metal anthems such as the mosh pit tribute of 'Bodies' and 'Tear Away' were incredibly popular on the back of being used in *WWE* Wrestling, and Drowning Pool's colossal debut album, *Sinner* – which went straight in at 14 on the *Billboard* 200 upon its release on 5 June – hit platinum certification by the end of 2001.

At this time, Drowning Pool was one of the hottest acts on the planet, but on 14 August 2002, lead singer Dave Williams was tragically found dead on his tour bus during the band's stint on Ozzfest. The cause was later confirmed as an undiagnosed heart condition, but the shock and sadness caused by his untimely passing within the nu metal community showed just how loved Dave Williams was both as a musician, but more importantly as a human being.

Intent on continuing with the incredible start which Williams had helped make possible, C.J. Pierce (guitar), Stevie Benton (bass) and Mike Luce (drums) pressed on and hired Jason 'Gong' Jones as Drowning Pool's new vocalist in 2003. Debuting on the sophomore record, *Desensitized,* in 2004, the band focused on a more accessible hard rock sound as opposed to the abrasive alternative metal heard on *Sinner*, and it was no surprise that the album failed to hit the heights of what came before it. 'Step Up' was a popular single, however, and the album still reached 17 on the *Billboard* chart, and other than the raucous album track, 'Bringing Me Down', there wasn't much else to write home about. In another bizarre twist of events, Jones left the band not long after the album's release-citing personal and musical differences; and once again, Drowning Pool was on the hunt for a new singer.

Leaving his original band to join the Pool in 2005, Soil's Ryan McCombs was a popular choice of replacement, and the metal community's first taste of hearing him at the helm came in the form of 'No More', which made its way onto the

Saw III movie soundtrack. After previously parting company with Wind-Up, Drowning Pool signed with Eleven Seven Music and released their third album in August 2007 – titled *Full Circle*. McCombs's instantly recognisable vocal snarl was evident from the off and highlights included the anthemic 'Shame', 'Soldiers' (dedicated to the US Army), 'Reason I'm Alive' (written by Mötley Crüe's Nikki Sixx) and the haunting ballad, '37 Stitches'. Becoming the first vocalist to appear on more than one Drowning Pool record, McCombs returned for a self-titled effort in 2011 where single releases included 'Feel Like I Do', 'Turn so Cold', and the groovy 'Let the Sin Begin'; and compared to *Full Circle* only reaching number 64 in the charts stateside, *Drowning Pool* fared much better this time around by peaking at 35.

Appearing as if Drowning Pool had found a consistent headspace, McCombs then left the band later in 2011, returning to his original position in Soil where anniversary shows were on the cards. Relatively unknown Jasen Moreno took over vocal duties, debuting on the 2013 album *Resilience* – which couldn't have been a more apt title for said record; and then following it up with 2016 album, *Hellelujah.*

Sadly, we will never know how big the Dallas four-piece could have become had it not been for the tragic and untimely death of Dave Williams. It appeared that the band was destined for greatness on the back of *Sinner*, a debut album which infected people's hearts and minds with a refreshing slab of nu metal unlike anything else that was coming out at that time. 'Bodies' remains one of the most iconic songs to come out of the whole nu metal era, and that tells you all you need to know about Drowning Pool's skill for crafting heavy and extremely catchy metal songs.

Killer Cuts – 'Bodies', 'Tear Away'

Dry Cell

Years Active: 1998-2009
Location: Los Angeles, California, USA
Main era line-up: Jeff Gutt (vocals, rhythm guitar), Danny Hartwell (lead guitar), Judd Guenbaum (bass), Brandon Brown (drums)
Albums: Disconnected (2002)

Still heavily talked about today even though they only semi-officially released one studio album, Beyond Control started out in 1998 and after earning the attention of Jeff Blue – a Warner Brothers A&R and the man who discovered Linkin Park, the band signed a development deal and enlisted Jeff Gutt at their new vocalist; before changing their name to Impúr.

Setting to work on their debut album in the summer of 2002 and with planned release dates coming and going with no sign of the finished product, the now known Dry Cell was released from their Warner contract after a heated argument between the label and one of the band members' fathers. Limited quantities of the album, *Disconnected,* were sold at the Locobazooka Festival in August, with advanced copies containing different artwork to that being distributed soon after, and the track 'Body Crumbles' remains Dry Cell's most recognised song. Earning the band decent exposure from its inclusion on the *Queen of the Damned* movie soundtrack, 'Body Crumbles' still packs a punch today, while 'Slip Away' and 'So Long Ago' were also used on various other platforms to promote the band. *Disconnected* would later be released on iTunes some seven years after its initial inception, which was a relief for many fans due to the physical CD becoming somewhat of a highly sought-after item.

In 2004, Jeff Gutt left the band before returning in 2006 and then walking away again in 2009; ultimately spelling the end for Dry Cell. In early 2010, *The Dry Cell Collection* turned up on iTunes and featured plenty of unreleased material to keep fans relatively content, and at the end of 2017, Gutt was announced as the new frontman for grunge icons, Stone Temple Pilots.

Killer Cuts – 'Body Crumbles', 'Slip Away'

Dry Kill Logic

Years Active: 1995-
Location: Westchester County, New York, USA
Main era line-up: Cliff Rigano (vocals), Scott Thompson/Jason Bozzi (guitar), David Kowatch (bass), Phil Arcuri (drums)
Albums: The Darker Side of Nonsense (2001), The Dead and Dreaming (2004), Of Vengeance and Violence (2006)

Forming under the name Hinge in 1995, this noisy quartet released two EPs (*Cause Moshing is Good Fun* and *Elemental Evil*) and opened shows for System of a Down and Coal Chamber before signing to the mighty Roadrunner Records. Due to a recording studio already owning the copyright to the name 'Hinge', Dry Kill Logic was born not long after signing their major label deal and by the summer of 2001, they had released their first record, *The Darker Side of Nonsense*.

The visceral vocal growls of Cliff Rigano were backed up by punishing metallic fury from the guitar and bass work of Scott Thompson and Dave Kowatch respectively, while Phil Arcuri's huge drum sections rounded off a devastating addition to the nu metal scene as Dry Kill Logic earned exposure from their 'Nightmare' single and the album track, 'Give Up, Give In, Lie Down' – which featured Primer 55 duo J-Sin and Bobby Burns. Global tours followed with fellow label mates Ill Nino and Spineshank, as well as the feisty felines in Kittie, and although *The Darker Side of Nonsense* went on to sell over 100,000 copies, Dry Kill Logic split from Roadrunner at the end of 2002 due to the label reportedly wanting a more commercial sound for the band's next record.

Via Psychodrama Music Group, *The Dead and Dreaming* followed in 2004 and it was led by the colossal single, 'Paper Tiger', which mixed heavy groove-laden metal with an incredibly catchy and melodic chorus. The album appeared to show the band going into metalcore territory, which Killswitch Engage and

Trivium were bringing firmly into the public eye around this time. However, Dry Kill Logic continued touring with nu metal bands such as Hed PE, Drowning Pool and Fear Factory.

A third album again featured a metalcore edge as 2006 effort, *Of Vengeance and Violence,* maintained the band's shift away from nu metal, but this was to be Dry Kill Logic's last release for some time as a period of inactivity pretty much confirmed the band were no longer together. Over the last couple of years, Dry Kill Logic has been putting out some strong singles ('Vices' and 'Don't See ghosts'), and it appears there may be more to come soon.

Killer Cuts – 'Nightmare', 'Paper Tiger'

Earshot

Years Active: 1999-
Location: Los Angeles, California, USA
Main era line-up: Wil Martin (vocals, guitar), Mike Callahan (guitar), Scott Kohler/Johnny Sprague (bass), Dieter Hartmann/Chas Stumbo (drums)
Albums: Letting Go (2002), Two (2004), The Silver Lining (2008)

Earshot began just before the new millennium but their flirtation with the mainstream came after signing with Warner Bros. and releasing their debut album, *Letting Go,* in 2002. 'Get Away' received significant airplay – reaching number 4 on the Active Rock Chart and remaining in the Top 100 for over a year, while 'Not Afraid' was a minor hit which had a strong accompanying promo video. 'Headstrong' was added to *The Queen of the Damned* movie soundtrack, and Earshot would earn further and welcome exposure when they went on tour with the likes of Staind, Kid Rock and Stone Temple Pilots.

2004 saw their second album, *Two,* get its release. 'Wait' was a breakthrough hit even though it didn't chart as successfully as 'Get Away', but it appealed to the mainstream by showcasing the band's intent on writing catchy hard rock/post-grunge anthems. Following in the same footsteps, *The Silver Lining* maintained Earshot's consistency upon its release in 2008 via Indegoot/Fontana/Universal. Only one single was officially put out – the made-for-radio 'MisSunderstood', but other strong songs such as 'Closer' and 'Don't Hate Me' showed that although there were some new band members on board for album number three, Earshot was still a force to be reckoned with. A new single titled 'The Ugly Truth' would be freely released through the band's official website in 2009, but it wouldn't be until 2014 that any further material would surface.

An EP titled *Aftermath* launched in May and was led by the singles 'Now That It's Over' and 'Let Me', and on the first day of this year, Earshot released their first original material in almost seven years in the form of the rousing single, 'Been a Long Time'.

Killer Cuts – 'Not Afraid', 'Wait'

Earthtone9

Years Active: 1998-2002, 2010-
Location: Nottingham, England
Main era line-up: Karl Middleton (vocals), Owen Packard (guitar), Joe Roberts (guitar), Dave Anderson (bass), Simon Hutchby (drums)
Albums: Lo-def(inition) Discord (1998), Off Kilter Enhancement (1999), Arc'tan'gent (2000), IV (2013)

After signing to Copro Records in 1998, earthtone9 released their major-label debut, *lo-def(inition) discord,* in the same year – consisting of tracks from earlier demos as well as a handful of newer recordings. The 1999 album, *Off Kilter Enhancement,* was a critical triumph despite its moderate sales. Showcasing a combination of alternative and progressive metal with softer textures and dynamic arrangements, the quintet earned quite a name for themselves in the British metal scene through their hard work and live performances. After their *Arc'tan'gent* album was released in 2000, the band attempted to secure a record deal in America in the hope their sound would suit the nu metal explosion that was firmly in motion at this time; however, a deal failed to materialise and in 2002, earthtone9 sadly announced their split. A reunion took place in 2010 and a new album followed in 2013 in the form of *IV*, where the song 'Preacher' reminded everyone exactly why earthtone9 was such a special and intriguing band in the first place.

Killer Cuts – 'Tat Twan Asi', 'Evil Crawling I'

Element Eighty

Years Active: 1998-2006, 2007-2010
Location: Tyler, Texas, USA
Main era line-up: David Galloway (vocals), Matt Woods (guitar), 'Roon' (bass), Ryan Carroll (drums)
Albums: Mercuric (2001), Element Eighty (2003), The Bear (2005)

Element Eighty mixed hard rock and alternative metal and self-released their first record, *Mercuric,* in 2001. Doing fairly well on the independent circuit, the four-piece soon caught the attention of Universal/Republic in 2003, and after signing a deal, they quickly put out their second album, which was self-titled, in October. 'Broken Promises' was added to the video game soundtrack for *Need for Speed: Underground*, and it also peaked just inside the Top 40 of the Mainstream Rock Tracks chart; while other standouts on *Element Eighty* were the popular stomps of 'Bloodshot' and 'Texas Cries'. Tours with the likes of Sevendust, Mudvayne, Ill Nino and 40 Below Summer enhanced the band's reputation across America, but at the end of 2004, Element Eighty split from Universal after not receiving the push they believed they deserved. Choosing to release their third record, *The Bear,* through their own Texas Cries Records label, limited distribution thwarted

Element Eighty from getting their new music out to a wider audience and by the end of 2007, the band was no more.

Killer Cuts – 'Broken Promises', 'Texas Cries'

Endo

Years Active: 1995-2007, 2012-2013
Location: Miami, Florida, USA
Main era line-up: Gil Bitton (vocals), Eli Parker (guitar), 'Zelick' (bass), Joel Suarez (drums)
Albums: Evolve (v3.0) (2001), Songs for the Restless (2003)

Endo shared stages with the likes of Static-X, Foo Fighters and Megadeth before signing to DV8/Columbia at the turn of the new millennium. Releasing their major-label debut in 2001 in the form of *Evolve,* the album showcased some explosive rap metal. 'Suffer' had an accompanying music video and the album track, 'Malice', was added to the *Dracula 2000* movie soundtrack before Endo ditched the rap metal sound for their second album, *Songs for the Restless*, which followed in 2003. Presenting hard rock and post-grunge anthems, lead single 'Simple Lies' was the high point and it also featured on the *Daredevil* movie soundtrack. To promote the album, Endo played Ozzfest (2003) and also opened up for heavyweights such as Korn, Marilyn Manson and Chevelle. After parting company with DV8/Columbia in 2004, the band had talked about a third record being in the works, but nothing came of it and, in 2007, Endo officially disbanded. In 2012, the band began playing shows in the Miami area once again and a new song titled 'Get Low' was uploaded to their YouTube page. However, Endo would part ways again the following year.

Killer Cuts – 'Suffer', 'Simple Lies'

Evanescence

Years Active: 1995-
Location: Little Rock, Arkansas, USA
Main era line-up: Amy Lee (vocals, keyboards), Ben Moody (guitar), John LeCompt (guitar, backing vocals), Will Boyd (bass), David Hodges (piano, keyboards), Rocky Gray (drums)
Albums: Fallen (2003), The Open Door (2006), Evanescence (2011), Synthesis (2017), The Bitter Truth (2021)

Upon their initial formation, Evanescence could never have imagined just how much of a global phenomenon their brand of gothic rock would become in the years to follow. From Little Rock, Arkansas, and led by the multi-talented Amy Lee, Evanescence released a number of EPs before their demo album *Origins*, which was limited to 2,500 copies, made music moguls stand up and take notice.

Signing to Wind-Up Records, their major-label debut *Fallen* stormed into the charts in 2003 by debuting at seven on the *Billboard* 200 – eventually peaking at 3 in June of the same year. The gigantic single, 'Bring Me to Life', featured 12 Stones vocalist Paul McCoy, and reached number 1 on multiple singles charts worldwide, having earned early recognition from when it was used as a *WWE* pay-per-view theme song.

Interestingly, Lee would reveal in 2021 that Wind-Up originally wanted Evanescence to be the 'female Linkin Park' by adding a male vocalist to the band as a full-time member. Refusing to bow to record label pressure, the already-signed deal was temporarily scrapped until Wind-Up came crawling back and pushed the band as the female-fronted rockers the world came to know and love. *Fallen* claimed top spot in eleven countries (including the UK) and the following singles, 'Going Under', Everybody's Fool' and the tearjerker of 'My Immortal', continued the band's chart dominance. Eventually going 7x platinum in the US, Evanescence received a staggering five Grammy nominations- winning two in the Best New Artist and Best Hard Rock Performance categories, in 2004.

In October 2003, guitarist Ben Moody left the band and was replaced by Terry Balsamo from Cold, and he featured on the 2004 live album, *Anywhere But Home,* which was recorded in Paris, France. Will Boyd left his bass duties in 2006, with ex-Revolution Smile member, Tim McCord, taking over; and in September of the same year, sophomore album *The Open Door* was unleashed. Debuting at number 1 on the *Billboard* 200, it was certified platinum within a month of its release thanks in part to the singles, 'Call Me When You're Sober', 'Sweet Sacrifice', 'Lithium' and 'Good Enough'. Confirming that demand was still there for catchy gothic rock, which was suitable for the mainstream, *The Open Door* would go on to sell over five million copies worldwide and reinforce Evanescence's global domination.

With Lee's vocals contributing to the moody, gothic, and latterly symphonic rock sound, the Arkansas band had played their part in releasing some of the many highlights which nu metal spawned, and a return in 2011 saw them put out their long-awaited self-titled third record. Predictably cruising straight to number 1 on the *Billboard* 200, the tried and tested formula of their previous albums shone through with the raucous 'What You Want', the weepy ballad 'My Heart is Broken' and the spine-tingling 'Lost in Paradise' providing just some of the high points.

With more changes to the line-up, Evanescence once again returned in 2016 with the B-sides compilation album, *Lost Whispers*, which was made available for streaming and download only (until it was released on vinyl as part of the band's *The Ultimate Collection* LP set). Then, towards the end of 2017, the incredible *Synthesis* became the band's fourth record, put out via BMG. Containing reworked versions of previous songs, orchestral arrangements and electronics were also added to make the likes of 'Bring Me to Life', 'My Immortal' and 'Lithium' sound all the more haunting and vibrant. Two new songs also made their way onto the tracklist- 'Hi-Lo' and the sensational 'Imperfection', which showed that Evanescence was still relevant and had an artistic edge capable of blowing much of their competition out of the water. Having just released another album in the form of *The Bitter Truth*, which went straight to number one once again in America, Evanescence remain one of the most successful bands to come out of the nu metal movement.

Killer Cuts – 'Bring Me to Life', 'My Immortal'

Factory 81

Years Active: 1997-2003
Location: Detroit, Michigan, USA
Main era line-up: Nathan Wallace (vocals), Bill Schultz (guitar), Kevin Lewis (bass), Andy Cyrulnik (drums)
Albums: Mankind (1999), Factory 81 (2019)- digital upload

Factory 81 deployed a variety of hardcore punk, metal, jazz fusion and world music elements into their sound. However, they would only ever release one official album. *Mankind* was first put out via Medea Records in 1999 before being reissued a year later through Motown/Universal; and then it got a third release by indie label, Mojo. 'Nanu' was the sole single pushed to try and promote the record, although 'Peace Officer' also deserves a special listen. The band was included on the compilation album, *Take a Bite Outta Rhyme: A Rock Tribute to Rap*, where Factory 81 covered Cypress Hill's 'Insane in the Brain', and in 2000 they would earn some exposure through touring with Mudvayne, Kittie and Apartment 26. Having then signed to Jive Records, Factory 81 would disband in 2003.

Killer Cuts – 'Nanu', 'Peace Officer'

Fallen To

Years Active: 2001-2004
Location: Cornwall, England
Main era line-up: James Norris (vocals), Christian Norris (guitar), 'Chinn' (guitar), Iain Moir (bass), Jez Marshall (drums)
Albums: The Mark (2001), Which Side of the Line? (2003)

A rap-tinged metal quintet who seemed destined for a successful career from the off, Fallen To quickly gained significant exposure on *MTV2* with their debut single, 'No Allies'. Distinctively heavy but with an edge capable of bothering the mainstream, 'No Allies' carried Fallen To into their debut album, *The* Mark, which was released through Rough Justice in 2002.

Also spawning a decent second single in the form of 'Bovine Calm', as well as the melodic tour de force of 'Dark Wounds', *The Mark* received critical acclaim and it appeared these likeable Brits could do no wrong. A follow-up release titled

Which Side of the Line? contained some new material as well as remixes and acoustic takes of tracks from the album before – split over two discs where one demonstrated the band's heavier side and the other leaned towards atmospheric and ambient musings. 'Smoke & Mirrors' and 'Lost No. 7' had accompanying music videos and then out of nowhere, Fallen To announced they were calling it a day. Leaving behind some shocked and upset fans, the band can take comfort in the fact that 'No Allies' remains one of the UK's premier nu metal anthems.

Killer Cuts – 'No Allies', 'Bovine Calm'

Fear Factory

Years Active: 1989-2006, 2009-
Location: Los Angeles, California, USA
Main era line-up: Burton C. Bell (vocals), Dino Cazares (guitar), Christian Olde Wolbers (bass), Raymond Herrera (drums)
Albums: Soul of a New Machine (1992), Demanufacture (1995), Obsolete (1998), Digimortal (2001), Archetype (2004), Transgression (2005), Mechanize (2010), The Industrialist (2012), Genexus (2015)

Fear Factory's early material ventured into death metal and grindcore territory, but it was with their third release, *Obsolete,* where the band introduced nu metal elements amongst a brutal slab of industrial metal. It also included the first use of 7-string guitars by Dino Cazares, giving a lower-toned sound that had not been heard on Fear Factory tracks prior to this. *Obsolete* was a concept album focusing on the future of mankind and how machines had taken over humanity, and to promote the record, Fear Factory toured with the likes of Spineshank, System of a Down, Hed PE and Static-X. *Obsolete* would go gold in the US with sales of over 750,000 copies and lead single, 'Resurrection', which was accompanied by a stunning promo video, saw Fear Factory creating a melodic and futuristic metal masterpiece (lead singer Burton C. Bell has reportedly called 'Resurrection' one of his favourite Fear Factory songs of all time). Goth rock hero, Gary Numan, would also appear on the record – singing on the album title track as well as on a cover of his own classic song, 'Cars', and 'Edgecrusher' also deserves an honourable mention as it remains one of the band's most popular songs today.

Digimortal followed in 2001, packed with industrial alternative metal, which contained a hugely accessible edge. B-Real of hip-hop superstars Cypress Hill appeared on the album track 'Back the Fuck Up', as Fear Factory followed other nu metal bands of that time by collaborating with hip-hop artists. Along with the pulsating lead single 'Linchpin' earning significant airplay, *Digimortal* reached a reputable 32 on the *Billboard* 200, but shortly after the *Digimortal* cycle, Fear Factory announced their split. Thankfully, within two years of their initial departure, they were back together and releasing *Archetype*, which returned to the band's heavier sound of old – leaving behind their period of nu metal-influenced anthems.

In the years since, Fear Factory has released further albums (*Transgression* in 2005, *Mechanize* in 2010, *The Industrialist* in 2012, and *Genexus* in 2015), before Bell would quit the band in 2020 after an apparent falling out with Cazares. One final album was released in 2021, having been reportedly recorded a couple of years before, and as it stands, that could be the last we hear from one of the most popular bands in all of heavy metal.

Killer Cuts – 'Edgecrusher', 'Resurrection'

Five Pointe O

Years Active: 1993-2003
Location: Joliet, Illinois, USA
Main era line-up: Daniel Struble (vocals), Eric Wood (guitar), Sharon Grzelinkski (guitar), Sean Pavey (bass), Tony Starcevich (drums), Casey Mejia (keyboards)
Albums: Untitled (2002)

Like so many others in the nu metal era, Five Pointe O only stuck around long enough to release one album, but it is an album that has truly stood the test of time. A six-piece entourage from Illinois, the band signed to Roadrunner Records off the back of two self-released EPs, and they brought a rap, scream and clean vocal concoction on top of some meaty riffs and subtle keys.

March 2002 saw Five Pointe O's self-titled debut come out and their one and only single, 'Double X Minus', received moderate airplay on the likes of *MTV2* and *Kerrang!* while the album track, 'The Infinity', would later be included on the *Resident Evil* movie soundtrack to enhance the band's notoriety a little more. Lead vocalist Daniel Struble, and guitarist, Sharon Grzelinski, announced their departure in 2003 and later got married, and although the rest of Five Pointe O vowed to continue, it wasn't long until they confirmed the band was over for good.

Killer Cuts – 'Double X Minus', 'The Infinity'

Flaw

Years Active: 1996-2004, 2006-
Location: Louisville, Kentucky, USA
Main era line-up: Chris Volz (vocals), Jason Daunt (guitar), Lance Arny (guitar), Ryan Juhrs (bass), Chris Ballinger (drums)
Albums: American Arrogance (1997), Flaw (1998), Through the Eyes (2001), Endangered Species (2004), Home Grown Sessions (2009), Divided We Fall (2016), Vol IV: Because of the Brave (2019)

Formed by Jason Daunt, Flaw rose to prominence on the back of the independently released albums, *American Arrogance* and *Flaw*, and then a strong EP titled *Drama*, which led to the band showcasing for some of the biggest record labels at New York's CGBG club.

After signing with Republic/Universal, the five-piece earned strong exposure from their major-label debut, *Through the Eyes*, which was recorded at Sound City studios and produced by David Bottrill. Arriving at the end of October 2001, the album launched the career of Chris Volz, who became revered for his melodic vocals and deeply personal lyrical content, and the record became an underground success with sales of over 150,000 copies. 'Payback' and 'Whole' were strong singles, and the powerful album tracks 'My Letter' and 'Only the Strong' (the latter of which featured on *The Scorpion King* movie soundtrack) became post-grunge classics-in-waiting.

Flaw returned in 2004 with their next album, *Endangered Species,* and it debuted at 42 on the *Billboard* 200. Daunt and drummer Chris Ballinger had departed the band by now, and although Micah Havertape had taken over on the drum kit, a replacement wasn't sought for Daunt. After some initial success with their sophomore release, Flaw was dropped by Universal and the four-piece confirmed their split. Volz went on to form Five.Bolt.Main before various Flaw reformations with the original line-up were attempted, and an independently released third record materialised in 2009 under the title *Home Grown Studio Sessions*. A deal was later penned with Pavement Entertainment which allowed a fourth record to come out in 2016 titled *Divided We Fall*, and after a tour with Dope and Motograter, an EP in 2017 was put out under the name *United We Stand*.

Constantly plagued by line-up changes and in-house fighting, Flaw continues on today with Volz being the only original member, however *Through the Eyes* remains one of nu metal's best albums – showing the band's true potential when all five members were on the same page and at their most creative.

Killer Cuts – 'Payback', 'Only the Strong'

From Zero

Years Active: 1998-2005
Location: Chicago, Illinois, USA
Main era line-up: Pauly Weiner (vocals), Peter Capizzi (guitar), Joe Pettinato (guitar), Rob Ruccia (bass), Johnny Dinu (drums)
Albums: One Nation Under (2001), My So-Called Life (2003)

Coming up alongside Soil in Chicago, From Zero's alt metal/hard rock direction saw them attempt to distance themselves from a lot of the rap metal which was coming out at the end of the 1990s. Building some momentum with an independently released EP in 1999, as well as support slots with Disturbed, Nothingface and Amen, From Zero would get their big break when they signed a deal with Arista Records and released their major-label debut in 2001. *One Nation Under* featured the strong singles of 'Check Ya' and 'Erase', as well as other tracks which had been re-recorded from the band's first EP, and although From Zero earned some decent coverage in certain parts of the US, nationwide success wasn't quite secured.

My So-Called Life followed in May 2003 and spawned the singles 'Sorry' and 'Fleeting Glimpse', and a cover of the Phil Collins classic 'I Don't Care Anymore' was also included on the album. Due to a lack of promotion by Arista the record sadly bombed, and less than a month after its release From Zero were dropped by their label. Two tracks were later put online which would have been included on a third record ('Middle of the Road' and 'My Own Destiny'), but by this time From Zero had already announced their split.

Killer Cuts – 'Check Ya', 'Erase'

Godhead

Years Active: 1994-2008
Location: Washington D.C., USA
Main era line-up: Jason C. Miller (vocals, guitar), Mike Miller (guitar), Ullrich Hepperlin (bass), James O'Connor (drums)
Albums: America Now (1994), Godhead (1995), Nothingness (1997), Power Tool Stigmata (1998), 2000 Years of Human Error (2001), Evolver (2003), The Shadow Line (2006), At the Edge of the World (2008)

Bringing some gothic-tinged industrial beats to the movement, Washington D.C. natives Godhead became the first and only band to sign to Marilyn Manson's short-lived Posthuman Records in 2000. Originally starting out in 1994, the quartet put out some independent releases as well as the acclaimed *Power Tool Stigmata* album in 1998, before Godhead broke through with *2000 Years of Human Error* at the turn of the new millennium. From the Nine Inch Nails-esque groove of 'The Reckoning' to their gloomy rendition of The Beatles' classic, 'Eleanor Rigby', the tracklist (which also saw Manson guest on 'Break You Down') helped *2000 Years* sell over 100,000 copies in the US. This newfound fame also caught the eye of Ozzy Osbourne, who gave Godhead the headline spot on the Levi stage of Ozzfest in 2001, while 'Eleanor Rigby' continued its strong rotation on *MTV2* and *Kerrang!* in the UK.

After the dissolution of Posthuman, the creepies from the capital penned a deal with Reality Entertainment in 2003, with whom they distributed another 100,000 plus seller in the form of *Evolver*. 'The Hate in Me' and 'Far Too Long' were singles that ensured Godhead's continued progression into mainstream territory, and Wayne Static turned up for a guest spot on the album track 'The Giveaway'.

Having left the band before *Evolver* and replaced by Static-X drummer, Ken Jay, James O'Connor took over from Jay for 2005 album, *The Shadow Line*, with high points coming in the form of 'Trapped in Your Lies' and 'Push'; however, O'Connor would leave the band again not long after its release. *At the Edge of the World* would prove to be Godhead's final studio album in 2008, although a remix record titled *The Shadow Realigned* emerged six years later. Including unreleased covers of Depeche Mode's 'Never Let Me Down Again' and 'God of

Thunder' by KISS, the album was designed to partner the original album, *The Shadow Line*.

Lead singer Jason Miller now focuses on country music, which seems a million miles away from what came before it, but sharing stages with nu metal's finest (Rammstein, Mudvayne and Orgy, for example) showed that Godhead were a welcome addition who backed up the hype raised by Marilyn Manson and latterly, Ozzy Osbourne.

Killer Cuts – 'The Reckoning', 'Eleanor Rigby'

Godsmack

Years Active: 1995-
Location: Lawrence, Massachusetts, USA
Main era line-up: Sully Erna (vocals, rhythm guitar), Tony Rombola (lead guitar), Robbie Merrill (bass), Shannon Larkin (drums)
Albums: Godsmack (1998), Awake (2000), Faceless (2003), IV (2006), The Oracle (2010), 1000hp (2014), When Legends Rise (2018)

One of the most consistent bands to rise up during the nu metal revolution, Godsmack independently released their first album, *All Wound Up*, but it would be remastered and re-released in 1998 and put out as a self-titled effort after the band had signed a huge deal with Universal/Republic Records. Containing a heavy/alternative metal sound which accommodated Sully Erna's throaty vocals, songs such as 'Whatever', 'Keep Away' and 'Bad Religion' helped to propel the record to 22 on the *Billboard* 200, and by December 2001 *Godsmack* had been certified a staggering 4x platinum.

Riding the waves of their major label debut, Godsmack played both Ozzfest and Woodstock in 1999, before touring Europe as direct support to metal masters Black Sabbath, and then a second album was unleashed at the end of October 2000 amongst a lot of hype and expectation. Selling 256,000 copies in its first week, *Awake* went straight to number 5 on the *Billboard* 200. The title track and 'Sick of Life' were frequently used in the mid-noughties for the US Navy's *Accelerate Your Life* commercials, while 'Greed' was another successful single. In another incredible feat, the album track, 'Vampires', earned a Grammy Award for 'Best Rock Instrumental' in 2001, and *Awake* would later be certified double platinum in the US.

Faceless followed in 2003 and sailed straight to number 1 on the *Billboard* 200, with the successful singles 'I Stand Alone' (which featured on *The Scorpion King* movie soundtrack) and 'Straight Out of Line' (which was also nominated for a Grammy in the 'Best Rock Performance' category) regularly featuring on the radio airwaves. A huge tour through America and Europe supporting Metallica followed before Godsmack switched things up a little and put out an acoustic EP (*The Other Side*) in 2004. Returning in 2006 with a new studio album, *IV* followed in the footsteps of *Faceless* by topping the *Billboard* 200 within a week of release. The lead single, 'Speak', probably had something to do with it, and later singles 'Shine Down' and 'The Enemy' kept the Boston mob fresh in people's minds.

With their ten-year anniversary just around the corner, a greatest hits compilation came out just in time for Christmas in 2007 *(Good Times, Bad Times ... Ten Years of Godsmack*) before the band took some time out to recharge their batteries. Thankfully returning in 2009, Godsmack supported Mötley Crüe on the hair metal legends' Crüe Fest 2 tour, before putting out the single 'Whiskey Hangover' ahead of entering the studio to work on their fifth record. *The Oracle* arrived in May 2010 and it became the band's third consecutive number 1 charting album. Harking back to Godsmack's heavier early years, the fist-pumping single 'Cryin' Like a Bitch' (reportedly written by Erna about Mötley Crüe's Nikki Sixx after a spat on the Crüe Fest 2 tour) was the standout track, while 'Love-Hate-Sex-Pain' and 'Saints and Sinners' were also strong promos. As with *IV*, *The Oracle* has since earned gold certification.

Tours with Disturbed and Staind ensued before Godsmack dropped a live album (*Live & Inspired*) which was recorded in 2010 at a show in Detroit, while a bonus disc accompanied the release, which featured cover songs such as 'Come Together' by The Beatles, and Metallica's 'Nothing Else Matters'.

In August 2014, Godsmack roared back with *1000hp* which debuted at number 3 in the US, and in 2016 they announced a deal with BMG – thus ending a long-standing relationship with Universal/Republic. In the first quarter of 2018, the band marked their intent to include more melody in their songs with the stunning 'Bulletproof', which whetted fans' appetites for Godsmack's newest studio album, *When Legends Rise* – released in May of the same year. Hard rock anthems aplenty, it remains Godsmack's last album release, but there is sure to be more to come from these Boston badasses in the future.

Killer Cuts – 'Awake', 'I Stand Alone'

Grade 8

Years Active: 1996-2008
Location: Los Angeles, California, USA
Main era line-up: Ryan Tooker (vocals), Dustin Tooker (guitar), Guy Couturier (bass), Scott Carneghi (drums)
Albums: Grade 8 (2003), Resurrection (2004)

A rap metal crew who signed to Lava Records in 2002, Grade 8 immediately set about working on their first album, which would follow in February 2003. A self-titled effort led by the popular single 'Brick by Brick' and a cover of Rare Earth's hit song 'Celebrate', a club tour followed with rising stars Spineshank in order to maintain Grade 8's elevation. A stint on the second stage of Ozzfest in 2003 was then cut short due to Lava reportedly refusing to fund the band's needs to get from city to city, so to make up for lost audiences, the quartet went out on a short tour with the rising Chimaira.

Disappointing album sales contributed to Lava later dropping Grade 8; however, they would return in the summer of 2004 with their appropriately titled second album, *Resurrection,* via Sound Barrier Records. A slightly darker alternative metal direction was shown on the title track, 'Demons' and 'Fallen Angel' especially, and then a period of inactivity followed which ultimately led to Grade 8 officially announcing their end through a MySpace blog in 2008.

Killer Cuts – 'Brick by Brick', 'Celebrate'

Guano Apes

Years Active: 1994-2006, 2009-
Location: Gottingen, Germany
Main era line-up: Sandra Nasic (vocals), Henning Rumenapp (guitar), Stefan Ude (bass), Dennis Poschwatta (drums)
Albums: Proud Like a God (1997), Don't Give Me Names (2000), Walking on a Thin Line (2003), Bel Air (2011), Offline (2014)

A fine export from Germany – within two years of Guano Apes' formation, the band won a 'local heroes' competition with their future fan favourite song, 'Open Your Eyes', as the quartet overcame a thousand other entrants. In October 1997, their debut album, *Proud Like a God,* was released via BMG and GUN/Supersonic Records to critical acclaim. Sandra Nasic led the line with her energetic vocal displays, and musically, Guano Apes fused together alternative metal, funk and rapcore to create crushing ensembles such as the popular singles 'Rain', 'Lord of the Boards', and the song that got them noticed in the first place, 'Open Your Eyes'. *Proud Like a God* would later go platinum in Germany and unsurprisingly, Guano Apes became somewhat of a national treasure.

Don't Give Me Names followed in May 2000 and gained gold certification, partly due to the hugely successful singles 'Dödel Up', 'No Speech', 'Living in a Lie'; and a cover of German synthpop band Alphaville's 'Big In Japan'. *Walking on a Thin Line* would be the Apes' last album for some time when in 2003, it went straight to number 1 on the German album chart; before earning another gold disc. A 'best of' collection (*Planet of the Apes*) followed at the end of 2004 before a final tour in early 2005 saw the band go on an indefinite hiatus upon its conclusion.

Sharing stages with the likes of Marilyn Manson, Linkin Park and Slipknot showed how highly thought of Guano Apes were within the nu metal community, and their first three albums remain strong favourites. The band has since returned with the albums *Bel Air* in 2011 and *Offline* in 2014, both of which saw a change in direction as Guano Apes ventured into pop rock territory.

Killer Cuts – 'Open Your Eyes', 'Rain'

Headplate

Years Active: 1993-
Location: Gothenburg, Sweden
Main era line-up: Magnus Klavborn (vocals), Daniel Granstedt (guitar), Hakan Skoger (bass), Niklas Osterlund (drums)
Albums: Bullsized (2000), Delicate (2002), Pieces (2003), 12-12-12 (2012)

Headplate originally began in 1993, but they didn't really become productive until 1999, when their Limp Bizkit-esque rapcore earned them a deal with Gain Productions. Debut album, ***Bullsized,*** was released in 2000 and spawned two singles – the title track and then the groovy 'Feel Like Porn', both of which had accompanying music videos before their standout track 'Jump the Bridge' followed in 2002. Included on the band's sophomore release, ***Delicate***, the album also included 'Retina', 'Breathing', and the explosive title track, and it is fair to say that had Headplate been an American act, their music would have grasped a much larger and wider demographic which in turn, would have elevated them to the level of many of their contemporaries.

A third album titled *Pieces* came in 2003, and in 2005 vocalist Magnus Klavborn left the band to join Swedish melodic death metal band, Engel. A fourth album emerged in 2012 (*12-12-12*) with a new frontman on board, but Headplate's main moments came in the early 2000s with rap metal of the finest European quality.

Killer Cuts – 'Feel Like Porn', 'Jump the Bridge'

Hed PE

Years Active: 1994-
Location: Huntington Beach, California, USA
Main era line-up: Jahred Gomes (vocals), Chad 'Chizard' Benekos (rhythm guitar), Wesley Geer (lead guitar), Mark 'Mawk' Young (bass), B.C. Vaught (drums), DJ Product (turntables, samples)
Albums: Hed PE (1997), Broke (2000), Blackout (2003), Only in Amerika (2004), Back 2 Base X (2006), Insomnia (2007), New World Orphans (2009), Truth Rising (2010), Evolution (2014), Forever! (2016), Stampede (2019), Class of 2020 (2020)

Also known as (hed) Planet Earth, (hed) p.e, and Hed PE, this is a band that has remained a constant throughout the nu metal movement and beyond, and they are also one of the more original bands to emerge from the scene, with a sonically diverse sound which incorporated hip-hop, reggae, ska and metal; on records where you simply had no idea what was going to come next.

Their self-titled debut album was released in 1997 through Jive Records and the singles 'Ground' and 'Serpent Boy' helped the accompanying record sell over 100,000 copies. Largely consisting of tracks that were originally included on their independent release, ***Church of Realities***, Hed PE quickly ascended then hit the jackpot with their sophomore effort, ***Broke,*** in 2000.

Featuring the massively popular track 'Bartender', as well as guest spots from System of a Down's Serj Tankian and Kittie's Morgan Lander on 'Feel Good', *Broke* literally broke Hed PE into the mainstream by peaking at 63 on the *Billboard* 200 and selling over 250,000 copies worldwide. Frontman Jahred Gomes was thrown into the spotlight as he proved himself to be a hugely talented and diverse vocalist, and in 2001 the band played Ozzfest and toured with Korn and Static-X; before they released another popular single in the form of 'Killing Time' – also taken from *Broke.*

Returning to the studio and writing their third record with the intention of ambushing the mainstream further, the resulting *Blackout* arrived in March 2003. Led by the title track single, which gained heavy rotation on both radio and TV, the album peaked at a very healthy 33 in the US before the band left Jive and signed with Koch Records ahead of their fourth opus, *Only in Amerika*, which hit in 2004. Hardcore punk and heavy metal elements were introduced for the first time, with 'Represent' being the sole single released from the record. Within two years Hed PE had switched to Suburban Noize Records and returned to their rap rock roots on *Back 2 Base X*, which ironically came out on the same day that Jive put out a compilation of the band's material which had been written while on said label – without Hed PE's consent it must be mentioned.

Insomnia followed in 2007, then *New World Orphans* in January 2009, and within eighteen months *Truth Rising*; which meant Hed PE had incredibly released four records in a little over six years, with over 60 tracks of new material coming over the course of that period. Hed PE was certainly a band that refused to rest on their laurels.

Moving to Pavement Entertainment in time for their ninth album, *Evolution*, Hed PE included more of a reggae fusion sound which would also remain prominent on *Forever!* in 2016, which was arguably Hed PE's strongest release in over a decade. A more hip-hop orientated *Stampede* dropped in 2019, however the tracks 'NOAPOLOGIES' and 'DIEANOTHERDAY' are up there with the band's best material, and in 2020, Gomes and his latest band members returned with *Class of 2020*, which turned up the guitars once more and helped promote the 20th anniversary of the release of *Broke*. As this book goes to press, a new EP is on the way in the form of *Sandmine*, which has been co-written by the highly talented Dutch guitarist and producer, Remy Dovianus.

Although Gomes remains the only original member, Hed PE has remained a consistent machine turning out quality albums more frequently than most, all the while producing solid rapcore that only they are capable of creating.

Killer Cuts – 'Bartender', 'Blackout'

Hoobastank

Years Active: 1994-

Location: Aguora Hills, California, USA

Main era line-up: Doug Robb (vocals, rhythm guitar), Dan Estrin (lead guitar), Markku

Lappalainen (bass), Chris Hesse (drums)
Albums: They Sure Don't Make Basketball Shorts Like They Used To (1998), Hoobastank (2001), The Reason (2003), Every Man for Himself (2006), For(n)ever (2009), Fight or Flight (2012), Push Pull (2018)

And the winner of the award for worst band name goes to…! Reportedly getting their name from a long-standing joke stemming from the mispronunciation of a street name by vocalist Doug Robb, Hoobastank rose to prominence after signing with Island Records in 2001. Their self-titled major-label debut arrived later in the year, containing a hard rock/post-grunge approach which also incorporated small nu metal influences. Spawning the huge introductory single, 'Crawling in the Dark', Hoobastank quickly broke into the mainstream by charting at 68 on *Billboard*'s Hot 100, number 3 on the Modern Rock chart, and 7 on the Mainstream Rock chart. A second single, 'Running Away', bettered its predecessor by peaking at 44 on the Hot 100 and 2 on the Modern Rock chart, while the album itself reached a high of 25 on the *Billboard* 200 and later went platinum in the US.

Next, Hoobastank recorded 'Losing My Grip' for *The Scorpion King* movie soundtrack and 'Right Before Your Eyes' for the *Daredevil* movie, and then came time to put out their second album, *The Reason,* in December 2003. Preceded by the lead single and moderate hit 'Out of Control', the album sold steadily to begin with, but the band themselves surely could never have predicted what would follow in 2004. First, they went out as main support to Linkin Park on the rap rockers' *Meteora* world tour at the turn of the New Year, before Hoobastank released the album title track as a single. A modern rock ballad that brought in many new fans due to its frequent rotation on rock and pop radio, 'The Reason' unsurprisingly became a worldwide hit and reached number 2 on the *Billboard* Hot 100, number 1 on the US and world Modern Rock charts, as well as 12 in the UK singles chart; while the song also helped the accompanying album re-climb the *Billboard* 200 all the way to number 3. 'Same Direction' and 'Disappear' followed as singles, and *The Reason* would eventually go twice platinum in the US and silver in the UK.

Seemingly anywhere and everywhere for the next year or so, Hoobastank then settled on a softer and more melodic rock orientation, and their third album, *Every Man for Himself,* underlined this in 2006. The band was also a trio for the first time after their bassist Markku Lappalainen had left in 2005, but the album still powered to number 12 on the *Billboard* 200 and spawned the popular singles 'If I Were You', 'Inside of You' and 'Born to Lead'. The fourth album, *For(n)ever,* came out in 2009 and reached 26 in the US, with the album track 'I Don't Think I Love You' finding its way onto the *Transformers: Revenge of the Fallen* soundtrack, and then an acoustic album was for some reason only released in Japan. Hoobastank's latest two releases *Fight or Flight* (2012) and *Push Pull* (2018), continue the band's steady momentum. However 'Crawling in the Dark' and 'The Reason' remain

Hoobastank's shining moments, and for a couple of years at least, they were one of the biggest bands in the world.

Killer Cuts – 'Crawling in the Dark', 'The Reason'

Human Waste Project

Years Active: 1992-1998
Location: Huntington Beach, California, USA
Main era line-up: Aimee Echo (vocals), Mike Tempesta (guitar), Jeff Schartoff (bass), Scott Ellis (drums)
Albums: E-Lux (1997)

In their early years, Human Waste Project opened up for the likes of Sublime, Helmet, Deftones and Korn around Los Angeles, before they went on to sign with Hollywood Records. Treks over to the UK gave the band arguably more publicity than in their native America, and when their debut album *E-lux* was released in June 1997, it earned the quartet a cult following. Produced by Ross Robinson, the record was a visceral slab of alternative metal that stood beside the latest material that Korn and Deftones had released; as the nu metal movement was beginning to gather pace. 'Powerstrip' and 'Disease' were the picks of the tracklisting, and with everything appearing to be in place for a strong assault, Echo would then leave the band, which ultimately caused Human Waste Project to call it a day in 1998.

Killer Cuts – 'Powerstrip', 'Disease'

Ill Nino

Years Active: 1998-
Location: Union City, New Jersey, USA
Main era line-up: Cristian Machado (vocals), Marc Rizzo (lead guitar), Jardel Martins Paisante (rhythm guitar), Lazaro Pina (bass), Dave Chavarri (drums), Roger Vasquez (percussion)
Albums: Revolution Revolucion (2001), Confession (2003), One Nation Underground (2005), Enigma (2008), Dead New World (2010), Epidemia (2012), Till Death, La Familia (2014)

Ill Nino brought a taste of Latin metal to the table after signing for Roadrunner and releasing their first album, *Revolution Revolucion,* in 2001. Playing the US Road Rage tour with Machine Head and Fear Factory, as well as Ozzfest in the same year, helped the sextet gain strong exposure, and with their combination of English and Spanish vocals gelling nicely with a largely melodic metal sound, the singles 'What Comes Around', 'God Save Us' and 'Unreal' helped the album sell over 375,000 copies in the US. In truth, the tracklisting for *Revolution* was littered with monstrous anthems, any of which could have been considered for single releases, such was the quality and skilful songwriting the band evidently possessed from the off.

Ahead of recording their follow-up album, guitarist Marc Rizzo left to join Soulfly and Roger Vasquez quit his percussion duties, and the duo were replaced by ex-Machine Head axeman, Ahrue Luster, and Danny Couto, respectively. *Confession* debuted at 37 on the *Billboard* 200 upon its release in September 2003 and it was promoted by the powerhouse single, 'How Can I Live', which featured on the *Freddy vs. Jason* movie soundtrack. This album also launched Ill Nino into headline status, as they topped the bills on tours with label mates Spineshank and Chimaira, while other highlights on the *Confession* record included 'Unframed', 'Cleansing', and the pulsating 'When It Cuts'.

Evolving with the times, the band's third release, *One Nation Underground,* saw Ill Nino beginning to bring metalcore elements into their sound with less of an emphasis on melody. 'What You Deserve' and 'This Is War' showcased their new direction, and perhaps people perceived the change as a little too far out as the album debuted at a lowly 101 in the US. Ill Nino then joined Cement Shoes Records after leaving Roadrunner, and their first effort for their new label was an EP titled *The Under Cover Sessions* in 2006. Covers of Faith No More's 'Zombie Eaters' and Nirvana's 'Territorial Pissings' were nicely done, and the EP served as an appetiser for *Enigma* – Ill Nino's fourth studio album, which emerged a year later. Continuing further into metalcore territory, *Dead New World* was put out via Victory Records in 2010, followed by *Epidemia* in 2012; and then *Till Death, La Familia* in 2014 – which would prove to be the band's final album.

In 2019, Cristian Machado, Diego Verduzco and Luster quit the band due to issues they had with founding member Dave Chavarri. The trio planned to continue with the Ill Nino name, as did Chavarri with his remaining bandmates and new additions. However, a settlement was agreed in 2020 and Machado, Verduzco and Luster announced a new metal project they were working on. Chavarri's Ill Nino saw Marcos Leal of Shattered Sun take over as lead singer, with the strong singles of 'Sangre' and 'Mascara' released thus far.

Killer Cuts – 'What Goes Around', 'How Can I Live'

Incubus

Years Active: 1991-
Location: Calabasas, California, USA
Main era line-up: Brandon Boyd (vocals, guitar), Mike Einziger (lead guitar), Alex Katunich (bass), Jose Pasillas II (drums), Chris Kilmore (turntables, synth, piano)
Albums: Fungus Amongus (1995), S.C.I.E.N.C.E. (1997), Make Yourself (1999), Morning View (2001), A Crow Left of the Murder... (2004), Light Grenades (2006), If Not Now, When? (2011), 8 (2017)

Incubus began to make waves with their 1995 album, *Fungus Amongus*, which was released on their own independent label – the hilariously titled,

Stopuglynailfungus Music On Chillum. Their infectious brand of funk metal led to Incubus signing with Immortal Records, which was to later become Epic Records, and Incubus's first release for their new label was a six-track EP called *Enjoy Incubus* which was presented during a European tour supporting Korn. In 1997, they released *S.C.I.E.N.C.E.*, which incorporated heavy metal, electro, jazz, funk and hip-hop into the band's sound, and the album was to be certified gold by the RIAA thanks in part to the singles 'A Certain Shade of Green', 'Redefine' and 'New Skin'. Plenty of high-profile tours followed including another stint alongside Korn, as well as runs with 311, System of a Down and Ultraspank; and Incubus was also part of the Ozzfest and Family Values tours as they relentlessly promoted their music in the live environment.

In 1999, the band's hard work finally paid off upon the release of their sophomore album, *Make Yourself*, which peaked at 47 on the *Billboard* 200 and went on to sell over two million copies in the US alone. Containing down-tuned guitars with lots of additional electronics, the popular singles 'Pardon Me', 'Stellar', and the acoustic ballad 'Drive' received heavy rotation. 'Drive' hit the number 1 spot on the US Modern Rock Chart as well as eventually getting into the top 10 of the *Billboard* 100, and in October 2000, *Make Yourself* received its first platinum certification. After going on tour with Deftones, *Fungus Amongus* was re-released in 2000 due to popular demand, and then another studio album landed in October 2001 – titled *Morning View*.

With a mix of ambience, aggression, and groove, it stormed to second spot in the US by selling 266,000 copies in its first week, turning Incubus into a mainstream favourite. Four diverse singles were released in the forms of 'Wish You Were Here', 'Nice to Know You', 'Warning' and 'Are You In?', as Incubus dominated the airwaves so much that *Morning View* went double platinum just as their previous album had.

Next, one of the band's founding members, Alex Katunich (stage name Dirk Lance), was replaced on bass by Ben Kenney in time for *A Crow Left of the Murder...* released in 2004 and focusing on an art rock and alternative metal sound. Debuting at number 2 on the *Billboard* 200 and also reaching a highly respectable 6 in the UK, the excellent 'Megalomaniac' was the perfect choice of lead single. However, it was *Light Grenades* which earned Incubus their first number 1 album in 2006. Featuring the singles 'Anna-Molly', 'Dig', 'Love Hurts' and 'Oil and Water', *Light Grenades* is perhaps more famously known for being the record to have the biggest drop from number 1 in US chart history as it slipped to 37 in its second week – beating the two-year record which had been reluctantly claimed by Marilyn Manson after *The Golden Age of Grotesque* fell twenty places in 2003.

Releasing the greatest hits compilation (*Monuments and Melodies*) in 2009, which also contained a second disc of B-side material, and then the softer and alternative rocking *If Not Now, When?* album in 2011, Incubus then dropped a four-track EP titled *Trust Fall (Side A)* in 2015 before returning to a slightly heavier sound on the eighth record, *8*, in 2017. Containing some of Incubus' best material in years, the brilliant 'Nimble Bastard' sounded like classic Incubus and the engrossing 'State of the Art' caught people's imagination with its ballad-feel; as the best band from Calabasas continued to remain extremely popular and hugely relevant in the modern rock world.

Although Incubus has always shunned the nu metal tag, *'S.C.I.E.N.C.E.'* and *'Make Yourself'* continue to be included in many nu metal discussions, the first of which appears to be the true fan favourite record.

Killer Cuts – 'Pardon Me', 'Drive'

InMe

Years Active: 1996-
Location: Brentwood, Essex, England
Main era line-up: Dave McPherson (vocals, guitar), Joe Morgan (bass), Simon Taylor (drums)
Albums: Overgrown Eden (2003), White Butterfly (2005), Daydream Anonymous (2007), Herald Moth (2009), The Pride (2012), Trilogy: Dawn (2015), Jumpstart Hope (2020)

Originally going under the name Drowned in 1996, British trio InMe emerged in 2001 after signing to Music For Nations, where they released their major-label debut, *Overgrown Eden,* in 2003. Promoted by the pre-album singles 'UnderDose', 'Crushed Like Fruit' and 'Firefly', all of which earned heavy rotation on *Kerrang!* in the UK, InMe's energetic alternative metal and post-grunge anthems gained themselves a strong following from the offset. *Overgrown Eden* reached 15 on the UK album chart and number one on the Rock Chart, while a fourth single titled 'Neptune' continued the band's mainstream radio challenge.

White Butterfly followed in 2005 via V2 Records- after the Music For Nations label had gone out of business, and the album was produced by Josh Abraham, who had previously worked with the likes of Limp Bizkit, Staind, Orgy and Coal Chamber. *White Butterfly* (like the record before it) reached top spot in the UK Rock Chart, and the singles 'Faster the Chase', '7 Weeks' and 'So You Know' had strong exposure, and although the music continued with the same formula as its predecessor, Dave McPherson's vocals were delivered with a cleaner English accent as opposed to the Americanised stylings on *Overgrown Eden*.

Later albums, *Daydream Anonymous* (2007), *Herald Moth* (2009), *The Pride* (2012) and the first part of a trilogy titled *Dawn* (released in 2015) have since followed with limited success; and in 2020, InMe returned from the wilderness with another strong and guitar-driven album, in the form of *Jumpstart Hope*.

Killer Cuts – 'UnderDose', 'Neptune'

Insolence

Years Active: 1995-
Location: San Jose, California, USA

Main era line-up: Mark Herman (vocals), Mike Rowan (guitar), Paul Perry (bass), Armando Cardenas (drums), Jerry Dalalo (turntables)
Albums: Vicious Circle (1995), Within (1997), Universal (1999), Poisonous Philosophy (2000), Revolution (2001), Stand Strong (2003), Audio War (2007), Project Konflict (2010)

Insolence are another band that produced a hybrid of rap, hardcore, metal and reggae, and the San Jose massive has been going since 1995. Over the years, they have toured with the likes of Papa Roach, Hed PE, Cypress Hill and Skindred, and their biggest moments came on the major label albums *Revolution* (2001) and *Stand Strong* (2003) – released via Maverick and Warner Bros. Records, respectively. Listen to the songs 'Death Threat' and 'Poison Well' to hear Insolence at their most vital, and although further records have been released, it was the during early new millennium which saw the band's defining moments.

There are currently two versions of Insolence – the first being the Powerslave Records-signed band that includes original members such as vocalist Willis 'Mecha' Rosenthal, while the other features Armando Cardenas – who quit the band in 2001 but still holds the copyright to the Insolence name.

Killer Cuts – 'Death Threat', 'Poison Well'

Kid Rock

Years Active: 1988-
Location: Romeo, Michigan, USA
Main era line-up: Kid Rock (vocals, guitar, bass), Twisted Brown Trucker Band- Joe C. (backing vocals), Jason Krause (guitar), Kenny Olson (guitar), Stefanie Eulinberg (drums), Uncle Kracker (turntables), Jimmie Bones (keyboards
Albums: Grits Sandwiches for Breakfast (1990), The Polyfuze Method (1993), Early Mornin' Stoned Pimp (1996), Devil Without a Cause (1998), Cocky (2001), Kid Rock (2003), Rock n Roll Jesus (2007), Born Free (2010), Rebel Soul (2012), First Kiss (2015), Sweet Southern Sugar (2017)

Born Robert James Ritchie, Kid Rock already had a considerable following from his hip-hop days in the early 1990s, but it was in 1998 and when nu metal was really exploding that Rock forced his way into the mainstream. Through Atlantic Records, *Devil Without a Cause* came out in August – a rap metal masterpiece that spawned the massive nu metal hit, 'Bawitdaba'. Sales for the album were slow to begin with, however, with the first two singles released being 'Welcome 2 the Party…' and 'I Am the Bullgod', before Rock supported the record by playing on the Vans Warped Tour. 'Bawitdaba' wouldn't get a release until April 1999, but once the single dropped, Kid Rock became more of a household name. With the help of various performances on *MTV*, *Devil Without a Cause* went gold by the end of the month, and by the end of May, it had gone platinum. In the summer, Rock went out on his first major tour, joining Limp Bizkit and Staind, then followed a successful performance at Woodstock; and by July 1999, the album he was touring had gone double platinum. 'Cowboy' and 'Only God Knows Why' were also put out as singles, the second of which became the highest-charting single from its accompanying album by reaching 19 on the *Billboard* Hot 100, and in 2000, 'Wasting Time' became the sixth and final single taken from *Devil Without a Cause*. As of 2015, the ground-breaking rap rock album had been certified a staggering 11x platinum – with sales of over nine-and-a-half million copies in the US alone.

After acquiring the rights to his older material, Kid Rock released *The History of Rock* in 2000 which featured remixed and re-recorded tracks from earlier albums. Debuting at 2 on the *Billboard* 200, the brand-new hit, 'American Bad Ass', sampled Metallica's 'Sad But True' classic, and it would go on to become the entrance music for *WWE* superstar, The Undertaker. The other new track to make its way onto *The History of Rock* was 'Fuck That' which would later be included on the *Any Given Sunday* movie soundtrack.

After the Summer Sanitarium Tour with Metallica, Korn, System of a Down and Powerman 5000, Rock ventured into southern rock and country waters on his 2001 release, *Cocky*. The song 'Picture' saw Sheryl Crow provide guest vocals, and although the album went 5x platinum, Rock was clearly prepared to leave rap metal behind. A self-titled effort in 2003 and *Rock n Roll Jesus* in 2007 featured country and blues elements, while *Born Free* (2010) and *Rebel Soul* played around with heartland rock and soul. *First Kiss* (2015) saw country rock being prominent once more before *Sweet Southern Sugar* followed at the end of 2017. Containing country and blues rock but with a greater hip-hop influence once again, the swaggering 'Greatest Show on Earth' and 'Po-Dunk' saw Kid Rock on fine form once more.

While he remains hugely popular all around the world, it was *Devil Without a Cause* that undoubtedly put Kid Rock on the map with incredible sales that few others could ever compete with back then.

Killer Cuts – 'Bawitdaba', 'American Bad Ass'

Kill II This

Years Active: 1995-2005, 2016-

Location: Stockport, Lancashire, England

Main era line-up: Nick Arlea/Matt Pollock (vocals), Mark Mynett (guitar), Caroline Campbell (bass), Ben Calvert (drums)

Albums: Another Cross II Bare (1996), Deviate (1998), Trinity (2001), mass.(down)-sin(drone) (2003)

Kill II This brought some extreme metal to the nu metal scene, which included flourishes of industrial, electronica, hip-hop and even classical music. Yes, you read that last one right. The first incarnation of the band comprised founding member, Mark Mynett, Pete Stone on bass, Jeff Singer on drums and American vocalist, Nick Arlea; and their debut album, *Another Cross II Bare,* earned Kill II

This a strong following in 1996; and it ultimately led to them supporting thrash metal legends Megadeth on their *Cryptic Writings* European tour. Standout moments on the band's first record included the bruising 'Blessed are the Blind' and 'The Wicker Man', but by the time a second album emerged in 1998, Mynett was the only original member in the band's line-up.

On *Deviate*, Matt Pollock had taken over vocal duties, Caroline Campbell picked up the bass and Ben Calvert took his seat behind the drums after Singer had completed recording. Despite all the changes, *Deviate* received excellent reviews, with many praising a much more cohesive sound. 'Funeral Around My Heart' and 'The Flood' became essential listening due to the inclusion of some intriguing classical elements, which highlighted the band's knack of being brutally heavy in one moment and then melodic and subtle the next. Supporting the album, Kill II This went out on their own headline tour of the UK where they were supported by fellow Brits Earthtone9 and Italian nu metallers Linea 77; before a third album, *Trinity* (2001), saw Fear Factory's Burton C. Bell guest on a cover of Frankie Goes to Hollywood's 'Two Tribes'. Tours with metal superstars-in-waiting Slipknot, Anthrax and Machine Head, to name just a few followed, before *Mass.[Down]-sin(Drone)*, which saw the band name stylised as Kill 2 This, emerged in 2003. Joining Mynett was Phil Bretnall (vocals), Steve Rooney (drums) and the returning Pete Stone, and this fourth studio album would be the last to be put out under the band's original moniker.

Instead, when it was time to return, the band was known as City of God, and they were led by vocalist Simon Gordon, while Singer came back in to join Mynett and Stone. *A New Spiritual Mountain* was released in 2005 and featured more pounding metal with Kill II This' stamp all over it, and a return at the Bloodstock festival in 2016 under their original name went down a storm. A couple of new songs have dropped since, as the musicianship supplied by Kill II. This continues to show a band who, in many ways, have always been well ahead of their time.

Killer Cuts – 'Blessed are the Blind', 'Funeral Around My Heart'

Kittie

Years Active: 1996-
Location: London, Ontario, Canada
Main era line-up: Morgan Lander (vocals, guitar), Fallon Bowman (guitar), Tanya Chandler (bass), Mercedes Lander (drums)
Albums: Spit (2000), Oracle (2001), Until the End (2004), Funeral for Yesterday (2007), In the Black (2009), I've Failed You (2011)

Four noisy young ladies from Canada emerged in 1996 with the intent of changing the rock and metal world forever, and in some ways, Kittie (often stylised KiTTiE) did just that – by taking the emphasis away from a male dominated genre for a short time and giving more females the confidence to embark on their own metallic dreams and journeys.

Releasing their debut album, *Spit,* on 11 January 2000 through Artemis Records, Kittie combined heavy and abrasive thrash-tinged metal with Morgan Lander's deathly screams and harmonious melodies separating the band from the rest of the nu metal crowd. Throwing in some pro-feminist lyrics for good measure, visceral tracks such as 'Brackish', 'Charlotte' and 'Paperdoll' became hugely popular, helping *Spit* sell over 600,000 copies in the US. *Oracle* followed in 2001 and edged towards a harsher death metal sound, but it still peaked at 57 on the *Billboard* 200. As well as the lead single, 'What I Always Wanted', a cover of Pink Floyd's 'Run Like Hell' was also an interesting inclusion.

The explosively anthemic 'Into the Darkness' featured on the 2004 album, *Until the End*, which contained a gloriously addictive pop metal chorus, yet the album itself only reached 105 on the *Billboard* chart and Kittie would then part ways with their record label. Forming their own X of Infamy Records to release their next album, *Funeral for Yesterday,* in 2007, the band used EMI for distribution, but with record sales taking a nosedive across the whole industry, the band's fourth record sold less than 9,000 copies in its first week. The title track fared better though, getting to 40 on *Billboard*'s Mainstream Rock Tracks chart and earning Kittie their best ever chart position in America. Further albums followed after Kittie signed to E1 Music – *In the Black* in 2009 and *I've Failed You* in 2011, the latter of which has been considered by some as the band's best record of their whole career.

With Morgan Lander and her sister Mercedes being the two constants throughout Kittie's career, this band of fiery females look like they can go on for as long as they want – if they want; and if you missed them the first time around, check out their career-spanning documentary, *Kittie: Origins/Evolutions,* which includes interviews with all members past and present, who have helped Kittie prove that females had just as much right as men to be in the nu metal spotlight.

Killer Cuts – 'Brackish', 'Charlotte'

Fallon Bowman speaks:

> When Mercedes and I got together, we didn't actually start out as a heavy band. I was hugely influenced by Nirvana and the full Seattle grunge scene, so my main influence to start a band was grunge, not metal. I think it was with the addition of Morgan when I started being introduced to heavier music. It wasn't that we set out to be a band that was a female band, we never thought about it like that at all, and it was only when we started to get popular that people started to point that out; and it was men that pointed it out. 'Oh, but you are females doing this…' The fact we were also very young was something that people pointed out at first, too. So, the impetus of Kittie's sound was grunge in the beginning, and then later when our music influences changed, when Korn, Sepultura and Deftones' records were coming out – it just changed the game for us.
>
> I didn't know that what was happening was necessarily called nu metal at the

time; I just knew what I liked. Being associated with what was happening was an honour – to be associated with the people that I was personally listening to. I think the difference too was that I was, as a young person, the target demographic for all these bands that were out and who were a lot older than us. It was an interesting mix in the fact that I was the people they were playing to, but I was also playing alongside them.

At the time it was such a novelty to actually have bands who were all-female. There wasn't anybody to compare Kittie to, and journalists were taking major liberties with 'They sound like this and this mixed together…' and I was like, 'No, not at all!' I don't think consciously that was what we were doing; we just wanted to be considered human beings playing music that we liked. We wanted people to think of us regardless of gender, to just think of us as musicians playing music in our favourite genre. The gender thing kept being brought up, which at the time I didn't want to be the focus, but now I'm realising how much of a lasting effect it had on emerging artists and that is mind-blowing to me. People were like, 'I picked up a guitar because of you' or 'As a female, in my case sometimes as a female of colour, you made me feel like I could pick up a guitar and play in a genre that is not welcoming necessarily to women, or inclusive to women – and especially people of colour as well,' so gradually we saw the impact we were making.

Originally, we signed with NG Records and they were a 100% indie label out of New York with a very small but dedicated team. They dedicated all their resources to us and a large portion of what they were doing was for us. Orange 9mm was on the roster; they had a punk band, they had a very eclectic mix of people, so I think they took a chance with us, but they saw what was happening in the wider scope of things with the emergence of nu metal. Then they merged with Artemis Records, which I don't know if you would consider as a major label, maybe more of a mid-range label, I guess. They absorbed all the resources and all the bands of NG Records and became Artemis Sheridan Square Entertainment. Danny Goldberg ran an artist management company called Gold Mountain Entertainment which included Nirvana at one time, and that was awesome because I was a disgustingly huge Nirvana fan, so it was life-changing to meet Danny.

Before signing to NG, we showcased for other labels, but we got rejected. None of them wanted to take a chance on us except NG. Jason Weiner was essentially the one who discovered us and he was a visionary. He just saw things and saw potential in us to be something really great and long-lasting, so kudos to him for taking a major risk for a label that may not have had the reach of a major label, but he put the whole team behind us and it was fantastic; and I think the risk paid off. We were touring; I was pretty much living in New York, and remember, I was only fourteen or fifteen years old.

Our debut album, *Spit*, sold over 600,000 copies and I can say for myself that it was incredibly overwhelming. You really had to take a deep breath and jump into what was happening because it was all happening very quick. The release was in January 2000 and I was a little bit surprised that people dug it, and I still have that awe when people say, 'Man, when I first heard that song, it was amazing!' and I'm like, 'Man, we wrote that song in my friend's basement!' I had never taken a guitar lesson in my life, I was self-taught, and I think that was effective in its simplicity. You didn't have to try and complicate it too much; it was just heavy, punch you in the face kind of music, and that is what we wanted to do. It was overwhelming and surprising but also 100% fulfilling to know that this music we nurtured up until that point was being received tremendously well; and that is a very intensely satisfying feeling.

We had a lot of good tours, but Slipknot was the best tour. Going back to the gender thing about being a woman in this industry – generally the guys and the bands you play with fall into two categories at this point and remember – we were also very young. They fell into the 'I wanna be your big brother and protect you and make sure everything is okay,' or 'I'm a fucking creep!' Thankfully, everybody on the Slipknot tour was very professional. They fell into the big brother category, 100%. They were protective of us, but they didn't infantilise us. They treated us with respect, and I will just say that on other tours, that was not the case.

Slipknot was a treat to watch every night because this was when their first record had just come out and they were playing relatively small clubs. People were losing their fucking shit seeing this band, and I was so honoured to be a part of that journey with them and to see how big they were becoming. That was a highlight tour, and of course, there was Ozzfest 2000. It was like a travelling high school. You got to hang out with some of the most amazing musicians who were people I looked up to, like Pantera and Soulfly. You became very comfortable with everybody and you all stick together. Reveille was on the tour with us, and they were around the same age as us, so that was nice, and it was the same with Apartment 26. It was probably the highlight of my life.

I have many great memories of being part of the nu metal movement, but probably my favourite; I will preface it by saying that prior to being on the Ozzfest tour, I wasn't a huge Pantera fan. I just wasn't exposed to them as much as I probably should have been. *Reinventing the Steel* had come out that year, so they were on Ozzfest with us and to hang out with Phil Anselmo every single day was one of the highlights. The guy is kind of out there, but in a good way, so he would go on these tangents and talk for hours about his favourite black metal bands. The first night of the tour was somewhere in Northern Florida, and I tell this story a lot because it is a cautionary tale of knowing your limits. We were sitting there, and I didn't drink alcohol at this point. Pantera fell into that big brother category in that they really wanted to take care of you, but then they were also like 'Here, have this drink!' and of course, I drank too much, and it was my first induction into the rock & roll Hall of Fame, as it were- with some of the most influential musicians ever; especially Dimebag Darrell. He came over to me and said, 'I like you, you're a good guitar player' and he was putting his arm around me, saying 'You guys are so young and so great, it's so fucking awesomc ... here, have a Black Tooth Grin!' That memory has been all the more meaningful too since his death – it really means a lot to me.

Korn

Years Active: 1993-
Location: Bakersfield, California, USA
Main era line-up: Jonathan Davis (vocals, bagpipes), Brian 'Head' Welch (guitar, backing vocals), James 'Munky' Shaffer (guitar, backing vocals), Reginald 'Fieldy' Arvizu (bass), David Silveria (drums)
Albums: Korn (1994), Life Is Peachy (1996), Follow the Leader (1998), Issues (1999), Untouchables (2002), Take a Look in the Mirror (2003), See You on the Other Side (2005), Untitled (2007), Korn III: Remember Who You Are (2010), The Path of Totality (2011), The Paradigm Shift (2013), The Serenity of Suffering (2016), The Nothing (2019)

Becoming the reluctant founders of the nu metal movement, Bakersfield, California natives Korn (generally stylised as Ko n) emerged in the early 1990s with a completely new sound which would forever change the landscape of heavy metal.

Forming after James 'Munky' Schaffer, Reginald 'Fieldy' Arvizu, and David Silveria's first band, L.A.P.D., and latterly Creep, ceased to exist, they enlisted Brian 'Head' Welch and Jonathan Davis to form a quintet who gained a decent following early on by playing shows in the Huntington Beach area. The band released a less than well received demo titled *Neidermayer's Mind*, but by this time Korn had already been spotted by an Epic Records A&R employee. By May 1994, they had started recording their debut album with Ross Robinson, who ultimately gained from the success of the record too as he launched his own career as a renowned record producer.

Simply titled *Korn*, the eponymous release introduced a uniquely dark and twisted vibe to an unsuspecting world. Even the album cover looked sinister, depicting a young girl sitting on a swing looking up at an adult figure who was only visible by a shadow in the sand; and to make the cover even more disturbing, the band logo (featuring the backwards R) sees the shadowed head of the girl looking as if she is hanging from the bottom of the K. Visual imagery was certainly going to be a big thing in nu metal.

Distorted 7-string guitars and deep slapping bass tones accompanied Davis' at times horrifying lyrics of child abuse and emotional torture, not to mention his angst-filled vocals, which often verged on the sadistic. Tracks such as 'Faget' and 'Clown' became anthems for kids going through troubled times, whether it be in school or at home, and the opening to possibly the greatest nu metal song – 'Blind', featured the now classic and famous line, 'Are you ready?!'

Incredibly, a metal band using bagpipes became a reality with Davis playing them on the nightmarish nursery rhyme renditions of 'Shoots and Ladders', but strangely enough, the sound worked; however it was the final song on the album which truly shook the metal world. Suffering from child abuse in his younger years, Davis sheds real tears as his emotions pour out of every orifice on 'Daddy' – a track that still makes listeners today feel very uncomfortable to listen to. This was just another reason why people flocked to buy *Korn* – an album unlike anything released before, and it provided a form of salvation for many listeners. Hitting the *Billboard* 200 also, it was further proof that *Korn* had started something and heavy metal was finally ready to challenge the mainstream once again.

After a huge touring cycle, Korn returned to the studio with Robinson and recorded *Life Is Peachy,* which followed in 1996. Featuring 'Good God', 'No Place to Hide' and 'A.D.I.D.A.S.' (All Day I Dream About Sex – if you didn't already know), the album was harsh and heavy but still featured undercurrents of hip-hop groove, and it was a suitable follow-up to the hype caused by Korn's 1994 debut. The sophomore album also gave the first introduction to Davis's scat singing on the intro track, 'Twist'. A rabid and schizophrenic vocal, this was something only Davis could do and along with the bagpipes, he would use it on various other tracks in the years to come.

It was *Follow the Leader* though, which would become the major breakthrough album for Korn, and ultimately for nu metal. Released on the Immortal/Epic label in 1998, the album was huge in production and further explored the band's love of hip-hop, with the song 'Children of the Korn' featuring N.W.A. icon, Ice Cube. Duelling vocals between Davis and Cube, on top of metallic riffing and a funky drumbeat may have been a new experience for some, but it showed that nu metal was daring to try new things at every turn. More Korn classics appeared on *Follow the Leader* with 'Freak on a Leash' and 'Got the Life' becoming mainstays in the band's live setlist. 'Got the Life' had a disco rock feel, and its promo video showed the band celebrating their newfound superstardom with smart suits and even smarter cars. Fred Durst from fellow nu metal poster boys Limp Bizkit guested on the explicit 'All in the Family', while songs such as 'Dead Bodies Everywhere' and 'Pretty' kept elements of prior releases with dark lyrical content detailing sex abuse and personal alienation. *Follow the Leader* reached number 1 on the *Billboard* 200, as well as in Australia, New Zealand and Canada, while a top 5 spot in the UK wasn't to be sniffed at either. Times were indeed a-changing, and to this day *Follow the Leader* remains Korn's most successful album, having sold over fourteen million copies worldwide.

Not far behind it in sales was the quintet's fourth studio album, *Issues*, which dropped in 1999, less than eighteen months since *Follow the Leader*. 'Falling Away from Me' and 'Make Me Bad' were to become further fan favourites, and the interlude '4 U' acted as a dedication from the band to their fans. The album cover depicted a rag doll – which was the winning design in a competition set up by the band, and it would be more imagery which became synonymous with Korn. Although the tracklist wasn't quite as strong as its predecessor, *Issues* still packed a groovy punch, and with over thirteen million copies sold, it confirmed Korn to be one of the biggest bands in the world at the time, and already well on their way to reaching legendary status.

Taking their time to follow-up the massive success of their last two records, it wasn't a surprise when hype had reached fever pitch by the time *Untouchables* announced itself in June 2002. Standout moments came in the form of the Grammy Award-winning lead single, 'Here to Stay', and the emotive promo video for second single, 'Thoughtless', which told the story of a high school student building up to his high school prom, intent on taking revenge on his bullies. Reportedly costing millions of dollars to make, *Untouchables* gained relatively positive reviews, but it failed to beat Eminem's hip-hop album, *The Eminem Show* to number 1 on the *Billboard* 200, with Davis allegedly blaming internet piracy for lower than projected album sales after it had leaked online more than two months before its official release date.

Take a Look in the Mirror fared dramatically worse when it was released at the end of 2003, reaching ninth spot in the US and 53 in the UK album charts. The release date was pushed forward due to it leaking online, but tracks such as 'Right Now' and 'Did My Time' (which was included in the *Tomb Raider* movie) were released as singles and found Korn on decent form. Rap star, Nas, featured on the track 'Play Me' – thus continuing Korn's collaborations with hip-hop – and 'Alive' was finally given an official release, having only previously been found on the band's *Neidermayer's Mind* demo a decade before. Concluding their partnership with Immortal and Epic, a *Greatest Hits Vol. 1* compilation was put out in 2004, before Korn began what would prove to be the most challenging decade of their entire career.

In mid-2005, Welch shocked the metal world when he announced he was quitting the band he had helped form. Choosing to focus on his newfound spirituality as well as raising his young daughter, but perhaps, more importantly, to finally get himself sober after years of drug and alcohol abuse, Welch was a highly acclaimed guitarist and many were interested to see what Korn would come up with next, especially after Shaffer vowed to take on sole guitar duties on the band's next studio album.

Months after Welch's departure, Korn released their first album through EMI/Virgin – *See You on the Other Side.* The production team of The Matrix were enlisted by Korn, despite them generally being known for working with pop artists, and the likes of 'Twisted Transistor', 'Coming Undone' and 'Politics' saw some industrial elements being introduced into Korn's blueprint; while Shaffer offered his first samplings of life as lead guitarist. There was an overall sense that Korn's nu metal sound was being left behind in favour of experimentation, perhaps in an attempt to remain contemporary in an ever-changing musical climate. Fans remained supportive, however, so much so, that *See You on the Other Side* debuted in the top 3 in the US and reached platinum status within four months of its release.

The fragility of the band's lineup took another hit when Silveria was next to depart Korn in 2006. Various stories have been thrown around as to why he left, and it is fair to say there has been a fair amount of animosity from both camps ever since. Silveria claimed to have gone hiatus with the intention of returning to the band at a later date; however, Korn pressed on without him and now two integral pieces of the band's puzzle were missing. Remaining defiant as always, Davis, Shaffer and Arvizu soldiered on and for the first time, Korn would be recognised as a three-piece band – the results of this coming in 2007 with their *Untitled* record (and occasionally referred to as *Korn II*). Not officially given a title, it was intended for fans to call the record whatever they desired, and due to the lead single 'Evolution' receiving heavy rotation, the album debuted at a maybe somewhat surprising number 2 on the *Billboard* 200. Shaffer continued as the sole guitarist, while drumming duties were undertaken by Terry Bozzio, who was known for his work with Frank Zappa, and current Avenged Sevenfold and ex-Bad Religion and Suicidal Tendencies hitter, Brooks Wackerman. Moderately received due to its heavily experimental nature, further singles such as 'Kiss' and 'Hold On' polarised fans and critics. Despite being maligned, *Untitled* still reached gold status after only being on the shelves for a few months.

In the next three years, Korn would play countless live shows around the globe, confirm Ray Luzier (ex-David Lee Roth) as the band's new full-time drummer, and sign with the renowned Roadrunner Records, before reuniting with Ross Robinson with the intention of bringing back some of the classic Korn heaviness.

In May 2010, 'Oildale (Leave Me Alone)' confirmed that Korn was close to being on top form once again with a storming lead single featuring their customary heavy down-tuned guitars. Leading the band's ninth studio album, *Korn III: Remember Who You Are*, the release once again peaked at number 2 in the US with first-week sales of over 63,000 copies and included later popular numbers such as 'Let the Guilt Go' and 'The Past'.

Clearly showing a creative second wind, Korn revealed another album within eighteen months, but this would be one of the most incredible swerves the metal community had ever seen. Instead of continuing with the metallic sound of *Korn III,* Davis showcased his love of electronic music to link up with a plethora of dubstep artists on *The Path of Totality*. Dubstep and drum and bass meets nu metal – it was the most insane that Korn had ever sounded, but like they always did, they made the concoction sound legitimate. The thriving first single 'Get Up!' featured Noisia, 'Narcissistic Cannibal' featured Skrillex, who was one of the biggest dubstep artists around at that time, while other guests to appear on the album included Kill the Noise, Downlink, and 12th Planet. Produced in Davis' own studio in Bakersfield, *The Path of Totality* peaked at 10 in the US, and after years of destroying mosh pits, Korn was now taking over dancefloors too.

To cement 2011 as a year to remember, *Kerrang!* welcomed Korn into their Hall of Fame at their annual awards show, underlining the band's influence on heavy music over the last two decades, and in 2012 the reunion most Korn fans had probably dreamed of yet barely thought was ever possible, came true. Welch joined his former bandmates on stage at the Carolina Rebellion to play guitar on a couple of songs, and it was like he had never been away from the fold. His performances became more frequent until, in May 2013, Welch officially re-joined the band; and with that came the announcement that Korn was already writing a brand-new record.

Five months later, *The Paradigm Shift* dropped and combined a heavier sound but with flourishes of electronica. 'Never Never' and 'Spike in My Veins' were chosen as singles, while 'Prey for Me' and 'Love & Meth' were Korn classics-in-waiting. The album debuted at 8 in the US, and it would later get a re-release which spawned the incredible new track, 'Hater', with an accompanying music video containing a strong anti-bullying theme. For what may well have been the first time, the whole band was sober, in charge of their lives and careers, and the music they were making together remained effortlessly engrossing. In 2016, *The Serenity of Suffering* proved to be the heaviest and possibly most consistent Korn record since *Issues* way back in 1999, and 'Rotting in Vain', 'Insane' and 'Black is the Soul' were three tracks that will surely make the next greatest hits compilation. Slipknot's Corey Taylor turned up for a long-overdue guest spot on 'A Different World', and topped off by Nick Raskulinecz's production skills, *The Serenity of Suffering* confirmed once and for all that Korn was indeed here to stay.

In September 2019, the five-piece once again teamed up with Raskulinecz and released their thirteenth album, *The Nothing*, which continued the band's renewed momentum and received critical acclaim. Peaking just inside the *Billboard* 200's top 10 and with powerful songs such as 'You'll Never Find Me', 'The Ringmaster' and 'Cold' – the whole album written by Davis in response to his former wife's passing – Korn confirmed themselves to be one of the best heavy metal bands in history and forever be the kings of nu metal; whether they want the tag or not. Korn's sound broke boundaries left, right and centre, with heavy riffs, a bass sound which seemed ridiculous until you actually heard it, bombastic drumming; and lyrical themes deep and dark enough to shake a generation to its very core. The term 'ground-breaking' was made for the likes of Korn.

Killer Cuts – 'Blind', 'Freak on a Leash'

Level

Years Active: 2002-2004
Location: Bakersfield, California, USA
Main era line-up: Bobby Reeves (vocals), Ed Faris (guitar), Alley Useless (bass), Nicco Villalobos (drums), DJ Primer (turntables, samples)

Going on to earn somewhat of a cult status years after their demise, LeVeL came out in 2002 and sported some catchy rapcore which may have come a couple of years too late to truly make its mark. Led by Bobby Reeves, who would later front Adema in 2007, LeVeL released their only album in November 2003, and if you want to pick up a copy of the self-titled effort, be prepared to spend some serious Yen because it only seems to be available to buy in Japan these days. 'Living Inside of Me', 'Unstable', 'Down', and an interesting take on Portishead's 'Wandering Star' were the high points on an album that featured plenty of turntable action and thumping instrumentation. 'Disaster Proof' was included on the *Twisted Metal: Head On* video game, and although the band showed strong cohesiveness, LeVeL called it quits in 2005.

Killer Cuts – 'Living Inside of Me', 'Disaster Proof'

Lifer

Years Active: 1999-2002, 2018-
Location: Wilkes-Barre, Pennsylvania, USA
Main era line-up: Nick Coyle (vocals), Aaron Fink (guitar), Mark Klepaski (bass), Chris Lightcap (drums)
Albums: Lifer (2001)

One of the more interesting starts to a career, Lifer began as Strangers With Candy and played cover songs of various nu metal bands. In 2000, they entered *MTV*'s *Ultimate Cover Band* contest and gained a strong following from their rendition of Limp Bizkit's 'Nookie', amongst others. By the summer, the band had signed a six-album deal with Universal/Republic before briefly changing their name to Driver, and then finally settling on Lifer.

Generally featuring alternative metal instrumentation and a DJ, Lifer's self-titled debut came out in 2001 and included the excellent songs 'Boring' (the lead single and only rap-tinged rocker on show), 'Not Like You' and 'Breathless'; the latter of which was added to *The Scorpion King* movie soundtrack. Tours with Cold and Dope ensued; however, the album sold poorly, and to add salt to the wound, founding members Aaron Fink and Mark Klepaski would then leave to join the up-and-coming Breaking Benjamin.

An independently released EP, *IV*, emerged in 2002 and saw the band going into melodic hard rock territory, and this resulted in lead singer Nick Coyle changing Lifer into myDownfall; however, the band announced their end less than a year later. Coyle has played guitar in Cold for a few years now, and over the last couple of years, he has reformed Lifer with Fink, now releasing some alternative rock numbers which seem to have gone down well with the band's most dedicated fans.

Killer Cuts – 'Boring', 'Breathless'

Limp Bizkit

Years Active: 1994-
Location: Jacksonville, Florida, USA
Main era line-up: Fred Durst (vocals), Wes Borland (guitar), Sam Rivers (bass), John Otto (drums), DJ Lethal (turntables, samples)
Albums: Three Dollar Bill, Y'all (1997), Significant Other (1999), Chocolate Starfish and the Hot Dog Flavored Water (2000), Results May Vary (2003), The Unquestionable Truth, Part 1 (2005), Gold Cobra (2011)

As Korn gained more of a following, a whole host of bands came out of the woodwork in the hope of achieving similar success that the Bakersfield five were slowly achieving, and in 1997, a band led by a cocky and expletive-filled-baseball-cap-wielding Fred Durst brought their brand of rap metal to the masses.

Originally forming in 1994 in Jacksonville, Florida, the quintet named their band Limp Bizkit – which was designed on repelling listeners (and it certainly worked). Gaining an underground cult following, Limp Bizkit attracted crowds by word of mouth, covering songs such as George Michael's 'Faith' and Paula Abdul's 'Straight Up'. Whilst still an unsigned act, they went on two tours with Korn which earned heightened exposure, and after enlisting former House of Pain member DJ Lethal, for turntable duties, Limp Bizkit signed to Flip Records and was taken under the wing of Jordan Schur.

After fighting off Mojo – who tried to steal the band from Flip – Korn's bassist, 'Fieldy', persuaded Ross Robinson to check out Limp Bizkit's demo, and clearly impressed with what he heard, the flourishing record producer took the helm to work on the band's debut album, *Three Dollar Bill, Y'all*. An abrasive and angry sounding record which featured a cover of 'Faith' (against Robinson's early wishes), the album was met with minimal response in the early days; but nu metal making steady waves, promo singles and videos were made for 'Faith' and 'Counterfeit' to help get the Bizkit's name out there. 'Faith' became a successful radio hit and it led to the band getting a slot on the bill of Ozzy and Sharon Osbourne's Ozzfest, as well as Korn's Family Values Tour.

Building their fanbase and growing in stature, their sophomore album *Significant Other* followed in 1999, and was produced by Terry Date, who had previously worked with bands such as Pantera and fellow up-and-comers Deftones. The album allowed Durst and DJ Lethal to revisit their hip-hop backgrounds, recording 'N 2 Gether Now' with Wu-Tang Clan member Method Man and 'Turn Me Loose' with Eminem, although the latter was left off the album's final tracklisting. The energetic anthems of 'Break Stuff' and 'Nookie' propelled Limp Bizkit higher, and their commercial success grew off the back of them; and before long, the band was featured on the front covers of music magazines and the album received generally favourable reviews. 'Nookie' hit the top spot on the *Billboard* singles chart, and *Significant Other* followed suit on the *Billboard* 200. In the summer of 1999, Limp Bizkit played Woodstock in front of nearly 200,000 people, where violence occurred during and after their set and several sexual assaults were reported, as well as plywood being torn from walls during the performance of 'Break Stuff'. Durst felt that his band was being made scapegoats for the controversy at the event, and the music video for 'Re-Arranged' saw them responding to the criticism by depicting themselves being given life sentences for their participation at the festival. Despite the controversy, *Significant Other* remained at number 1 on the *Billboard* chart, thus cementing Limp Bizkit's growing popularity to levels even they probably never expected.

In the year 2000, it was announced that *Chocolate Starfish and the Hot Dog Flavored Water* would be the title of Limp Bizkit's third studio album, with the *Chocolate Starfish* wording referring to, in part, Durst himself, who was frequently being labelled an 'asshole' from all sides. The summer saw them go on a tour sponsored by the file-sharing service Napster, with Durst becoming an outspoken advocate of file-sharing, and later they embarked on a 'Guerilla Tour' which involved the band setting up illegal and impromptu public gigs in places such as on rooftops and in alleyways; leading to some being shut down by local police forces.

Chocolate Starfish was released on 17 October 2000 and it set a then-record in the US for the highest first-week sales of a rock album. With over 400,000 sales on the very first day and over one million copies in its first week, it became the fastest-selling rock album ever made, ending the seven-year record held by Pearl Jam's album, *Vs*'. The hugely popular songs 'Rollin', 'My Way' and 'My Generation' bothered singles charts across the globe, as did the *Mission: Impossible II* theme song, 'Take a Look Around'; all of which helped *Chocolate Starfish* earn gold, platinum, and later on, 6x multi-platinum status. The album was also known for the amount of expletives included. Featuring more swearing than your average episode of *The Sopranos*, this was underlined by the lyric in the second track, 'Hot Dog', where Durst stated, 'If I say fuck two more times, that's 46 fucks in this fucked up rhyme…' Enough said. Further controversy hit Limp Bizkit in 2001 when their performance at the Big Day Out festival in Sydney, Australia, saw fans in the mosh pit rush the stage, resulting in the death of a teenager by asphyxiation. Durst later testified in court and said he was left 'emotionally scarred' by the teenager's death.

Wes Borland and Limp Bizkit parted ways later in the year, with Snot guitarist Mike Smith replacing him ahead of the recording of the band's next album. However, a fall out later led to Smith upping sticks, and much of the recording sessions were scrapped. *Results May Vary* was finally released in September of 2003 – receiving largely unfavourable reviews. Still, it peaked at number 3 on the *Billboard* 200, and featured on the album was the storming anthem, 'Eat You Alive'. Featuring Hollywood stars Bill Paxton and Thora Birch in the accompanying music video, it was easily the heaviest song on the record, but overall, *Results May Vary* had a much more mature sound to it than people were used to hearing when it came to Limp Bizkit. Still, a strong release which included further highlights such as 'Creamer (Radio is Dead)', 'Lonely World', 'Let It Go' and a delicate cover of The Who's 'Behind Blue Eyes', Limp Bizkit's appeal seemed to be dwindling around the same time that nu metal itself was also on a downward slide.

Borland returned to the fold for the 2005 release, *The Unquestionable Truth (Part 1)* (as did Ross Robinson for production duties), and it was a big departure from the mainstream sound, which helped Limp Bizkit's rise to superstardom. Everything was heavier, darker and raw, with more than just a hint of Rage Against the Machine influence to the songs. 'The Truth' was the standout moment and lyrical themes included propaganda and catholic sex abuse cases (see the brutally honest, 'The Priest'). Known in the New York hardcore scene, Sammy

Siegler provided his drum talents on the release instead of original member, John Otta, and although there was very little advertising or promotion for it, *The Unquestionable Truth* still managed to debut at 24 in America.

With the nu metal movement pretty much done and dusted by now, Limp Bizkit put out their *Greatest Hitz* compilation at the end of 2005 and then they went on hiatus, and it wouldn't be until 2009 that we would see the original band back together. Showing people what they had been missing, Durst and the rest of the line-up toured around the world before heading into the studio to work on a brand-new album, and that album finally surfaced in 2011, titled *Gold Cobra*. Returning to the established sound of their *Significant Other* and *Chocolate Starfish* records, Limp Bizkit sounded as good as ever as they rifled through explosive anthems such as 'Shark Attack', 'Douche Bag', 'Shotgun', and the incredible ballad, 'Walking Away'. Although the album was critically successful, *Gold Cobra* only managed to peak at 16 in America, which underlined the fact that although Limp Bizkit still had a hefty following, their appeal to a much wider audience wasn't as strong as it once was. That could however also be blamed on the changes in the music industry and lack of support from radio and TV channels who, only years before, couldn't get enough of Limp Bizkit and the rest of the nu metal roster.

After cutting ties with Flip/Interscope, the band raised a few eyebrows when in 2012, they signed with Cash Money Records. Distributed by Republic, Cash Money was a label which generally catered for hip-hop artists such as Lil' Wayne. DJ Lethal left the band in the same year, and in 2013, Limp Bizkit debuted some new material. First, they leaked 'Lightz (City of Angels)', which was very much a hip-hop/r&b orientated track, then 'Ready to Go', which was put out as a single and featured Lil' Wayne; before a cover of Ministry's 'Thieves' brought the industrially heavy sound back. In the years since, the band has done a lot of touring, especially overseas, and they did put out another single titled 'Endless Slaughter' in 2014 before leaving Cash Money. DJ Lethal is back on board once again, as is Sam Rivers, having taken some time away due to various health issues, and talk remains incessant of the long overdue and much-promised record with the working title of *Stampede of the Disco Elephants*. Whether it ever sees the light of day remains the big question. A co-headline tour of the UK with Korn at the end of 2016 brought back pleasant memories of the nu metal era in its prime when both Limp Bizkit and Korn were the kings of a movement that made sure rock and metal music would never be the same again.

Killer Cuts – 'Nookie', 'Rollin'

Linkin Park

Years Active: 1996-2017 (Hiatus)

Location: Agoura Hills, California, USA

Main era line-up: Chester Bennington (lead vocals), Mike Shinoda (vocals, rhythm guitar, keyboards), Brad Delson (lead guitar), Dave 'Phoenix' Farrell (bass), Rob Bourdon

(drums), Joe Hahn (turntables, samples)
Albums: Hybrid Theory (2000), Meteora (2003), Minutes to Midnight (2007), A Thousand Suns (2010), Living Things (2012), The Hunting Party (2014), One More Light (2017)

Originally starting off as Xero before changing their name to Hybrid Theory upon the arrival of lead vocalist Chester Bennington, the future global megastars emerged out of California in 1999 with their debut self-titled EP. Showing their early promise with pristine rap rock anthems such as 'Step Up', 'And One' and 'High Voltage', Hybrid Theory caught the eye of Warner Bros. A& R, Jeff Blue, who only took the job with the label providing the band got a record deal too. After a British band by the name of Hybrid threatened to sue the Americans, Linkin Park was born and they released their debut album – ironically titled Hybrid Theory – in October 2000. Blue's guidance and persistence helped drive the band to new heights of popularity.

A less than 40-minute rap rock rager, the potential hits kept coming one after another as sales rocketed and Linkin Park took the world by storm. Fusing together Mike Shinoda's rapping with Bennington's melodic vocals and harsh screams, 'One Step Closer', 'Crawling', 'Papercut' and 'In the End' punished charts all over the globe. *Hybrid Theory* became the best-selling album of 2001, even though it just missed out on the top spot of the *Billboard* 200. Initially shifting more than 4,500,000 copies, by 2014, US sales had exceeded a staggering ten million, thus putting Linkin Park in an exclusive club of artists to earn diamond certification.

Trying something different, Linkin Park next decided to release a remix album in 2002. Titled *Reanimation*, the record featured tracks from *Hybrid Theory* which were revamped and given a new slant, with fellow nu metal musicians such as Orgy's Jay Gordon, Staind's Aaron Lewis, Stephan Richards from Taproot; and Korn's very own Jonathan Davis contributing vocals on various tracks. David 'Phoenix' Farrell also returned to the Linkin Park fold for bass duties, having previously left the band before their major label inception, while lead single, 'Pts.OF.Athrty', (Originally 'Points of Authority') reached number 9 in the UK. *Reanimation* peaked at number two on the *Billboard* 200. However, it was a record of new material that fans were really craving and on 25 March 2003, *Meteora* was met with sheer euphoria.

Coming out fighting with more of what brought them to the dance on their first album, singles including the leading 'Somewhere I Belong', the mosh pit frenetic 'Faint', 'Numb', 'From the Inside' and 'Breaking the Habit' proved there was plenty of strong and diverse tracks containing stadium-sized choruses to pick potential hits from. The album bulldozed its way to number 1 in the US and UK, and as of 2014, *Meteora* had sold over six million copies in America and over twenty million worldwide.

As with a growing trend during the nu metal era, Linkin Park next joined forces with a hip-hop superstar. Jay-Z collaborated with the band to release the *Collision Course* EP, which came out in November 2004 and featured six tracks of mashups of each artist's songs. 'Numb/Encore' (which went on to win a Grammy in 2006 for Best Rap/Sung Collaboration) was chosen to be released as a single, and the EP quickly sold more than seven million copies and earned the title of best-selling EP worldwide. Becoming heavyweights in mainstream music and not just in the rock and metal genres, Linkin Park hooked up with Rick Rubin to produce the band's third album, *Minutes to Midnight*, which was originally planned for a 2006 release but eventually surfaced in May 2007.

Moving into alternative rock territory, the singles of 'What I've Done' (included on the first *Transformers* movie), 'Shadow of the Day' and 'Leave Out All the Rest' incorporated softer guitar textures and predominantly clean vocals, although 'Given Up' and 'No More Sorrow' threatened a small nu metal renaissance with punchy riffs and some of Bennington's trademark harsh screaming. Despite potentially threatening to divide Linkin Park's fan base, *Minutes to Midnight* still cruised to number 1 in both the US and UK (as well as many other countries), and it wasn't long before it had gone 3x platinum in the band's native homeland. Also in 2007, Linkin Park collaborated with Busta Rhymes on the rapper's single, 'We Made It', and in the summer, they headlined the Download Festival in the UK. At the end of 2008, a live CD/DVD was released titled *Road to Revolution: Live at Milton Keynes,* and to accompany the latest *Transformers* movie, *Revenge of the Fallen*, the band released the incredible single, 'New Divide', which instantly became a fan favourite for its gigantic chorus and *Hybrid Theory* era instrumentation.

2010 saw a spanner thrown into the works when the band's fourth album, *A Thousand Suns,* emerged. Once again produced by Rubin and with the assistance of Shinoda, the record polarised fans with its experimental and electronically focused direction. Still debuting at number 1 in the US and UK, it showed that Linkin Park's music was capable of reaching a much wider audience than just the heavy demographic; however, the band's original followers didn't seem convinced. 'The Catalyst', 'Waiting for the End', 'Burning in the Skies' and 'Iridescent' were chosen as singles, and *A Thousand Suns* remains a hotly debated album to this day due to its lack of guitars and crashing drum sections. Less than two years later, Rubin and Shinoda took the reins again and it seemed Linkin Park was back on form for *Living Things*. While it still contained strong electronic elements, some of the classic Linkin Park crunch had also returned – as proven by the storming numbers of 'Lost in the Echo', 'In My Remains', 'Burn It Down' and 'I'll Be Gone'. Unsurprisingly, *Living Things* continued Linkin Park's trend of topping both the US and UK album charts, before another remix album followed a year later titled *Recharged.*

In 2014, the heaviness returned for the band's sixth album, *The Hunting Party*. Produced by Shinoda and fellow band member Brad Delson, this was the heaviest and most raw Linkin Park had ever sounded, with brash guitar rhythms and punk rock energy empowering the whole record. For the first time ever, guests were enlisted to feature on various tracks, as Helmet's Page Hamilton stole the show on 'All or Nothing', System of a Down's Daron Malakian performed some guitar wizardry on 'Rebellion', Rage Against the Machine axeman Tom Morello put his own spin on 'Drawbar', and rap artist Rakim vocal-led on 'Guilty All the Same'. Receiving largely positive reviews, it was clear that fans and critics alike were pretty happy with Linkin Park's latest effort, although *The Hunting Party* became the band's first album since their debut to miss out on the top of either the UK or US album charts.

Releasing another swerve in the form of *One More Light* in mid-2017, an album which fitted more into the pop category than any other (see the ironically titled 'Heavy' and 'Battle Symphony' for confirmation), one thing you can say about Linkin Park is that variety is the spice of life and throughout their successful career, you never quite knew what you were going to get with them from one album to the next.

And then came one of the biggest tragedies the rock and metal world had suffered in quite some time, when on 20 July 2017, Chester Bennington was found dead of an apparent suicide at his home in California. Having openly admitted for many years of his struggles with depression and addiction, it was still something that no one saw coming, and his passing left everyone in a state of shock and mourning for days on end. Only a matter of weeks prior, Chester's friend and rock icon, Chris Cornell (Soundgarden, Audioslave) had passed away, also through suicide, and the bone-chilling similarities were there to be seen by all. Unsurprisingly, sales of Linkin Park's back catalogue went through the roof, and physical copies of *One More Light* virtually sold out in every record store; as people revisited the album and its lyrical content in an attempt to see if Bennington's lyrics revealed a struggle which was becoming too hard to fight.

A benefit show was performed at the Hollywood Bowl in October 2017, with various musicians joining the rest of the band to perform Linkin Park classics. Guests included Korn's Jonathan Davis, Daron Malakian and Shavo Odadjian from System of a Down, and ex-Orgy duo Amir Derakh and Ryan Shuck, and the show was streamed live and viewed by millions of people all over the world; providing a fitting goodbye to one of the brightest lights that nu metal ever had to offer, and one of the greatest vocalists of all time.

From unknowns to heavyweights within three years of their inception, Linkin Park were the frontrunners of nu metal's post-millennium breakthrough. Many rap metal bands attempted to jump on the bandwagon, but most failed to meet the grade, and although Linkin Park went on to mix up their sound on later albums, both *Hybrid Theory* and *Meteora* remain essential listening when it comes to hearing the best of what nu metal had to offer.

Killer Cuts – 'One Step Closer', 'In the End'

Machine Head

Years Active: 1991-
Location: Oakland, California, USA
Main era line-up: Robb Flynn (vocals, guitar), Ahrue Luster (guitar), Adam Duce (bass), Dave McClain (drums)

Albums: Burn My Eyes (1994), The More Things Change... (1997), The Burning Red (1999), Supercharger (2001), Through the Ashes of Empires (2003), The Blackening (2007), Unto the Locust (2011), Bloodstone & Diamonds (2014), Catharsis (2018)

Machine Head started off as a thrash and groove metal band who quickly signed to Roadrunner Records and released the immensely popular *Burn My Eyes* and *The More Things Change...* albums, before incorporating nu metal elements into their sound for their third release – 1999's *The Burning Red*. Another album produced by Ross Robinson, *The Burning Red,* featured rapping vocals from Robb Flynn and strong choruses with singalong capabilities. The change in direction brought heavy criticism from fans of the band's earlier material, but thanks in part to the groovy singles 'From this Day' and 'The Blood, the Sweat, the Tears', as well as an excellent cover of The Police's 'Message in a Bottle', *The Burning Red* would sell close to 135,000 copies in the US and over 60,000 in the UK; and it remains Machine Head's second-biggest selling album in America today.

Continuing to tread the nu metal waters on their next album, Machine Head returned in 2001 with *Supercharger*, which in its own right was a very good record. Unfortunately, it was released a few weeks after the 9/11 terrorist attacks and the lead single, 'Crashing Around You', had been removed from *MTV* and radio due to its lyrical content and music video. Unsurprisingly, *Supercharger* was a commercial failure due to its lack of promotion, with reported sales of only 50,000 copies in America up to the present day. Sadly taking the focus away from the content, blistering numbers such as 'Bulldozer', 'All in Your Head', and the breathtaking 'Deafening Silence' deserved to be given more attention, and even today, they remain essential Machine Head listening.

To the delight of many, the Bay Area quartet returned to their thrash metal roots with *Through the Ashes of Empires* in 2003 (check out the incredible 'Imperium'), the much-lauded masterpiece *The Blackening* in 2007 and *Unto the Locust in* 2011. The slightly more experimental *Bloodstone & Diamonds* followed in 2014 before Machine Head revisited *The Burning Red* era with rap metal included once again on the monstrous 2018 epic, *Catharsis*. Huge statements were made on the likes of 'California Bleeding', 'Triple Beam' and 'Kaleidoscope', while the folky 'Bastards' also received heavy plaudits upon its release.

Machine Head has become one of the biggest heavy metal bands on the planet, and both *The Burning Red* and *Supercharger* remain important parts of the band's legacy. Now adding *Catharsis* to their discography, as well as the bruising but accessible 2020 single, 'Circle the Drain', Machine Head has shown the power nu metal had of being able to influence bands from all areas of heavy metal who wanted to try something new; even if it was for just one or two records- without ever forgetting where they originally came from.

Killer Cuts – 'From this Day', 'The Blood, the Sweat, the Tears'

Methods of Mayhem

Years Active: 1999-2000, 2009-2011
Location: Los Angeles, California, USA
Main era line-up: Tommy Lee (vocals, guitar, bass, drums), plus guests
Albums: Methods of Mayhem (1999), A Public Disservice Announcement (2010)

A project formed by Mötley Crüe drummer, Tommy Lee, after he had temporarily quit the iconic hair metal band in the late 1990s, Methods of Mayhem was a decent rap rock band which encompassed much of what was happening in mainstream music at the time. A collaboration of sorts with the rapper TiLo, Methods of Mayhem's self-titled debut album was released in December 1999 through MCA Records, and it featured guest spots from Fred Durst on 'Get Naked', Kid Rock on 'New Skin', as well as a host of hip-hop and r&b stars on further songs. Earning gold certification, the album proved to be a quick flash in the pan as Lee would soon return to his original band; however, in 2009, he revived Methods of Mayhem to release the harder rocking *A Public Disservice Announcement* through Roadrunner Records.

Enlisting a new line-up of musicians which included Sevendust's Morgan Rose on drums for some tracks, the energetic 'Fight Song' and 'Time Bomb' were popular singles and perfect examples of Lee's ability to write his own valid music. Another hiatus ensued while he set to work on Mötley Crüe's final few years of touring, but the two albums released under this project include many a song worthy of popping on repeat to rock out to.

Killer Cuts – 'Get Naked', 'New Skin'

Motograter

Years Active: 1995-2005, 2008-2011, 2013-
Location: Santa Barbara, California, USA
Main era line-up: Ivan 'Ghost' Moody (vocals), Matt 'Nuke' Nunes (guitar), J.R. Schwartz (guitar), Bruce 'Grater' Butler (motograter), Chris Binns (drums), Joey Krzywonski (percussion), Zak Ward (samples, electronics)
Albums: Motograter (2003), Desolation (2017)

Named after a DIY instrument made by Bruce Butler called the (you guessed it) 'Motograter', which had an unusual bass sound produced from industrial cable and guitar pieces, the band started out releasing a couple of EPs – *Hugh Chardon* in 1998 and *Indy* in 2000. Often painting themselves in tribal designs, Motograter has often been mentioned in the same breath as Mudvayne, Mushroomhead and Slipknot for having an instantly recognisable appearance in the rock and metal world.

Coal Chamber vocalist Dez Fafara, then signed the band to his recently formed record label, Sever, before more line-up changes occurred, which included Ivan 'Ghost' Moody becoming the new vocalist. Motograter then signed to No Name/

Elektra Records to release their self-titled full-length in 2003. 'Suffocate' was included on the soundtrack for *The Texas Chainsaw Massacre* movie remake and 'Down' – a melodic metal opus featured on the *NASCAR Thunder 2004* video game. To add to the band's oddness, the album featured eleven tracks, all of which had an intro of the same name but spelt backwards, although nothing should have really surprised us about Motograter. Ahead of touring the record, the band added a second guitarist (J.R. Swartz) and welcomed back Zak Ward to handle electronics/sampling and backing vocals, therefore making Motograter a seven-piece behemoth, but more line-up changes would plague the band before they went on hiatus in 2005. A one-off reunion show took place in 2006 before Motograter officially disbanded, only for them to return two years later with another new line-up.

An EP emerged at the beginning of 2009 (*Pre-Release*), which featured Michael 'Angel' Woodruff on vocals (Moody had left to join future metal favourites, Five Finger Death Punch), and the new incarnation toured until 2011 when Motograter called it quits once again. Like a proper soap opera, another reunion occurred in 2013, which saw The Browning drummer, Noah Robertson, come on board, and the band played the 2014 Knotfest. James Anthony Legion then replaced Woodruff on vocals and a new album titled *Desolation* was finally unleashed in the summer of 2017 – some fourteen years after the band's debut release. A melodic metal delight with some pretty impressive vocal displays, the single 'Dorian' had an accompanying video which was filmed in the same prison used in the classic *The Shawshank Redemption* movie, while other highlights such as 'Bleeding Through', 'Rise (There Will Be Blood)' and 'Daggers' mixed heavy guitar rhythms with some strong singalong choruses.

Seemingly looking to have built some strong foundations at last, Robertson then departed the band at the end of 2017 and more chaos has followed since. Whether Motograter can truly turn themselves around and have a much-belated career of consistency remains to be seen, but you wouldn't bet on it.

Killer Cuts – 'Down', 'Suffocate'

Mudvayne

Years Active: 1996-2010
Location: Peoria, Illinois, USA
Main era line-up: Chad Gray (vocals), Greg Tribbett (guitar), Ryan Martinie (bass), Matt McDonough (drums)
Albums: LD.50 (2000), The End of All Things to Come (2002), Lost and Found (2005), The New Game (2008), Mudvayne (2009)

Mudvayne was one of the more unusual acts to emerge during the nu metal storm, but they were also one of the most popular as they would become known for using sonic experimentation, face and body paint for their startling appearances and on occasions, masks and uniforms. Having built up a reputation around

Illinois from their frantic live shows and a 1997 self-released EP titled *Kill, I Outta,* the band's debut album, *LD.50* launched Mudvayne head-first at unsuspecting music fans in 2000. Released via Epic Records, it was an album which contained elements of death metal, hardcore punk, speed metal and jazz fusion; it was led by 'Dig', which became a nu metal favourite. Chad Gray's venomous rapping and deafening scream vocals also found some sultry cleans filter in, and the further singles of 'Death Blooms' and 'Nothing to Gein' increased the band's profile within the metal community. Also consisting of Greg Tribbett (guitar), Ryan Martine (bass) and Matthew McDonough (drums), *LD.50* reached 85 on the *Billboard* 2000 and was quickly certified gold while the band was out on tour promoting it.

On the back of successful tours with Nothingface, Slipknot, Sevendust and Slayer, Mudvayne returned with their second album, *The End of All Things to Come,* in 2002. Exploring more dynamic sounds such as progressive metal, as well as a wider vocal range from Gray, 'Not Falling' and 'World So Cold' were extremely melodic numbers that showcased the frontman's cleaner deliveries, and the album peaked at 17 on the *Billboard* 200 chart. Mudvayne's second album to go gold, the band members also changed their appearance for album number two by choosing to ditch the face paint for a rather spooky extra-terrestrial image, and as their stock rose, Mudvayne earned a spot on the Summer Sanitarium Tour in 2003 which was headlined by thrash metal kings Metallica.

2005 saw *Lost and Found* debut at 2 in the US – courtesy of the hugely popular singles 'Determined' and 'Happy?', both of which had been circulating for a few months prior to the record's unveiling. Still combining elements of thrash and alternative metal, *Lost and Found* was an album that only Mudvayne could come up with, and further highlights included 'Forget to Remember', 'Fall into Sleep', and the eight-minute epic, 'Choices'. Selling over one million copies, *Lost and Found* became Mudvayne's most commercially successful record, even if it wasn't as popular with fans compared to their earlier releases.

After putting out a compilation titled *By the People, For the People* in 2007, where fans chose the songs to be included and the band decided which version would appear, Mudvayne set about their next studio album, *The New Game*, which emerged in 2008. The first single, 'Do What You Do', received strong airplay to hype the accompanying record, and upon release, *The New Game* debuted at 15 in the US album chart, with sales of over 48,000 copies in its first week. Ditching much of the experimentation and sticking with a more straightforward hard rock/alternative metal sound, 'Fish out of Water' and 'Dull Boy' were popular additions to the tracklist; and just over a year later, Mudvayne followed *The New Game* with a self-titled effort which would prove to be the last album put out by the nutty quartet. Reportedly written around the same time as its predecessor, *Mudvayne* boasted the fan-favourite single, 'Scream With Me', but sales of the record were low due to the band choosing not to promote it or tour it.

With Gray fronting the heavy metal supergroup Hellyeah since their inception in 2000 (Tribbett was also in the band until 2014), Mudvayne has been inactive up until 2021, when they sent their dedicated fan base into raptures with the announcement of some reunion shows later in the year on the US festival circuit. At time of writing it was unknown whether this would convince the band to return to the studio, but it certainly made a new Mudvayne album more likely.

Killer Cuts – 'Dig', 'Not Falling'

Mushroomhead

Years Active: 1993-
Location: Cleveland, Ohio, USA
Main era line-up: Jason 'J Mann' Popson (vocals), Jeffrey 'Nothing' Hatrix (vocals), Dave 'Gravy' Felton (guitar), Marko 'Bronson' Vukcevich (guitar), Jack 'Pig Benis' Kilcoyne (bass), Steve 'Skinny' Felton (drums), Rick 'St1tch' Thomas (samples, electronics), Tom 'Schmotz' Schmitz (keyboards)
Albums: Mushroomhead (1995), Superbuick (1996), M3 (1999), XIII (2003), Savior Sorrow (2006), Beautiful Stories for Ugly Children (2010), The Righteous & the Butterfly (2014), A Wonderful Life (2020)

Another strangely named metal band who could rival Hoobastank for worst band name (but not quite), Mushroomhead began all the way back in 1993. Originally a side project for the band members, Mushroomhead became a full-time gig in 1995 after releasing their self-titled (and self-financed) debut album through Filthy Hands Co. Raising many eyebrows, the band wore costumes and masks as well as going under pseudonyms rather than their own names (sound familiar?), with the octet playing an abrasive mix of alternative, industrial and experimental metal which bred an influx of followers.

Superbuick (1996) and *M3* (1999) would be the final albums financed by themselves before Mushroomhead released a compilation titled *XX* on the independent label Eclipse Records. Featuring tracks from the band's first three outings, strong sales of the mix caught the attention of Universal Records, who signed the band and proceeded to remaster and re-release *XX*. Further elements incorporated into the music included gothic rock, punk, techno and hip-hop, and Mushroomhead earned further exposure through the video for the single 'Solitaire/Unraveling', as well as a vital spot on Ozzfest in 2002.

The fifth album, *XIII,* announced itself in October 2003, debuting at 40 on the *Billboard* 200. Featuring the singles 'Eternal', 'Kill Tomorrow', and the leading 'Sun Doesn't Rise', which was also included on the *Freddy vs. Jason* movie soundtrack, vocalist J Mann then announced his departure from the band in August 2004 – with Waylon Reavis replacing him. After signing with Megaforce Records in December 2005, the band's next release would be *Savior Sorrow* in September 2006. 'Simple Survival', 'Just Pretending' and '1200/Save Us' were mildly successful single releases, and although the album originally debuted at 45 in the US, it was later placed at 50 due to uncertainties over the amount of actual records sold.

Above: Record producer extraordinaire and along with Korn, the man who brought nu metal to the masses. (*Ross Robinson*)

Below: An incomparable duo – Chester Bennington and Mike Shinoda spearheaded Linkin Park's march to worldwide fame. (*Stefan Bending*)

Left: Who knew these smooth criminals would deliver a platinum record with *ANThology*? (*DreamWorks*)

Right: One of the most successful artists in US history, *Human Clay* by Creed went 11 x platinum. (*Wind-up*)

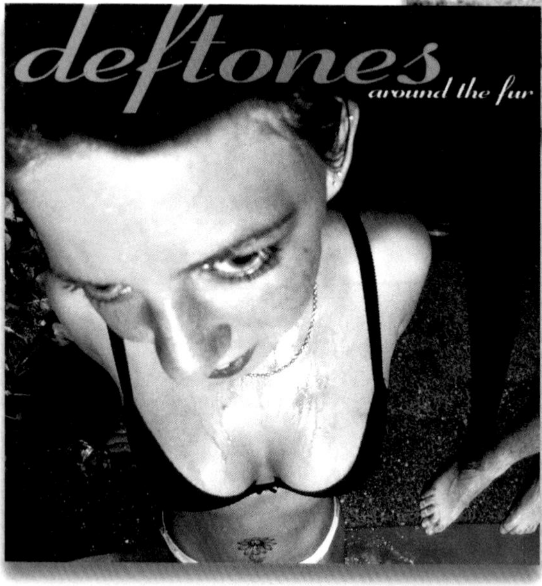

Left: Taking Deftones into the big time, *Around the Fur* offered the first glimpses of the band's artistic genius. (*Maverick*)

Right: A nu metal classic, Drowning Pool offered much on their bruising debut album. (*Wind-up*)

Left: Adding a touch of goth to nu metal, Evanescence also became massive on the back of *Fallen*. (*Wind-up*)

Right: *Faceless* continued Godsmack's relentless assault on the mainstream charts. (*Universal*, *Republic*)

Above: Coal Chamber. These LA ghouls looked and sounded different from anything else coming out in the late 1990s. (*Roadrunner*)

Below: From alt-metal masters to hard rock heroes, Cold went from strength to strength as their career progressed. (*Geffen*)

Right: The leader of a generation, Disturbed's David Draiman became a symbol for angsty teens all over the world. (*Razvan Orendovici*)

Left: Dope. These felons and revolutionaries blasted out of New York with attitude and swagger. (*Epic, Flip*)

Left: Cementing their place in the mainstream, Incubus' third studio album went double platinum in no time. (*Epic*, *Immortal*)

Right: A slow burner that eventually earned diamond certification, Kid Rock's fourth opus saw him reach superstardom. (*Atlantic*)

Left: A spicy debut album from these femme fatales was as good as anything their male counterparts were producing at the turn of the new millennium. (*Artemis*)

Right: A nu metal necessity, Mudvayne's major-label debut spawned the pulsating anthem 'Dig' and metal would never be the same again. (*No-Name*, *Epic*)

Left: Thought to rival Slipknot but always playing second fiddle, Mushroomhead still created some solid albums, such as *XIII*. (*Universal*)

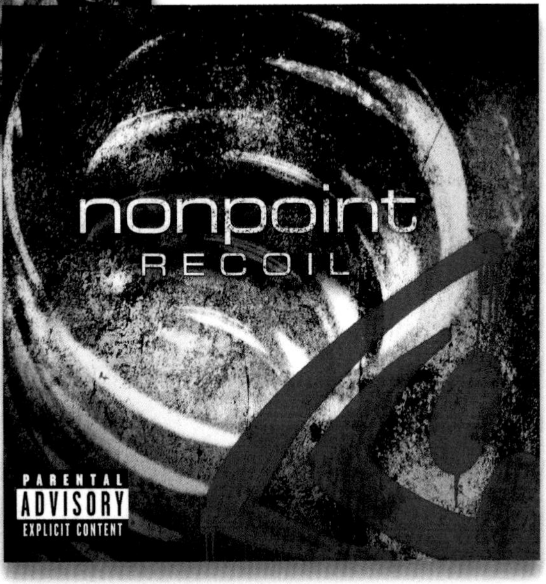

Right: A Phil Collins cover put Nonpoint on the map, but *Recoil* turned them into nu metal heavyweights. (*Lava*)

Above: Ill Nino brought their Latin metal with style and aplomb. (*Shawn Michael Webb*)

Below: Korn. Innovators and nu metal godfathers, who are still putting out immense music today. (*Sebastian Paquet*)

Above: Making red caps cool since 1997, Fred Durst drove Limp Bizkit to unimaginable heights. (*Achim Raschka*)

Below: Rage Against the Machine - spokesmen for a new generation with their brand of highly-charged rap metal. (*Penner*)

Above: Still going strong almost three decades on, Sevendust are one of the most respected bands in all of heavy music. (*Rise*)

Below: Led by Corey Taylor, Slipknot brought destruction to Nu Metal like no other band. (*Jose Goulao*)

Above: Snot. These funky punks emphasised nu metal's diversity with a sound all of their own, before tragedy struck. *(Geffen)*

Below: Thanks to Spineshank, industrial metal had never sounded so damn catchy. (*Roadrunner*)

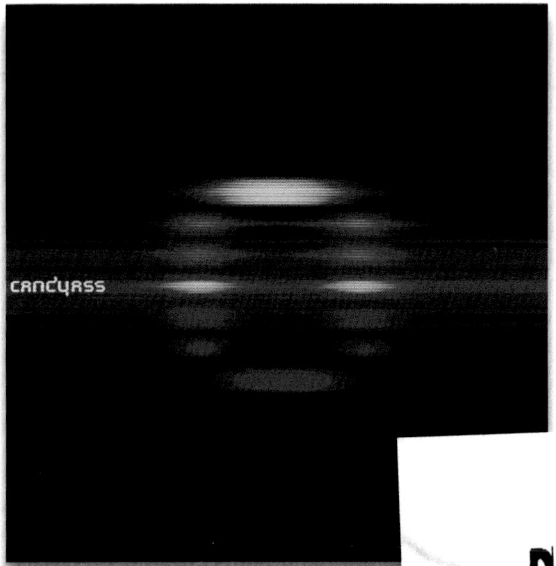

Left: With their form of 'death pop', Orgy raced out the gate with this catchy platinum seller, *Candyass.* (*Elementree*, *Reprise*)

Right: Part of nu metal's second wave, Papa Roach's major-label debut saw them *Infest* the mainstream with some mighty rap metal. (*DreamWorks*)

Left: Christian-tinged rap-metal sent from above, *Satellite* found P.O.D. anywhere and everywhere in the early 2000s. (*Atlantic*)

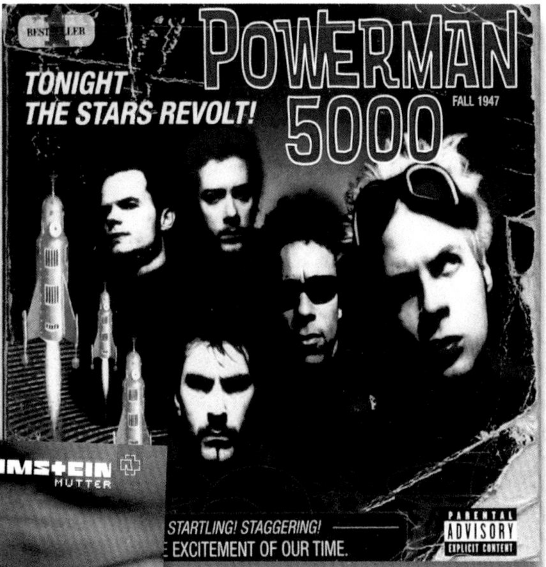

Right: A surprising platinum seller, Powerman 5000 went from underdogs to major players on the back of this 1999 powerhouse album. (*DreamWorks*)

Left: Stunning industrial metal from Germany's favourite sons. (*Motor*, *Universal*)

Right: Saliva's debut effort went platinum quicker than you can say 'Click Click Boom'. (*Island*)

Left: More melodic and radio-friendly, Slaves on Dope took a different approach on album three, but it still rocked hard. (*Bieler Bros., MCA*)

Right: Trying to follow up *Scars* was a tough task, but Soil did it and then some with *Redefine.* (*J*)

Left: Max Cavalera left Sepultura and formed Soulfly, and this debut effort found him in the form of his life. (*Roadrunner*)

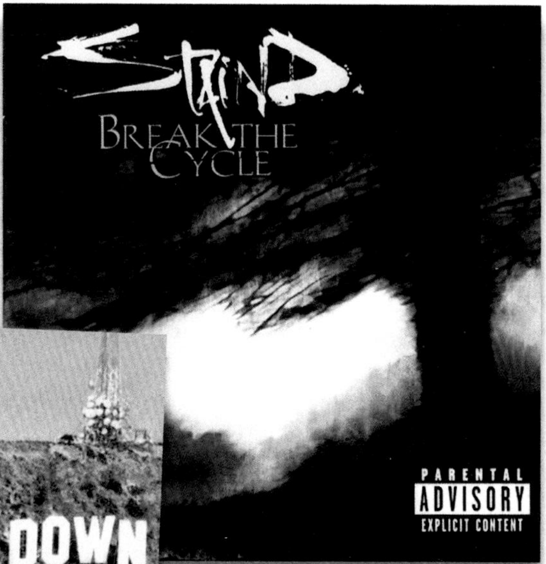

Right: Breaking the cycle and breaking records, Staind cruised to number on with this absolute stunner. (*Flip*, *Elektra*)

Left: Complete nutters but masters of their craft, SOAD were the new heroes on the block when *Toxicity* dropped in 2001. (*American*)

Right: Can a band have more than one magnum opus? Tool do and *Lateralus* is the latest of many. (*Volcano*)

Left: The late and great Wayne Static, doing what he did best. (*Shadowgate*)

Below: Highly respected by many, Taproot has never put a foot wrong during a highly accomplished career. (*Atlantic*)

At one stage pre-millennium, it was reported that Roadrunner Records were interested in signing the Ohio natives. However, the band passed on the deal and paved the way for another costume and mask-wearing metal band to sign with the popular label instead. Most interestingly and rather unsurprisingly, a small feud broke out between Mushroomhead and Slipknot, although it was more between the fans of each band who argued which one had started out first due to the many similarities between the two acts. After the untimely passing of Slipknot's Paul Gray, the feud was instantly ended when Mushroomhead sent their condolences to the Iowans, showing that life was too short for silly arguments. Common sense had prevailed and Mushroomhead was free to continue on their own path, and in 2010 their next record, *Beautiful Stories for Ugly Children,* took the number 1 spot on iTunes' metal albums chart. 'Come On' and 'I'll Be Here' were promoted as singles before a new song called 'Your Soul is Mine' made its way onto the *SAW VI* movie soundtrack. Various line-up changes ensued, which included a return for J Mann, who shared vocal duties with Reavis on the band's eighth album, *The Righteous & the Butterfly,* released in May 2014. It was to be the band's highest-charting album to date as it peaked at 20 on the *Billboard* 200, and it was thanks in part to the popular single, 'Qwerty'.

In the years since, Reavis left the band and set up a new project under the name A Killer's Confession, and more comings and goings have left drummer, Steve 'Skinny' Felton, and J Mann as the longest-serving members ahead of Mushroomhead's latest album, *A Wonderful Life*, which dropped in 2020 via Napalm Records. Despite never reaching the heights of their one time rivals Slipknot, it is safe to say that Mushroomhead has still left a frenzied imprint on the nu metal movement.

Killer Cuts – 'Solitaire/Unraveling', 'Sun Doesn't Rise'

Neurotica

Years Active: 1995-2002
Location: Sarasota, Florida, USA
Main era line-up: Kelly Shaefer (vocals), Chris Rollo (guitar), Shawn Bowen (guitar), Migwell Przybyl (bass), Jason West (drums)
Albums: Seed (1998), Living in Dog Years (1999), Neurotica (2002)

Neurotica started out in 1995 after Kelly Schaefer decided to put his popular death metal band, Atheist, to bed. Shows in the Sarasota area of Florida quickly caught the attention of AC/DC singer Brian – who was residing in the region at the time – and he would help Neurotica find a management deal as well as produce the band's debut album, *Seed*. A second release titled *Living in Dog Years* was again produced by Johnson, and the record earned Neurotica a deal with *WWE* Wrestling's Smackdown! Records – thus becoming the first actual band to join the label.

Departing from their grungier beginnings, the quintet moved into nu metal territory for their self-titled third album in 2002, and the songs consisted largely of updated versions of tracks from the *Seed* record. The pulsating 'Ride of Your Life' earned the band some decent exposure due to its inclusion on *WWE*'s *Forceable Entry* compilation. However, Neurotica would later split from the label after having the Smackdown! laid on them. Schaefer would unsuccessfully audition for the vacant vocal position in Drowning Pool following the tragic death of Dave Williams, and after he announced Neurotica was no more, he would revive Atheist and return to his death metal roots.

Killer Cuts – 'Ride of Your Life', 'All My Friends Crush You'

No One

Years Active: 2000-2003, 2010-2014
Location: Chicago, Illinois, USA
Main era line-up: Rick Murawski (vocals), Bob Bielarz (guitar), Mike Flaherty (bass), Billy Kassanits (drums)
Albums: No One (2001)

Coming up alongside fellow Chicago bands such as Soil and From Zero, No One played their first show in the summer of 2000 before subsequently producing a three-track demo with popular producer, Johnny K. Record labels soon came calling after a manager in California reportedly threw the demo around without the band's consent, but the quartet went with it anyway and elected to sign to Immortal Records; releasing their self-titled debut in mid-2001. The spikey singles of 'Chemical' and 'Down on Me' received moderate airplay (although neither charted), and to further promote their record, No One opened for Slaves on Dope and Dry Kill Logic on small club tours.

Led by Rick Murawski, the alt metal crew then played ten dates of Ozzfest in 2001 before joining Slipknot on part of their *Iowa* world tour, but No One would soon be dropped by Immortal because of disappointing album sales. Demos of new material were posted on the band's website and received decent feedback from fans. However, No One would officially split up in 2003. A handful of reunion shows took place in 2010, before founding bassist Bob 'Larz' Bielarz, tragically died along with his wife and a friend in a boating accident in 2014. Since then, No One has fallen back into the shadows.

Killer Cuts – 'Chemical', 'Down on Me'

Nonpoint

Years Active: 1997-
Location: Fort Lauderdale, Florida, USA
Main era line-up: Elias Soriano (vocals), Andrew Goldman (guitar), Ken MacMillan (bass), Robb Rivera (drums)

Albums: Separate Yourself (1997), Struggle (1999), Statement (2000), Development (2002), Recoil (2004), To the Pain (2005), Vengeance (2007), Miracle (2010), Nonpoint (2012), The Return (2014), The Poison Red (2016), X (2018)

Nonpoint was formed by Robb Rivera and Elias Soriano in Fort Lauderdale, Florida, and by the end of 1997, the four-piece (completed by Andrew Goldman and Ken MacMillan) had self-released their first album, *Separate Yourself*. Indie label, Jugular Records, distributed their follow-up release, *Struggle,* in 1999, before Nonpoint signed a major label deal with MCA Records.

The year 2000 was where Nonpoint truly emerged, releasing the groove metal, funk and hardcore infused *Statement*. Lead single 'What a Day' received heavy rotation which helped to reach a high of 24 on *Billboard*'s Mainstream Rock listings, before Nonpoint embarked on an eighteen-month tour cycle which saw them share stages with Hed PE, Taproot, Disturbed and Drowning Pool; as well a second stage slot on Ozzfest in 2001.

In 2002, *Development* was released with 'Your Signs' being a great choice of single, and another stint on Ozzfest followed before tours with Sevendust and Papa Roach endeared Nonpoint to even bigger audiences. After leaving MCA, Lava Records became the band's new home, and possibly the biggest moment in their career came in 2004 upon the release of *Recoil*. A solid record based around hard rock foundations, the singles 'The Trust' and 'Rabia' went down well, but it was the cover of the Phil Collins classic, 'In the Air Tonight', which really put Nonpoint on the map. A powerful interpretation of an already highly esteemed song, Nonpoint's version would go on to be hugely successful when it was included in the *Miami Vice* movie a couple of years later. By this time, it was 2006 and the band was already promoting another album (*To the Pain*) when 'In the Air Tonight' became more than just a cover song and album track, and it still remains one of Nonpoint's go-to songs today.

At the end of 2006, the quartet released a live CD/DVD (*Live and Kicking*) which was recorded during a hometown show they had played earlier in the year, and then a fifth album followed in 2007 in the form of *Vengeance*. An acoustic EP was all for 2009 and then *Miracle* was unleashed less than a year later, as Nonpoint proved how hard-working a band they were and always have been. A first venture over to Australia occurred in 2012 before a cover of Michael Jackson's 'Billie Jean' was recorded and released, and three more records were later put out (*Nonpoint* in 2012, *The Return* in 2014 and *The Poison Red* in 2016). In 2018, Nonpoint released their tenth studio album, *X,* which was considered one of the best albums of the band's career, and with plenty of touring seeing the band cover most of America, Nonpoint continue to be a highly popular band that have stood the test of time, emerging from nu metal's shadow with much admiration and respect.

Killer Cuts – 'What a Day', 'In the Air Tonight'

Robb Rivera speaks:

When Andy, Ken, Elias and I got together, we came from so many backgrounds of music that pretty much our genre, how we called it, was 'Anything goes'. I am a metalhead and I like thrash and hardcore – that is where I came from. Andy was into Metallica and blues, Ken was into hip-hop and hardcore, and Elias was completely r&b and hip-hop, and so we kind of mixed all those styles together. We had a song that was techno style with a blues bridge, we would go from one genre to another in the same song, and that is how we liked to do things. The one thing people used to call us when we started out was 'Rage Against the Machine on steroids', but we just decided to do whatever felt good at the time. It was never aimed at being this or that. I would put in thrash beats, hardcore beats, but then in the middle of the song, we would throw in a hip-hop part, because we wanted to be different and stand out from all the other bands when we lived in Fort Lauderdale. No one sounded like us and we didn't sound like them.

I think that what we brought different to other bands in nu metal was that we mixed all these styles, whereas a lot of bands had a DJ, or they were just rapping and singing. Elias was rapping and screaming, and Andy was singing and screaming, and a lot of bands didn't have that. We didn't even consider ourselves nu metal, we just considered ourselves a band that moulded as many styles as possible, and the only reason they put us in nu metal was because we had a guy who rapped.

Musically, I don't think we had anything in common with any of those bands, and to me, Korn was never nu metal – they had a completely different sound. When they came out there was nothing like that out there with those down-tuned guitars. Sevendust also gets thrown in that category but they are just a metal band. To me, nu metal has always been the guys who had a rapper and a DJ. I think if Nonpoint had come out now we wouldn't have been called nu metal, we just came out at that time. All we wanted was to be different from everybody else, we wanted to have an explosive live show, and if something was going on like a technical difficulty, we would just go into a blues jam which doesn't sound very nu metal to me at all. Another thing we had that was different was a guitar player who could play blues solos, and no one around that time was doing guitar solos in nu metal.

If you put Nonpoint in the company of Deftones, Incubus (with their *S.C.I.E.N.C.E.* record), System of a Down, Tool – those are the bands we actually listened to, but at the time we came up, the bands around were Orange 9mm, Stuck Mojo, Pressure 4-5; the first Taproot record we thought was fucking brilliant. We got put in that category and I was fine with it. We were friends with most of those bands and we enjoyed their music.

Getting record label interest was great and we sat down with Universal, Lava and MCA on the same day. We went out to breakfast with Lava, lunch with MCA and dinner with Universal (or vice versa), and MCA had the best plan for us.

They basically said, 'We're going to put you out there and you're going to tour for eighteen months'. They were more focused on trying to build the band, whereas the other two labels were more focused on our singer being the star. MCA bought us a van and a trailer and put us out on the road, and then five months later, we released the single, 'What a Day', and it was a great cycle. We got to play with a lot of killer acts, and we got incredible exposure. Who knows what would have happened if we had signed with the other labels, but we knew that MCA had the best plan for Nonpoint.

Being on Ozzfest in 2001 was, to me, single-handedly still my favourite tour I have ever done, just for the fact that the line-up was so incredible. We went into that tour knowing almost 80% of the bands on the bill. Nonpoint was the first band confirmed on the Streetwise stage and I remember getting that phone call. I had attended three Ozzfests prior and I was like 'One of these days, I'm gonna do Ozzfest' and I did it and it was an incredible experience. There are so many memories of that tour and it was an incredible community. I don't remember feeling any weirdness from other bands with egos or anything like that, and still to this day, we are friends with Drowning Pool, Mudvayne, the Taproot guys, Spineshank ... a lot of those bands aren't together anymore but we're all still very tight.

I got to see Black Sabbath every day, who are one of my favourite bands of all time, and getting to hear those songs that helped make me who I am – and here I am opening for them. Slipknot and Marilyn Manson put on incredible shows every day, I would go and watch pretty much all the bands I could every day, and one of the best memories of that tour was the very first day in Chicago. Disturbed headlined the second stage and it was so packed over there. I believe they had already gone platinum by then and there was maybe 10,000 to 15,000 people in attendance. They had to be moved to the main stage for the rest of the tour because there were so many people who wanted to see Disturbed play. Another cool thing was watching Hatebreed. We had to follow them every day and that absolutely sucked, but it was very inspiring. Jamey Jasta is one of the best frontmen I have ever seen in my life and he just knew how to get that crowd pumped. Their music is just so brutally heavy and the crowd would go off hard all the time, and following them was a challenge every day. Another thing that happened was we were in catering in Indianapolis, Indiana, and Marilyn Manson and Twiggy Ramirez walked in and the entire room went silent at the same time. That was one of the most incredible experiences because people didn't see him a lot and he didn't come out a lot. Outside of stage in those two months, I may have seen him only two or three times in total. That tour was killer and that whole cycle was killer. We did Hed PE, Spineshank, Stereomud, Glassjaw, Machine Head, Nothingface, Fuel, Sevendust; I couldn't have asked for a better time in my life. Those were the most fun eighteen months ever.

Covering 'In The Air Tonight' was a suggestion by one of my drum techs. We had obviously heard the song a million times, and when we went to record *Recoil* and record that song, it went through five versions before we got to the one that everyone knows. One day, Ken came in with the bassline and it just grew from there. We put it together pretty quickly and still, to this day, that song gets played everywhere. Any tour we are on and we play that song – everyone is singing it even if they have never seen Nonpoint before. Who doesn't know the lyrics to that song? It has been played at Baseball stadiums all over the country, a couple of players come out to bat with that song, the Miami Dolphins run out to that song; it has been on movie trailers. I could not be more thankful for Phil Collins, but we've played 'In the Air Tonight' so many times and for so long now that it feels like it's our song.

We had actually heard that Phil had given the thumbs up when he heard it, and we were going to do a video for the song that was going to feature him in it because Lava was part of Atlantic Records and Phil was on Atlantic. There was talk about it, but it never materialised, and I'm bummed out because I thought it was going to be the greatest thing in the world to work with this iconic artist. I really wish it had worked out. When it got into the *Miami Vice* movie, we were actually on the *To the Pain* record, and when they released the soundtrack it was the first track on the CD, so the song has brought an insane amount of exposure to the band. I don't think we're ever going to stop playing it live.

When I got into this, I was that kid of sixteen years old, learning to play instruments and joining bands. I dropped out of school for this because music was what I wanted to do. Now I have been in Nonpoint for over twenty years, and I have a family (I have two children). Me and Elias made a pact to ourselves a few years ago after we lost the original guys and we said we are going to do this shit forever. We've consistently been able to release records, labels still sign us, and if they don't sign us then we'll release the damn thing ourselves. We love playing music, Elias is singing better than ever, and he has got to a point where his ideas these days blow me away. To think that over twenty years later you can still blow someone else away…some people just run out of gas, but it's just desire to continue doing what we love.

I am a musician – there is no other option. I don't know how to do anything else, so if I'm not a musician, I'll be a band manager, a booking agent, or I'll do something else music-related. Me and Elias still have that fire after all this time; we take this band very seriously, which I think has resulted in some line-up changes over the years. Nonpoint is a full-time job and this is how we pay our bills, so we are going to continue doing this until our legs fall off.

My favourite memory is just the fact that I got signed. My dream came true. That first cycle for *Statement* was everything I had imagined it was going to be. Having crazy parties, the camaraderie between the bands; sometimes you would bump into a couple of egotistical people, but the memory is, to me, that I was living the dream I had wanted since I started playing music; and I am still living that dream today. I am still here, still relevant to our fans, still making music and making a living from what I love to do – that is something not a lot of people can say these days. We've had some incredible people who have worked for us over the years and I have a family who understands I have to leave, band members who I know will give 100%, a manager who kicks ass for us, and fans I know will always be there for us.

Nothingface

Years Active: 1993-2004, 2005-2009
Location: Washington D.C., USA
Main era line-up: Matt Holt (vocals), Tom Maxwell (guitar), Bill Gaal (bass), Chris Houck/ Tommy Sickles (drums)
Albums: Nothingface (1995), Pacifier (1997), An Audio Guide to Everyday Atrocity (1998), Violence (2000), Skeletons (2003)

Nothingface began as a grunge band before moving to a heavier sound upon the arrival of vocalist Matt Holt in 1995. Replacing David Gabbard, Holt helped the band produce some alternative and robust metal, which led to a self-released and self-titled debut album later in 1995. It wouldn't be long before the quartet signed to DCide Records, and in 1996 they released *Pacifier*, which included six tracks from the original first album as well as four new tunes. Following it up with *An Audio Guide to Everyday Atrocity* in 1998, the record was distributed by Mayhem Records and featured the stirring singles of 'Breathe Out' and 'Sick'. To promote the album, Nothingface toured the US with rap metal pioneers Stuck Mojo, alternative metal pioneers Helmet, and industrial powerhouses Ministry; and having finally earned some strong recognition, the band entered their most successful period at the turn of the new millennium when they joined TVT Records.

Unleashing their third album, *Violence*, in September 2000, it still featured the band's customary brash alternative metal. However, melodic influences began to creep in and the lead single, 'Bleeder', made it to 32 on the Mainstream Rock Charts. Often considered Nothingface's most successful record, *Violence* even made VH1's '12 Most Underrated Nu Metal Albums' list.

Becoming more diverse with possible mainstream exposure in mind, *Skeletons* followed in 2003 and it was led by the tender but tough 'Ether', as well as the fan favourite anthem, 'Murder Is Masturbation'. *Skeletons* earned Nothingface a spot on Ozzfest in the same year; however, it was a tour that would ultimately lead to the band's downfall. In early 2004, Nothingface announced they would be disbanding after partly blaming their record label for a lack of support. Reportedly stemming from an incident during Ozzfest when the band needed money for gas in order to be able to get to the next city on the tour, TVT refused to pay, and so Nothingface called out the label during one of their live shows on the tour. Holt later stated that TVT would give them the cash to finish the stint, however the band would take the money and go home with it before Ozzfest was over.

A reformation took place in late 2005 and Nothingface supported Disturbed for a one-off show in 2006, debuting the new line-up of Holt, Maxwell, Jerry Montano on bass and Tommy Sickles on drums. Two new songs were then released online before the band went on a small US club tour, and then Bill Gaal and Chris Houck returned to the band to re-complete Nothingface's original line-up. Teasers began to be uploaded online showing the members recording in the studio, but in 2009 Nothingface called it quits for good. Maxwell went on to help form the heavy metal supergroup Hellyeah alongside Mudvayne's Chad Gray, and in April 2017, the enigmatic and immensely popular Holt passed away after suffering from an undisclosed degenerative illness.

Killer Cuts – 'Bleeder', 'Ether'

One Minute Silence

Years Active: 1995-2003, 2011-2015
Location: London, England
Main era line-up: Brian 'Yap' Barry (vocals), Massimo Fiocco (guitar), Glen Diani (bass), Martin Davies (drums)
Albums: Available in All Colors (1998), Buy Now...Saved Later (2000), One Lie Fits All (2003)

One Minute Silence would become one of the most outspoken bands of the nu metal era by delivering an infectious slab of rap metal with lyrics full of political messages which have often been interpreted as anti-capitalist and anarchistic. *Available In All Colours* dropped in 1998 after the band had signed to Big Cat Records, but it was the band's 2000 release, *Buy Now...Saved Later,* where the quartet broke through with a more metallic sound. The album peaked at 61 in the UK album chart and the popular singles of 'Holy Man' and 'Fish out of Water' received strong airplay – especially on *Kerrang!* TV who supported their fellow countrymen.

By touring America with the likes of Slipknot and Mudvayne, with the latter supporting the Brit heroes on their own headline tour of the UK, One Minute Silence had built up some strong momentum in time for their next album, *One Lie Fits All,* which was released via Taste Media in 2003. Spearheaded by the fantastically heavy but catchy 'I Wear My Skin' which hit 44 in the UK singles chart, as well as other highlights such as 'Revolution', 'We Bounce' and 'You So Much as Move', it seemed that One Minute Silence was destined to feature alongside the big hitters of the nu metal movement; however the band would later announce in a press release that they were splitting up to focus on other projects which included frontman, Brian 'Yap' Barry, starting up a spoken word career.

In 2010, One Minute Silence confirmed their reformation with three of the original four members on board – the only line-up change seeing Martin Davies replace original drummer, Eddie Stratton. In 2013, the stirring EP, *Fragmented Armageddon,* was released and featured the popular tracks 'Fruit from the Lie' and 'Pandemic Schizophrenia', as One Minute Silence showed they hadn't lost their knack of producing some pounding metal to go with Barry's venomous rap vocals. The EP appears to have been the band's final swansong, but anyone who has ever listened to One Minute Silence will know they were one of the most important and dangerous bands to come out of the nu metal era. Having something different to say with a 'Don't give a fuck attitude' which endeared them to fans much further afield than their UK base, how we could do with them returning now to confront the chaos surrounding the world.

Killer Cuts – 'Holy Man', 'I Wear My Skin'

Onesidezero

Years Active: 1997-2003, 2004-
Location: Los Angeles, California, USA
Main era line-up: Jasan Radford (vocals, guitar), Levon Sultanian (lead guitar), Brett Kane (guitar), Cristian Hernandez (bass), Rob Basile (drums)
Albums: Is This Room Getting Smaller (2001), onesidezero (2007)

Performing heavy but melodic rock and containing deep and dark lyrical content, onesidezero made a promising start when they caught the eye of Maverick Records and signed to the label in 2000. Releasing their debut album a year later, *Is This Room Getting Smaller* propelled the band into the public eye and an almost three-year touring cycle saw them sharing stages with Incubus, Sevendust, Static-X, Soulfly, Soil and Linkin Park; and even though strong singles were released to promote the album ('Instead Laugh' and 'New World Order'), *Is This Room Getting Smaller* failed to sell significant numbers.

Asking to be released from their deal with Maverick, onesidezero called it quits in 2003 so band members could set about their own projects, however they would reform in 2004 and get back on the touring circuit. A second album followed in 2007 via Corporate Punishment Records – an Ulrich Wild-produced self-titled effort which included the appealing rockers of 'My Confession' and 'Sleep'. In the years which have passed, more new music has supposedly been in the works and onesidezero's social media pages remain active, but nothing has emerged music-wise in quite some time. It is also worth noting that VH1 listed the band's debut album in their twelve 'underrated nu metal albums' list, which shows onesidezero did have some effect on who they came across during the nu metal movement.

Killer Cuts – 'Instead Laugh', 'New World Order'

Orgy

Years Active: 1994-2005, 2010-
Location: Los Angeles, California, USA
Main era line-up: Jay Gordon (vocals), Amir Derakh (lead guitar, synthesizers), Ryan Shuck (rhythm guitar), Paige Haley (bass), Bobby Hewitt (drums)
Albums: Candyass (1998), Vapor Transmission (2000), Punk Statik Paranoia (2004)

Orgy shared their combined love of new wave music to produce an industrial rock sound full of synth and electronica, all the while wearing leather trousers and platform boots, as well as a healthy dose of eyeliner. Earning a name for themselves before ever playing a live show, it wouldn't be long before the five-piece signed to Elementree – the label which had recently been set up by Korn. In 1998, the Orgy's debut album, *Candyass,* was released and it was led by the introductory single 'Stitches'; however it was the second single which really brought people's attention to Orgy. A cover of New Order's 'Blue Monday' suited the quintet both musically and visually, and its accompanying promo video earned heavy rotation on TV while the song itself lit up the radio airwaves. Jonathan Davis guested on the album track 'Revival', 'Stitches' was re-released on the back of the success of 'Blue Monday', and all of this culminated in *Candyass* selling close to two million copies in America.

Riding the wave of success, Orgy featured on the Family Values tour later in the same year alongside Limp Bizkit, Rammstein, Ice Cube, and the headlining Korn, and it appeared the quintet was destined for even bigger things to come. After severing ties with Elementree, Orgy signed with Warner to put out their second album, *Vapor Transmission,* which arrived in October 2000. Concentrating on a more melodic sound while still being heavily reliant on synth, the brilliant 'Fiction (Dreams in Digital)' and 'Opticon' (included in the horror movie *Valentine*) were ideal choices of singles, and the album reached gold status in the US thanks to further radio releases of 'Suckerface' and 'Eva'.

The following year, Orgy contributed the song 'Faces' to the official soundtrack of Ben Stiller's *Zoolander* movie, and their next new material surfaced in 2004 when the heavier *Punk Statik Paranoia* came out on Gordon's own D1 Music label. 'Vague' and 'Pure' were excellent songs up there with anything the band had created before but with nu metal on a decline, album sales of only 5,000 copies were reported in the first week of release. It didn't help that by now, Orgy was on the verge of breaking point, and the band would go on hiatus to focus on various side-projects. Shuck and Derakh formed the electronic rock band Julien-K (which would also include Bobby Hewitt at a later date), and the duo also joined together with Linkin Park's Chester Bennington to unleash the alt metal project, Dead by Sunrise – putting out their *Out of Ashes* album in 2009.

Over the last few years, Gordon has continued to perform under the Orgy name with a brand-new line-up of musicians, and in 2015 they released the *Talk Sick* EP, which featured some strong and energetic electro rock ('Wide Awake and Dead' being the pick of the bunch), but nothing has followed since.

A solid cog in the nu metal machine, Orgy offered something different with their sound and look, and even though it was a cover song, the Californian's version of 'Blue Monday' remains a constant addition to any nu metal playlist or countdown.

Killer Cuts – 'Stitches', 'Blue Monday'

Otep

Years Active: 2000-
Location: Los Angeles, California, USA
Main era line-up: Otep Shamaya (vocals), Rob Patterson (guitar), Jason McGuire (bass),

Mark Bistany (drums)
Albums: Sevas Tra (2002), House of Secrets (2004), The Ascension (2007), Smash the Control Machine (2009), Atavist (2011), Hydra (2013), Generation Doom (2016), Kult 45 (2018)

Otep wasn't even signed to a record label when Sharon Osbourne welcomed the powerful quartet onto the Ozzfest 2000 tour – having witnessed one of the band's explosive live performances. Becoming more popular because of their stage performances, Otep (an anagram of Poet) hadn't made a single demo when Capitol Records came calling, and after signing with the label, the *Jihad* EP became the band's first release.

Next, a debut full-length album titled *Sevas Tra* announced itself to the world in June 2002. Reading *Art Saves* backwards, it was produced by Terry Date and featured track-after-track of punishing alternative metal, with Otep Shamaya's death metal growls and delicate tortured vocals adding an element of intrigue to proceedings. A handful of tracks were reworked from the *Jihad* EP, and songs such as the bludgeoning 'Blood Pigs' and 'T.R.I.C.' showcased poetic lyricism on top of some unforgiving metallic fury. *Sevas Tra* put Otep firmly on the map with a sound that never should have threatened the mainstream, but somehow it did, and the sophomore album, *House of Secrets,* followed in 2004. Spearheaded by the single *'Warhead',* whose accompanying promo video made the top 10 on *MTV*'s *Headbanger's Ball*, 'Buried Alive' also became a fan favourite single, while Slipknot's Joey Jordison featured on drums for a number of the album's tracks. After signing to KOCH, 2007 album, *The Ascension,* included a cover of Nirvana's 'Breed', while guitar duties were performed by Karma Singh Cheema from American Head Charge. Songs such as 'Ghostflowers' and 'March of the Martyrs' were popular singles and continued Otep's deliverance of brash, alt metal devastation.

Following extensive touring with Static-X, the band signed with Victory Records and released their next effort, *Smash the Control Machine,* in August 2009. Rob Patterson and Mark Bistany returned for the record after being out of the fold for almost five years, but they would soon leave the band again, and Jason McGuire followed in 2010. Shamaya remained busy and she enlisted new members ahead of recording and releasing *Atavist* in 2011, followed by their *Sounds Like Armageddon* album a year later. At the beginning of 2013, Shamaya announced that Otep's upcoming sixth album, *Hydra,* would be the last, however, in 2015, a deal was signed with Napalm Records and that led to the release of *Generation Doom* in April 2016. Remaining heavily active, the rap metal-focused *Kult 45* emerged in July 2018 and featured some of Otep's best songs in years.

From the early anthems of 'Blood Pigs' and 'T.R.I.C.' to newer material such as 'Fists Fall' and 'Apex Predator', Otep has always oozed brutal heaviness. Whether it be alternative, gothic, groove, thrash, death or extreme metal, at one stage or another, this band has provided it all with sheer precision and an abundance of passion.

Killer Cuts – 'Blood Pigs', 'T.R.I.C.'

P.O.D

Years Active: 1992-
Location: San Diego, California, USA
Main era line-up: Sonny Sandoval (vocals), Marcos Curiel (guitar), Traa Daniels (bass), Wuv Bernardo (drums)
Albums: Snuff the Punk (1994), Brown (1996), The Fundamental Elements of Southtown (1999), Satellite (2001), Payable on Death (2003), Testify (2006), When Angels & Serpents Dance (2008), Murdered Love (2012), The Awakening (2015), Circles (2018)

Payable On Death formed as a Christian band that effortlessly fused together rap and alternative metal. P.O.D. (as they are more commonly known) went largely under the radar with their early *Snuff the Punk* and *Brown* albums until they signed with Atlantic Records in 1998. *The Fundamental Elements of Southtown* reached 51 on the *Billboard* 200 upon its release in August 1999 and it was led by the heavy rotation of the singles 'Southtown', and latterly 'Rock the Party (Off the Hook)' on *MTV2*. Proving to be the perfect kind of band to continue nu metal's ascension, P.O.D.'s major label debut would later go on to be certified platinum.

On 11 September 2001 – a date forever remembered for the horrific 9/11 terror attacks – P.O.D. released their second major label record, *Satellite*, which debuted at 6 on the *Billboard* 200. 'Alive' hyped the record with frequent rotation on MTV2 and *Kerrang!* especially – a powerhouse anthem that introduced many new fans to the band from across the pond. 'Alive', as well as 'Youth of the Nation' and 'Boom', proved to be popular for their different styles – one being a ballad of sorts influenced by the Columbine shootings in 1999, and the other ('Boom') an adrenaline-fueled hard rocker. Eventually going 3x platinum and selling over seven million copies worldwide, *Satellite* proved to be the band's true breakthrough release by finishing the work that *The Fundamental Elements of Southtown* had started prior.

Next, P.O.D. produced the track 'Sleeping Awake' which was included on *The Matrix Reloaded* movie soundtrack, before a self-titled album followed in 2003. *Payable on Death* was to be the first release to feature new guitarist Jason Truby, who had replaced original member Marcos Curiel ahead of recording, and the album focused on an alternative metal sound that became less reliable on hip-hop influences. Vocalist Sonny Sandoval incorporated reggae stylings on a number of tracks and showcase singles 'Will You' and 'Change the World' helped to promote the record nicely, and while *Payable on Death* peaked at nine on the *Billboard* chart and sold 1.3 million copies worldwide, it ultimately failed to match the success of *Satellite* by a considerable margin.

Originally planned for a late 2005 release, the band's sixth album, *Testify,* debuted just inside the top 10 in America in January 2006. 'Goodbye for Now' featured backing vocals from the then-unknown pop star Katy Perry, as P.O.D. continued to attempt new things with their fashionable brand of mainstream metal. The second single, 'Lights Out', earned further success on the back of being the theme song for *WWE* Wrestling's *Survivor Series* event, before the quartet performed Rey Mysterio's entrance music at the *Wrestlemania* pay-per-view in April of 2006. Later in the year, P.O.D. announced they had left Atlantic Records and would soon be releasing a compilation dedicated to their Atlantic-era releases, and then Curiel returned to the fold and replaced his original successor, Truby.

When Angels & Serpents Dance dropped in 2008 through INO Records and featured Mike Muir from Suicidal Tendencies on the track 'Kaliforn-Eye-A' and Helmet's Page Hamilton on 'God Forbid'; while the singles 'Addicted' and 'Shine with Me' were put out either side of the album's issue. It would be over four years before P.O.D. returned with another record, and by July of 2012, the band had signed to Razor & Tie and announced *Murdered Love*. Produced by Howard Benson, who had worked on *The Fundamental Elements…, Satellite* and *Payable on Death* records, *Murdered Love* was a slightly heavier record than the last few.

Three singles were put out ('Lost in Forever (Scream)', 'Higher' and 'Beautiful'), Jamey Jasta of hardcore bruisers Hatebreed featured on the opening track, 'Eyez', and Cypress Hill's Sen Dog turned up on 'West Coast Rock Steady'. Continuing a highly productive spell around this time, P.O.D. then released an acoustic album titled *The SoCal Sessions* in late 2014, before creating their first-ever concept album, which arrived in 2015 and was titled *The Awakening*. Including voiceovers and skits, the story documented how the protagonist loses his way and later finds salvation, detailed across ten tracks where highlights included 'This Goes Out to You' and 'Criminal Conversations'. Rather disappointingly, *The Awakening* only reached 75 in the US, but during the nu metal years, P.O.D. dominated the airwaves with *Satellite* and the singles released from it. A 2017 single, 'Soundboy Killa', showed the band to be returning to their classic sound for their latest album, *Circles,* which did indeed include some heavier moments; however, 'Alive' and 'Youth of the Nation' will forever remain the tracks most synonymous with the San Diego crew.

Killer Cuts – 'Alive', 'Youth of the Nation'

Papa Roach

Years Active: 1993-

Location: Vacaville, California, USA

Main era line-up: Jacoby Shaddix (vocals), Jerry Horton (guitar), Tobin Esperance (bass), Dave Buckner (drums)

Albums: Old Friends from Young Years (1997), Infest (2000), Lovehatetragedy (2002), Getting Away with Murder (2004), The Paramour Sessions (2006), Metamorphosis (2009), The Connection (2012), F.E.A.R. (2015), Crooked Teeth (2017), Who Do You Trust? (2019)

Reportedly taking their name from Jacoby Shaddix's step-grandfather – whose name was William Roatch and given the nickname 'Papa Roach' – the band made a slow start before they finally solidified their line-up in 1996. Self-releasing their debut album, *Old Friends from Young Years,* in February 1997 via the now-defunct indie label, Onion Hardcore, Papa Roach went on to support other rising nu metal artists such as Incubus, Hed PE and Static-X before learning that Warner Bros. Records had decided against signing them, after checking out a new demo the band had put together in 1999. What a big mistake it would prove to be.

DreamWorks Records then offered the quartet a recording contract and in April 2000, Papa Roach's major-label debut, *Infest,* was released to the masses. Centring on a rap metal sound, the singles 'Last Resort', 'Between Angels and Insects' and 'Broken Home' were huge statements from a band who appeared to be both cocky and confident but had the talent and the songs to back it all up. *Infest* was certified triple platinum in July 2001, and as of 2010, the album has sold over eight million copies worldwide. Papa Roach would then embark on the Anger Management Tour with Limp Bizkit and rapper's Eminem, Xzibit and Ludacris, before playing Ozzfest in 2001, where they performed on the main stage of both the US and UK legs.

Lovehatetragedy followed in 2002, and although it still featured some of the rap-metal elements of its predecessor, cleaner singing vocals from Shaddix found Papa Roach evolving towards a straightforward hard rock sound. The album failed to match the success of *Infest*; however, it still gained gold status in the US and, latterly, Canada and the UK. 'She Loves Me Not' and 'Time and Time Again' were as good as any track the band had previously written, helping *Lovehatetragedy* sell over three million copies worldwide. The next album Papa Roach would release would be through Geffen, who absorbed DreamWorks and signed the band to their own label; and the platinum-selling *Getting Away with Murder* was unleashed in August 2004. The title track became a Papa Roach classic, the rock ballad of 'Scars' earned heavy rotation on both radio and TV, and with nu metal seemingly dying out, it was clear that Papa Roach's hard rock direction was the way forward as they continued on to 2006's *The Paramour Sessions*. The energetic '...To Be Loved' opened the record with precision and urgency, while the heart-wrenching 'Forever' and the sombre finale of 'Roses on My Grave' showed Papa Roach's ability to write relatable songs capable of leaving not a dry eye in the room. Debuting at 16 on the *Billboard* 200, *The Paramour Sessions* has sold well over two million copies; however, due to the sales being spread worldwide, it became the first Papa Roach album that failed to be certified at least gold.

Further into 2006, the band toured with Guns N' Roses, who were gearing up to release their first album in over a decade, then followed a stint with Deftones on a US tour which saw ticket sales go through the roof. In April 2007, Papa Roach would suffer their first line-up change when Dave Buckner decided to take some time off to address a few personal issues. Replaced by Unwritten Law drummer Tony Palermo, it would later be announced that the move was a permanent thing, and Palermo debuted on 2009's *Metamorphosis* album. Led by the sleazy single, 'Hollywood Whore', the album debuted at eight and further singles included 'Lifeline', and the gritty 'I Almost Told You That I Loved You'; while Mötley Crüe guitarist Mick Mars made a special guest appearance on the album track, 'Into the Light'.

After a huge touring schedule which saw Papa Roach share stages with Mötley Crüe, Staind, Seether, Buckcherry and Nickelback, the quartet returned to the studio and got to work on *Time for Annihilation*; which arrived in August 2010. The first release since signing to Eleven Seven Music, the album featured five brand-new tracks as well as nine live recordings. The newbies of 'Kick in the Teeth', 'Burn' and 'No Matter What' were put out as singles and around the same time, Geffen was putting out a greatest hits compilation – against Papa Roach's wishes. An eighth full-length record emerged in 2012, seeing *The Connection* debuting some electronic elements for the first time. Shaddix's rap vocals made a welcome return, and the album featured the fist-pumping anthem 'Still Swingin', as well as the gloriously catchy 'Where Did the Angels Go'. Produced by Sixx:A.M. vocalist, James Michael, the album peaked at 17 in the US, and with a nu metal revival on the cards around 2015, Papa Roach returned with arguably their best album since *lovehatetragedy* in the form of *F.E.A.R.* From the bruising opener of 'Face Everything and Rise' to the incredible hard rock ballad of 'Gravity' (featuring In This Moment's Maria Brink), as well as the closing 'Warriors' welcoming hip-hop star, Royce da 5' 9', *F.E.A.R.* was raw, honest and heavily addictive. Peaking at 13 in the UK and 15 in America, they were both respectable chart positions in a time where pop was once again reigning supreme over heavy music.

Papa Roach's momentum continued into 2017 on the hard-rocking *Crooked Teeth*, before the quartet went alternative for softer *Who Do You Trust?* album in 2019; however, *Infest* will forever be considered one of nu metal's most defining albums, which launched alongside Linkin Park's *Hybrid Theory* to cement nu metal's second wave, and ultimately the movement's rightful place in the mainstream eye.

Killer Cuts – 'Last Resort', 'Between Angels and Insects'

Pitchshifter

Years Active: 1989-2003, 2006-2008, 2018-
Location: Nottingham, England
Main era line-up: Jon 'JS' Clayden (vocals), Jim Davies (guitar), Mark Clayden (bass), Jason Bowld (drums)
Albums: Industrial (1991), Desensitized (1993), Infotainment? (1996), www.pitchshifter.com (1998), Deviant (2000), PSI (2002)

Pitchshifter's early days saw them as a deathgrind band before they turned their attention towards industrial metal which brought them some deserved success. The 1998 album, *www.pitchshifter.com,* was the band's major-label debut (through Geffen) and it featured the electronically smothered tracks 'Microwaved' and 'Genius'. Also incorporating drum and bass musings into the tracklist, the album sold a respectable 60,000 plus copies and provided a good foundation for Pitchshifter to launch from. Despite the excitement surrounding the band's follow-up album, *Deviant,* MCA/Universal expressed their disappointment at it only selling around 33,000 copies in America. However, the fan favourite 'Everything's Fucked' (released to radio as 'Everything Sucks') became one of Pitchshifter's most recognisable songs. The band later returned to minor label territory, choosing Mayan Records for the release of *PSI* in 2002. Less heavy than previous albums, the industrial rock on show was still sonically captivating and it was potentially the band's most consistent release, as the standout tracks 'Eight Days', 'Down' and 'Shutdown' proved. With rhythmic choruses suitable for the radio airwaves and a slight Americanised sound to proceedings, Pitchshifter earned decent traction from the record and gained further exposure, which somewhat boosted album sales. *P.S.I.* would be Pitchshifter's last studio album as they went on an indefinite hiatus soon after, but while they were around, the Brits effortlessly flew the flag for nu metal in the UK, and a twenty-year anniversary tour to celebrate *'www.pitchshifter.com'* at the end of 2018 was met with such a strong reaction that the band are going to do it all over again next year.

Killer Cuts – 'Genius', 'Everything's Fucked'

Pleymo

Years Active: 1997-2007, 2017-
Location: Fontainebleau, France
Main era line-up: Mike Maggiori (vocals), Erik De Villoutreys (guitar), Davy Portela (guitar), Benoit Juillard (bass), Fred Ceraudo (drums), Franck Bailleul (turntables)
Albums: Keckispasse? (1999), Episode 2: Medecine Cake (2002), Rock (2003), Alphabet Prison (2006)

A six-piece rap metal crew from France, Pleymo signed to Epic Records after the release of their 1999 debut, *Keckispasse?*. Singing almost entirely in their native tongue, Pleymo's second album, *Episode 2: Medecine Cake* came in 2002 and would go on to sell over 50,000 copies. An English version was also distributed under the title *Doctor Tank's Medicine Cake*, and a music video was produced for the excellently catchy lead single, 'New Wave'. A concept album titled *Rock* followed in 2003 which featured a less aggressive and more melodic sound, and 2006's *Alphabet Prison* would combine all of the band's previous styles within one highly impressive tracklist. A hiatus was announced in 2007 so band members could focus on new projects, but in 2017, Pleymo confirmed their comeback with a French tour taking place in the first quarter of 2018, and it was followed by a 'best of' compilation highlighting the band's finest moments.

Killer Cuts – 'Nawak', 'New Wave'

Powerman 5000

Years Active: 1991-
Location: Boston, Massachusetts
Main era line-up: Spider One (vocals), Adam '12' Williams (lead guitar), Mike 'M33' Tempesta (rhythm guitar), Dorian '27' Heartsong (bass), Al '3' Pahanish Jr. (drums)
Albums: The Blood-Splat Rating System (1995), Mega!! Kung Fu Radio (1997), Tonight the Stars Revolt! (1999), Anyone for Doomsday? (2001), Transform (2003), Destroy What You Enjoy (2006), Somewhere on the Other Side of Nowhere (2009), Builders of the Future (2014), New Wave (2017), The Noble Rot (2020)

Formed by Spider One, the younger brother of horror metal hero Rob Zombie, Powerman 5000 released the independent album, *The Blood-Splat Rating System*, before playing Ozzfest in 1996. The band then signed to DreamWorks Records and released a remastered version of *The Blood-Splat Rating System,* obscurely renaming it *Mega!! Kung Fu Radio*, which considerably built the band's reputation as the decade was nearing its end. PM5K's big break came in 1999 with the issuing of *Tonight the Stars Revolt!*, which would go on to sell over a million copies in the US. Spawning the hugely popular 'When Worlds Collide', and the second single, 'Nobody's Real', the material showcased accessible industrial metal with lyrical themes steeped in science fiction. Reaching 29 on the *Billboard* 200, special guests on the album included Rob Zombie on 'Blast Off to Nowhere' and Limp Bizkit's DJ Lethal on a cover of The Cars' 'Good Times Roll'.

Anyone for Doomsday? was supposed to be the much-anticipated follow-up album in 2001. However, Spider pulled the record two weeks ahead of its release, citing the material as sounding too similar to the songs on its predecessor. Line-up changes followed, which ultimately caused Spider to scrap the album altogether, but it would later turn up on the band's website through Megatronic Records; however, no sooner had it been uploaded, it had to be taken down due to legal issues.

Transform had a hassle-free release in 2003, but by now, Powerman 5000 had moved away from their industrial metal sound in favour of heading in a pop punk and rock direction. Still, the record peaked at 27 on the *Billboard* 200, with the singles 'Free' and 'Action' being released as promotion. A rarities collection titled *The Good, The Bad and The Ugly Vol. 1* followed in 2004, before the next studio album, *Destroy What You Enjoy,* would come in 2006 via DRT Entertainment. Only getting to 120 on the *Billboard* chart and continuing to flirt with pop punk rock, it was time for a change, and thankfully Powerman 5000 would bring back their classic sound in the years to come.

Two strong single releases ('Super Villain' and 'V is for Vampire') led up to the back-to-form record, *Somewhere on the Other Side of Nowhere,* in 2009, before a covers album followed in 2011 titled *Copies, Clones & Replicants*; where PM5K put their own spin on the likes of '20th Century Boy' by T-Rex, 'Jump' by Van Halen, and a great take of David Bowie's 'Space Oddity'. In 2014, the storming *Builders of the Future* came out via T-Boy Records and it was led by the catchy and breathless single, 'How to Be a Human', which helped the album reached a very positive 63 on the US album chart.

Continuing a second wind, 2017 saw another brilliant album in the form of *New Wave* which was released through Pavement Entertainment. With plenty of industrial flourishes and infectious singalongs, the rousing 'Footsteps and Voices', 'Sid Vicious in a Dress' and 'David Fucking Bowie' all helped to make *New Wave* arguably the band's best album since *Tonight the Stars Revolt!*, and in 2020, Powerman 5000 dropped *The Noble Rot,* which also went over well with their dedicated fanbase.

Killer Cuts – 'When Worlds Collide', 'Nobody's Real'

Pressure 4-5

Years Active: 1998-2003
Location: Santa Barbara, California, USA
Main era line-up: Adam Rich (vocals), Joe Schmidt (guitar), Mark Barry (guitar), John Miller (bass), Tom Schmidt (drums)
Albums: Burning the Process (2001)

Still highly thought of even though they only released one full-length album, Pressure 4-5 emerged out of Santa Barbara after college pals, Adam Rich and Mark Barry, decided to form a band. Lyle McKeany and brothers Joe and Tom Schmidt rounded out the line-up, and the band released an independent EP titled *Antechnology* before signing to DreamWorks Records in 2000. Coming a year later, *Burning the Process* brought a heavy rock sound which Pressure 4-5 made clear was their intention, as they attempted to steer clear of rap rock as much as they possibly could. Two singles were put out from the album – 'Beat the World' and 'Melt Me Down'; a second stage stint on Ozzfest took place later in 2001, and a sell-out show with Alien Ant Farm in New York was greatly received; but over 80,000 record sales weren't enough to save Pressure 4-5 from being dropped by DreamWorks, which led ultimately to the five-piece disbanding in the summer of 2003.

Killer Cuts – 'Beat the World, 'Melt Me Down'

Primer 55

Years Active: 1997-2003, 2007-2015
Location: Memphis, Tennessee, USA
Main era line-up: Jason 'J-Sin' Luttrell (vocals), Bobby Burns (guitar), Mike Christopher (bass), Josh McLane (drums)
Albums: Introduction to Mayhem (2000), (The) New Release (2001)

Louisville, Kentucky was the setting for Primer 55's formation when guitarist Bobby Burns and the charismatic Jason 'J-Sin' Luttrell combined their respective heavy metal and hip-hop influences to add themselves to a growing list of rap metal bands coming up around the same time. Primer released an independent EP, *As Seen on TV*, before signing to Island Records, and in 2000, the quartet re-recorded the EP and released it under the new title, *Introduction to Mayhem*, which spawned the massive anthem, 'Loose'. Primer would then go out on tour with heavy hitters such as Slipknot, Machine Head and Dope, before earning a second-stage stint on the year's Ozzfest extravaganza.

Some line-up changes occurred ahead of the band's second album, *(the) New Release*, which went to number one on *Billboard*'s Heatseekers chart in August 2001. The popular single 'This Life' was included on the heavier and alternative soundtrack to *The Fast and the Furious* movie, and although the record had some early success, Primer 55 was shelved by Island Records and the band would enter a hiatus in 2003. Burns joined metal heavyweights Soulfly, while 'J-Sin' battled addiction, however Primer 55 was revived in 2007 and an EP titled *Family for Life* came soon after, which contained unreleased material from a four-year period between 1998 and 2002.

After some poorly received live performances, 'J-Sin' was replaced by Heath Joyce, who was then ousted for Donny 'The DRP' Polinske, and a brand-new song titled 'Flexin'' was put out in 2009; but with a new album in the works, Burns reportedly fired the rest of his band. *As Seen on TV* was reissued under the fiery title *The Big Fuck You* in 2012, but any chance of an original line-up reunion was thwarted in August 2018, when Luttrell sadly passed away.

Killer Cuts – 'Loose', 'This Life'

Project 86

Years Active: 1996-
Location: Orange County, California, USA
Main era line-up: Andrew Schwab (vocals), Randy Torres (guitar), Steven Dail (bass), Alex Albert (drums)
Albums: Project 86 (1998), Drawing Black Lines (2000), Truthless Heroes (2002), Songs to Burn Your Bridges By (2004), ...And the Rest Will Follow (2005), Rival Factions (2007), Picket Fence Cartel (2009), Wait for the Siren (2012), Knives to the Future (2014), Sheep Among Wolves (2017)

A project created through the vision of Andrew Schwab, Project 86 combined elements of rapcore (early on), alternative metal, groove metal, post-hardcore, metalcore and Christian rock across a fairly productive discography thus far. With added dark and eerie atmospherics, the Orange County band toured early on with Linkin Park and P.O.D., while a deal was penned with Atlantic Records to make *Drawing Black Lines* Project 86's major-label debut. The 2002 release, *Truthless Heroes,* included the well-received single 'Hollow Again' before the Californian's returned to the Tooth & Nail label and put out the albums, *Songs to Burn Your Bridges By* (2004), *...and the Rest Will Follow* (2005), *Rival Factions* (2007) and *Picket Fence Cartel* (2009). *Wait for the Siren* was distributed independently in 2012, Team Black Recordings helped out with the 2014 effort, *Knives to the Future*, and to celebrate the twenty-year anniversary of Project 86, *Sheep Amongst Wolves* was released at the back end of 2017.

Schwab remains the only original member of a band with an ever-evolving sound. Highly creative and earning themselves a cult following without ever hitting the heights of many of the bands around them, Project 86 still had something important to say in the diverse and welcoming nu metal movement.

Killer Cuts – 'Pipedream', 'Hollow Again'

Puddle of Mudd

Years Active: 1991-
Location: Kansas City, Missouri, USA
Main era line-up: Wes Scantlin (vocals, rhythm guitar), Paul Phillips (lead guitar), Doug Ardito (bass), Greg Upchurch (drums)
Albums: Abrasive (1997), Come Clean (2001), Life on Display (2003), Famous (2007), Volume 4: Songs in the Key of Love & Hate (2009), Welcome to Galvania (2019)

Originally unknown when they released their first EP, *Stuck,* in 1994 and the self-released debut full-length, *Abrasive,* in 1997, Puddle of Mudd got their breakthrough when the first incarnation of the band split up. In early 1999, lead singer, Wes Scantlin, sent a demo to Fred Durst, who, upon hearing the tape invited the Kansas native to California in an attempt to put a new band together.

Puddle of Mudd version 2.0 formed with Scantlin, Paul Phillips, Doug Ardito and Greg Upchurch, and in August 2001, their major-label debut, *Come Clean,* took the world by storm. Released via Flawless/Geffen, fine-crafted hard rock and post-grunge anthems saw the band cruise straight into the mainstream on the back of the singles 'Control', 'Blurry', and the irresistibly catchy 'She Hates Me'. Peaking at nine on the *Billboard* 200 and with sales of over five million worldwide, *Come Clean* would go on to be certified 3x platinum in America.

Promising much, Puddle of Mudd returned in 2003 with the release of *Life on Display*, but it failed to maintain the quartet's rise due to a collection of largely underwhelming songs. To date, it has only sold around 700,000 copies, as heavier rhythms as heard on the singles 'Away from Me' and 'Heel Over Head' failed to grip listeners', and not long after the album's release, Upchurch left the band to join alternative rockers, 3 Doors Down, who quickly broke out with their debut single, 'Kryptonite'.

Puddle of Mudd welcomed Ryan Yerdon on drums for their next album, *Famous,* in 2007, and although it didn't sell massively, it was a strong return that contained some excellent songs. The energetic title track, 'Psycho', and the tender 'We Don't Have to Look Back Now' were as good as anything on *Come Clean*, and they helped *Famous* make it to a decent 27 on the *Billboard* 200. To promote the record, the band went out on tour with the hard rockers in Hinder and Papa Roach before returning to the studio to work on their fourth record- released in December 2009 and titled *Volume 4: Songs in the Key of Love and Hate*. Receiving mixed reviews once again, fans of Puddle of Mudd were left content with its material, such as the floor-filling singles 'Spaceship' and 'Stoned', and the record would go on to sell over 100,000 copies.

Trying their hand at a cover album in 2011, *re(disc)overed* included interesting renditions of Elton John's 'Rocket Man', 'Gimme Shelter' by The Rolling Stones and 'Old Man' by Neil Young; and in the years which have followed, band fallouts and Scantlin's apparent issues with alcohol saw Puddle of Mudd hit the skids. Ten years after their last studio album, Scantlin and a bunch of new musicians brought Puddle of Mudd back to release *Welcome to Galvania* in 2019. Despite a less than appealing band name, Puddle of Mudd's songwriting quality shone above most and they were a mainstay for a decent proportion of nu metal's mainstream heyday thanks to their pulsating major-label debut album.

Killer Cuts – 'Control', 'She Hates Me'

Pulse Ultra

Years Active: 1997-2004
Location: Montreal, Quebec, Canada
Main era line-up: Zo Vizza (vocals), Dominic Cifarelli (guitar), Jeff Feldman (bass), Maxx Zinno (drums)
Albums: Headspace (2002)

Initially starting out as Head Space, this Canadian four-piece became Pulse Ultra in 2000. After the band's guitarist, Dominic Cifarelli, handed a demo to Taproot following a live show he had seen them play, a deal was secured with Atlantic Records and Pulse Ultra released their debut album, *Headspace,* in July 2002. Containing alternative and progressive metal textures with unconventional time signatures, the record was littered with standout songs such as 'Never the Culprit', 'Put It Off', and the sole single to be put out, 'Build Your Cages'. Taproot vocalist, Stephen Richards, would also guest on the album track, 'Big Brother', which helped Pulse Ultra earn a little bit more of a following, and then an opening slot on the year's Ozzfest tour tried but ultimately failed to break the band into the mainstream. When Atlantic merged with AOL-Time Warner, low record sales was enough of a reason for the band to be dropped from their record label, and a much recorded second album sadly failed to see the light of day. Another promising band to only release one album despite having bags of talent at their disposal- Pulse Ultra officially disbanded in 2004.

Killer Cuts – 'Never the Culprit', 'Build Your Cages'

Ra

Years Active: 1996-
Location: Los Angeles, California, USA

Main era line-up: Sahaj Ticotin (vocals, rhythm guitar), Ben Carroll (lead guitar), Sean Corcoran (bass), Skoota Warner (drums)
Albums: From One (2002), Duality (2005), Black Sun (2008), Critical Mass (2013), Intercorrupted (2021)

Taking their name from the Egyptian sun god, Ra combined elements of alternative metal, funk, soul and hints of exotic Arabian textures into a highly intriguing sound. Led by Sahaj Ticotin, the LA quartet's early line-up made small gains with their 'Crazy Little Voices' song which was used as the end theme song for the movie, *The Rage: Carrie 2*. A brief stint signed to Edel Music ended when the label folded, and having written much of their debut album already, Ra set about trying to make their next play for the big time.

Over in Boston, 'Do You Call My Name' was getting significant radio exposure. A powerful anthem that encompassed everything that Ra had set out to achieve with their brand of contemporary metal, the band raised industry eyes after selling over 7,000 copies of their self-released EP, leading to Universal Records approaching the quartet with a two-album offer without even witnessing the band perform live. Naturally accepting the deal with such a lucrative label, Ra then teamed up with hip-hop producer, Paul Logus, to re-record the album they had pretty much already completed, releasing it in October 2002 under the title, *From One*. A more polished version of 'Do You Call My Name' became a national hit, 'Rectifier' continued momentum as the second single, while powerful hard rockers such as 'On My Side' and 'Sky' emphasised Ra's capability of writing songs which were perfect for arenas all around the world, given the chance.

Ticotin took on full production duties for Ra's follow-up album, *Duality*; however, Universal sought out Bob Marlette to come in and record some additional songs as they felt the album was missing those all-important radio hits. Finally releasing *Duality* in 2005 but with minimal promotion behind it, the album still shifted a decent 80,000 copies on the back of the songs 'Tell Me' and 'Fallen Angels', while a fun cover of 'Every Little Thing She Does is Magic' by The Police was also met with some strong plaudits.

Ra then left Universal at the end of their two-album contract and struck a deal with Cement Shoes Records in time for the release of their live album, *Raw*, in 2006, and in 2008, Ticotin's Sahaja Music Records distributed the band's third album, *Black Sun*. A couple more albums followed and in 2020, Ra awoke from their recent slumber to announce they had signed to Wake Up! Music Rocks. Releasing their new album, *Intercorrupted*, in March 2021, the material on show was arguably the band's best in almost fifteen years. Led by the storming title track as well as the catchy hard rockers of 'Jezebel', 'Let It Lie' and 'Nobody Loves You' (featuring Sevendust's Lajon Witherspoon); and with three-quarters of their original line-up back together, Ra's latest release could see them make a welcome return to the higher echelons of heavy music.

Killer Cuts – 'Do You Call My Name', 'Rectifier'

Rage Against the Machine

Years Active: 1991-2000, 2007-2011, 2019-
Location: Los Angeles, California, USA
Main era line-up: Zack de la Rocha (vocals), Tom Morello (guitar), Tim Commerford (bass), Brad Wilk (drums)
Albums: Rage Against the Machine (1992), Evil Empire (1996), The Battle of Los Angeles (1999), Renegades (2000)

Unaware of quite the superstars they would become in just a few short years, this LA band began back in 1991 when Tom Morello began jamming with Tim Commerford and Zack de la Rocha, and later they contacted Brad Wilk to complete the line-up. Naming themselves after a song that de la Rocha had written for a previous project, Rage Against the Machine was born and they eventually signed with Epic Records.

Containing leftist and revolutionary political views within their lyrical content, all spewed through the venomous rap vocals of de la Rocha, the entire world was put on notice when the band's self-titled debut album arrived in November 1992 – debuting at number one on the *Billboard* Heatseekers chart and 45 on the *Billboard* 200. The album cover was eye-catching, to say the least, featuring the iconic photo of the self-immolation of Thich Quang Duc – a Vietnamese Buddhist monk who set fire to himself in Saigon in 1963 in protest against the oppression of the Buddhist religion. Huge statements were made in the form of the singles 'Killing in the Name', 'Bullet in the Head', 'Bombtrack' and 'Freedom', all of which (as did the rest of the album) portrayed groove-laden rap metal which would go on to earn *Rage Against the Machine* 3x platinum certification in the US. 'Killing in the Name' featured a large amount of profanity (and included the renowned line 'Fuck you, I won't do what you tell me...' and in 1993, the unedited version was accidentally played on Radio 1 in the UK, leading to over 100 complaints from outraged listeners. To further promote the album, Rage played Lollapalooza in 1993 before supporting Suicidal Tendencies on a tour of Europe, and at the end of the year, they returned to the studio to start work on their sophomore record.

Evil Empire debuted at number one on the *Billboard* 200 in 1996 amongst a load of hype and expectation, confirming the band as the new heroes on the block. Singles released were 'Year of the Boomerang', the fist-pumping 'Bulls on Parade', 'People of the Sun', 'Down Rodeo' and 'Vietnow', however it was the album track of 'Tire Me' which would get the greatest exposure, winning a Grammy for Best Metal Performance in 1993. By May 2000, *Evil Empire* had also reached triple platinum status.

Rage supported Irish rockers U2 on their Popmart Tour in 1997, with all of Rage's profits going to support social organizations and later, they attempted a US tour with hip-hop superstars Wu-Tang Clan. However, some concerts were cancelled by local police who cited both bands' violent and anti-law enforcement philosophies as a potential security alert.

1999 began with Rage playing Woodstock, and then they released their third album, *The Battle of Los Angeles,* in November. Again debuting at number one in the US, the record sold 420,000 copies in its first week, and in total, four singles were released- 'Guerilla Radio', 'Sleep Now in the Fire', 'Testify' and 'Calm Like a Bomb'. While filming the video for 'Sleep Now in the Fire' in January 2000, the band members and a gathering of fans attempted to storm the New York Stock Exchange after director Michael Moore was arrested by the NYPD for allegedly not having the correct permits to shoot a video in the Wall Street area. Gaining entry through the first set of doors, the Stock Exchange's riot doors then came down, but it was enough to earn the band even more exposure and respect from their fans and music contemporaries. *The Battle of Los Angeles* went twice platinum, and Rage would win another Grammy Award in 2000 for 'Guerilla Radio', which took the Best Hard Rock Performance accolade.

Only a few months after winning their second Grammy, de la Rocha announced he was leaving Rage Against the Machine, stating that the band's 'decision-making process has completely failed.' Two months later, one last album was released – a collection of cover songs titled *Renegades*, where tracks included 'The Ghost of Tom Joad' (written by Bruce Springsteen) and 'How I Could Just Kill a Man' (Cypress Hill); as well as renditions of songs from other legendary artists such as Bob Dylan and The Rolling Stones.

Commerford, Morello and Wilk would later go on to join Soundgarden vocalist Chris Cornell and form the hard rock band Audioslave, while de la Rocha would embark on a solo career. After the 9/11 terrorist attacks, a document was distributed to radio stations called The 2001 Clear Channel Memorandum, featuring a long list of songs that were 'lyrically questionable'. Sent as a suggestion to radio stations not to play these songs, it was confirmed that all of Rage Against the Machine's tracks were on the list.

A successful reunion took place in 2007 when the band headlined the final day of the Coachella festival, before touring America, New Zealand, Australia and Japan, as well as partaking in headline slots on European festivals such as Reading and Leeds in the UK. A Facebook campaign was launched in December 2009 to get 'Killing in the Name' to the coveted Christmas number one spot in the UK, primarily to stop talent show *The X Factor* from having its winner take the accolade as it had done over the past few years. Over 900,000 people signed up for the campaign and amazingly, 'Killing in the Name' won the battle, therefore being number one on the singles chart at Christmas. Promised to fans after the success of the campaign, Rage performed a free show in London's Finsbury Park in the summer of 2010 and various live shows have continued since, but it remains to be seen if we will ever hear any new music from the band.

Revolutionary, inspirational and zero fucks given about the rules – Rage Against the Machine were true innovators who took political rap metal into the mainstream with unwavering success and style.

Killer Cuts – 'Killing in the Name', 'Bulls on Parade'

Raging Speedhorn

Years Active: 1998-2008, 2014-
Location: Corby, Northamptonshire, England
Main era line-up: John Loughlin (vocals), Frank Regan (vocals), Gareth Smith (guitar), Tony Loughlin (guitar), Darren Smith (bass), Gordon Morison (drums)
Albums: Raging Speedhorn (2000), We Will Be Dead Tomorrow (2002), How the Great Have Fallen (2005), Before the Sea Was Built (2007), Lost Ritual (2016), Hard to Kill (2020)

An extremely popular band during their early years, Raging Speedhorn burst out of the small town of Corby with an ear-splitting assault of what they called 'sludgecore'. A self-titled debut in 2000 told you all you needed to know before the non-album track, 'The Gush', became a fan favourite due to constant rotation on *Kerrang!* TV and also courtesy of its inclusion on an official *Kerrang!* compilation album.

We Will Be Dead Tomorrow should have been the record to send Raging Speedhorn global, with ferocious cuts like 'The Hate Song', and more melodic instances such as 'Heartbreaker' showing what the sextet were truly capable of. Also including elements of stoner metal, Raging Speedhorn had come out with a sound different to anything else within the nu metal movement, and tour slots with Rammstein and Ill Nino brought in more new fans. The band would later call it a day, however, before a reformation occurred in 2014 and a new album followed in 2016 (*Lost Ritual*). More new music has followed since – most recently another ball-busting album in the form of *Hard to* Kill – but it was with their early material where the beast that is Raging Speedhorn was at its most deadly and destructive and rightfully included amongst nu metal discussions.

Killer Cuts – 'The Gush', 'The Hate Song'

Rammstein

Years Active: 1994-
Location: Berlin, Germany
Main era line-up: Till Lindemann (vocals), Richard Kruspe (lead guitar), Paul Landers (rhythm guitar), Oliver Riedel (bass), Christoph Schneider (drums, percussion), Christian Lorenz (keyboards, samples, synthesizers)
Albums: Herzeleid (1995), Sehnsucht (1997), Mutter (2001), Reise, Reise (2004), Rosenrot (2005), Liebe ist für alle da (2009), Untitled (2019)

Originally starting off as a four-piece, Rammstein's early line-up entered a competition in their native Germany where the winners would receive the chance to record a four-track demo in a professional studio. Winning the competition and then adding Paul Landers and Christian Lorenz to their line-up, Rammstein soon signed to Motor Records and made their first steps towards national acclaim.

A brand of industrial metal that has been classed as 'Neue Deutsche Harte'

(New German Hardness), it is hard to disagree with such a label when you hear Rammstein's debut album, *Zerzeleid,* which arrived in September 1995. The front cover showed the whole band topless from the waist up, causing many critics to slam the band by claiming they were attempting to sell themselves as 'poster boys'; but as soon as the first track on the album kicked in, it was evident that Rammstein were anything but. *Herzeleid* directly translates to *Heartache*, but Kruspe later said it meant *Heartbreak*, but no matter what the idea behind the album title was, tracks such as 'Du Riecht So Gut' ('You Smell So Good') and 'Seemann' ('Seaman') laid the foundations for a band who only sang in German, to go on and become a worldwide phenomenon.

Rammstein's big breakthrough came when Trent Reznor of Nine Inch Nails was put in charge of producing the soundtrack to the David Lynch movie, *Lost Highway*, and he would choose two songs by the German sextet – 'Heirate Mich' ('Marry Me') and 'Rammstein' (no translation needed) – to be included on the compilation. Boosting the band's popularity just in time for their second album, *Sehnsucht (Desire),* in 1997, people were ready to grasp what Rammstein was selling them, and with the singles 'Engel' ('Angel') and 'Du Hast' (You have'), which continue to be live favourites to this very day, *Sehnsucht* was to become the only album sung entirely in German to be certified platinum in America. Continuing their success overseas, Rammstein joined the Family Values Tour of 1998 with Korn, Ice Cube, Orgy and Limp Bizkit, before the ground-breaking movie, *The Matrix,* included 'Du Hast' on its official soundtrack.

With nu metal firmly in the public eye by 2001, *Mutter (Mother)* became the band's most accessible album when it treaded gothic metal waters whilst still incorporating strong industrial flourishes. The dark but melodic anthems of 'Sonne' ('Sun') and the album title track received heavy rotation worldwide, as did the latter singles 'Ich Will' ('I Want'), 'Links 2-3-4' ('Left 2-3-4'), 'Mein Herz Brennt' ('My Heart burns') and the scorching 'Feuer Frei!' ('Fire at will!') – which opened up the equally scorching *XXX* movie soundtrack. *Mutter* dominated for well over a year before more touring further promoted both the band and their material, and Rammstein returned three years later with their next album, *Reise, Reise (Journey, Journey).*

Another well-received and successful selling record, the overall theme of the release was based on the fateful flight of Japan Airlines Flight 123, which crashed in 1985 and remains the deadliest single aircraft disaster in history. Including some of the band's best material to date, 'Amerika' became the first song to include some English lyrics, 'Mein Teil' ('My Part') was based on Armin Meiwes, a convicted killer and cannibal; and 'Ohne Dich' ('Without You') stepped into power ballad territory. *Reise, Reise* would go on to sell one-and-a-half million copies worldwide, and just over a year later, *Rosenrot (Rose Red)* followed. The first title for the record was reportedly *Reise, Reise Volume Two* as six out of the eleven tracks had been left off the previous album, but the singles 'Benzin' ('Fuel') and 'Mann Gegen Mann' ('Man Against Man') made listeners wonder why that hadn't been included on the previous record due to their staggering quality.

Four years later and after questions had been raised as to whether the band would continue on, Rammstein returned with a more tongue-in-cheek attitude on *Liebe Ist Für Alle Da (Love Is For All),* with more controversy to come. The artwork featured Kruspe spanking a naked woman, while the track, 'Ich Tu Dir Weh' ('I Hurt You'), contained sadomasochistic lyrical content. Both of these issues led to the accompanying record being placed on the index of the Federal Department for Media Harmful to Young Persons – banning sales of the album to anyone under the legal adult age. Also on the record was the addictively catchy 'Pussy' – sung partly in English and released with an X-Rated music video full of nudity and explicit sexual activity (stunt doubles were used to replace the band members in certain scenes). As 'Ich Tu Dir Weh' would later be, the 'Pussy' video was released on the adult website, Visit-X.

Rammstein's live performances have become legendary (check out their engrossing live DVD's, *Völkerball* and *Rammstein: Paris* to witness the band in all their glory), with the use of pyrotechnics from the band's very early days. An accident in 1996 led to the band hiring professionals to handle the pyrotechnics before Lindemann himself later became a licensed pyrotechnician and thus allowing himself to spend many a song engulfed in flames; all adding to the visual experience which Rammstein offer their legions of fans. As well as some already mentioned, a long list of controversies has followed Rammstein around over the years, with live shows featuring acts of simulated sodomy, liquid-ejecting dildos, and various dress ups which have included military uniforms, corsets, and butchers' wear. Away from the live scene, the *Mutter* album cover showed a photograph of a dead fetus, and in Germany, the band has faced accusations of having fascist sympathies due to the militaristic imagery of some of their past videos and concerts. Other promo videos have also caused concern, such as 'Ich Will', which saw the whole band depicted as robbers who hold up a bank until they get the media exposure they demand; while 'Mein Teil' took a dark and comical view of Armin Meiwes' cannibalism case, and of course later videos such as the one for 'Pussy' looked to top the lot.

Never ones to shy away from the spotlight, Rammstein truly are one of a kind and they are highly successful in everything they do. Leading the way for industrial metal over the last two decades, the German sextet continued their dominance with their 2019 album, which is sometimes titled *Rammstein* but more commonly known as an untitled release. 'Deutschland' and 'Radio' proved to be more classics-in-waiting, and despite regular stories from the band's camp about the end being nigh, they keep coming back with album after album of excellently consistent heavy metal.

Killer Cuts – 'Du Hast', 'Ich will'

Reveille

Years Active: 1998-2003
Location: Harvard, Massachusetts, USA

Main era line-up: Drew Simollardes (vocals), Greg Sullivan (guitar), Steve Miloszewski (guitar), Carl Randolph (bass), Justin Wilson (drums)
Albums: Laced (1999), Bleed the Sky (2001)

Reveille brought some rap metal out of Massachusetts in 1998 when a six-track demo attracted Elektra Records to their door. The quintet's first album, *Laced,* earned sales of over 100,000 copies when released in June 1999, and its accompanying artwork was designed by popular British author Clive Barker. Three strong singles in the forms of 'Flesh & Blood', 'Permanent (Take a Look Around)' and 'The Phoenix' were used to promote the record, while Cypress Hill's B-Real also guested on the track 'Splitt (Comin' Out Swingin')'. To further enhance the band's reputation, Reveille played the Warped Tour and Woodstock in 1999, Ozzfest in 2000, and then club tours with Godsmack, Machine Head and Powerman 5000 took place across America.

The sophomore album, *Bleed The Sky,* followed in September 2001, and it was produced by the acclaimed Howard Benson. Taproot's Stephen Richards supplied guest vocals on 'Plastic', while the 'Inside Out' single achieved some *Billboard* chart success. Before departing from Elektra, Reveille went on tour with Static-X, and then Sevendust, before shocking fans with the announcement that they had called it a day. A one-off reunion show in 2008 was performed to a sold-out crowd in the band's home state, while Reveille continue to be highly talked about on various nu metal forums in the present day.

Killer Cuts – 'Permanent (Take a Look Around)', 'Inside Out'

Saliva

Years Active: 1996-
Location: Memphis, Tennessee, USA
Main era line-up: Josey Scott (vocals), Wayne Swinny (lead guitar), Chris D'Abaldo (rhythm guitar), Dave Novotny (bass), Paul Crosby (drums)
Albums: Saliva (1997), Every Six Seconds (2001), Back into Your System (2002), Survival of the Sickest (2004), Blood Stained Love Story (2007), Cinco Diablo (2008), Under Your Skin (2011), In It to Win It (2013), Rise Up (2014), Love, Lies & Therapy (2016), 10 Lives (2018)

From a city famed more for its blues, Saliva surfaced out of Memphis with their self-titled rap metal debut in August 1997. Distributed by Rockingchair Records, the most notable tracks were '800' and 'Pin Cushion', which appeared on the movie soundtracks for *Resident Evil* and *Ginger Snaps,* respectively. The album helped Saliva catch the eye of Atlantic Records, and after quickly signing with them, the band released *Every Six Seconds* in March 2001. Going on to be certified platinum after initially peaking at 56 on the *Billboard* 200, the swaggering numbers of 'Your Disease' and 'Click Click Boom' gained extensive airplay through their associations with *WWE* Wrestling. Josey Scott's rapping vocals suited the hard and heavy instrumentation, underlined by the powerhouse anthem, 'Superstar', while the previously mentioned 'Your Disease' found its way on to the *Dracula 2000* movie soundtrack.

Saliva focused on a softer post-grunge sound for their 2002 album, *Back into Your System*, which hit 19 on the *Billboard* chart and ended up being certified gold by the RIAA. 'Always' was a storming hard rock ballad and ideal choice to be the lead single which reached the top spot on the Modern Rock Tracks chart in America, while second single, 'Rest in Pieces', was co-written by James Michael, and Nikki Sixx from Mötley Crüe. In support of the album, Saliva went on tour with rock behemoths KISS, and then Aerosmith, before returning to the studio to work on their next record.

Survival of the Sickest came out in 2004 and crept inside the top 20 in the US album chart. Sticking with their now preferred hard rock direction, Saliva chose the album title track as the lead single, even though its intro sounds scarily similar to Marilyn Manson's fan favourite, 'The Fight Song', while 'Razor's Edge' followed a little later on. *Survival of the Sickest* would be the last album to feature guitarist Chris D'Abaldo, who left the band citing 'creative differences' and was replaced by Jonathan Montoya, who debuted on *Blood Stained Love Story* in 2007. The single, 'Ladies and Gentlemen', had already reached number 2 on the Mainstream Rock Chart at the end of 2006, and upon its release, the accompanying album went straight in at 19 on the *Billboard* 200. 'Broken Sunday' was another highlight, and a guest appearance from ex-Marilyn Manson guitarist, John 5, saw him perform on 'Black Sheep'. During 2008, Saliva toured South Korea and Japan with fellow US hard rockers, Sevendust, before returning home to work on and release their next album, *Cinco Diablo,* just in time for Christmas. Perhaps surprisingly, the album only reached 104 on the *Billboard* chart, but the single, 'Family Reunion', still showed Saliva was packing a forceful punch. The *Moving Forward in Reverse: Greatest Hits* compilation followed in 2010 and after Montoya left, the band continued on as a four-piece to put out *Under Your Skin* in March 2011. Scott then shocked the world by announcing his departure from the band he helped build up, choosing to focus on a solo career playing Christian music.

The relatively unknown Bobby Amaru was announced as Scott's replacement at the beginning of 2012, and after the band signed to Rum Bum Records, the new version of Saliva came fighting back with *In It to Win It* a year later. Since then, they have continued with *Rise Up,* which featured re-arranged versions of songs from their previous release, and then *Love, Lies & Therapy* in June 2015. Over the last few years, Saliva has toured with fellow nu metal survivalists such as Alien Ant Farm, Crazy Town, Drowning Pool and P.O.D., proving furthermore that they have, like many of their contemporaries, no desire on slowing down any time soon.

Killer Cuts – 'Your Disease', 'Click Click Boom'

Sepultura

Years Active: 1984-
Location: Belo Horizonte, Brazil
Main era line-up: Max Cavalera (vocals, rhythm guitar), Andreas Kisser (lead guitar), Paulo Xisto Pinto Jr. (bass), Igor Cavalera (drums)
Albums: Morbid Visions (1986), Schizophrenia (1987), Beneath the Remains (1989), Arise (1991), Chaos A.D. (1993), Roots (1996), Against (1998), Nation (2001), Roorback (2003), Dante XXI (2006), A-Lex (2009), Kairos (2011), The Mediators Between Head & Hands Must Be the Heart (2013), Machine Messiah (2017), Quadra (2020)

Although predominantly a thrash and death metal band throughout their lengthy career, Sepultura deserve to be included in this book purely for their classic 1996 album, *Roots*. The Belo Horizonte group was formed by Max and Igor Cavalera in the mid-1980s, and after their 1993 record, *Chaos A.D.*, put them firmly on the map, Sepultura went global with a masterpiece which incorporated down-tuned guitars, Latin and Brazilian percussive stylings and world music influences; while still bringing their customary groove, thrash and death metal elements which made the band what they were.

Produced by Ross Robinson and reportedly inspired by Korn's eponymous debut from 1994, *Roots* contained a barrage of metallic fury best showcased by the brash singles, 'Roots Bloody Roots', 'Attitude' and 'Ratamahatta'; the latter of which featured Korn drummer, David Silveria. Jonathan Davis, Faith No More's Mike Patton and Limp Bizkit's DJ Lethal guested on the album track 'Lookaway', as the breath-taking record reached 24 on the *Billboard* 200 and a fabulous number 4 in the UK album chart.

Roots would later be certified gold in over ten different countries, but it would also prove to be Cavalera's last album with Sepultura, as he left the band in rather acrimonious circumstances at the end of 1996. But we all know what happened next as the mighty Soulfly rose to prominence with Max at the forefront while Derrick Green took over vocal duties and debuted on Sepultura's 1998 release, *Against*.

An album that was so heavy yet so diverse and captivating, *Roots* remains a classic album not just in terms of nu metal, but in heavy metal in general.

Killer Cuts – 'Roots Bloody Roots', 'Ratamahatta'

Sevendust

Years Active: 1994-
Location: Atlanta, Georgia, USA
Main era line-up: Lajon Witherspoon (vocals), Clint Lowery (lead guitar), John Connolly (rhythm guitar), Vince Hornsby (bass), Morgan Rose (drums)
Albums: Sevendust (1997), Home (1999), Animosity (2001), Seasons (2003), Next (2005), Alpha (2007), Chapter VII: Hope & Sorrow (2008), Cold Day Memory (2010), Black Out the Sun (2013), Time Travelers & Bonfires (2014), Kill the Flaw (2015), All I See is War (2018), Blood & Stone (2020)

Sevendust was formed by Vince Hornsby and Morgan Rose, who were previously in a band together called Snake Nation. John Connolly then joined before the trio found Lajon Witherspoon and Clint Lowery; and as a five-piece, they renamed the band Rumblefish. After finding another band with the same name, they became Crawlspace, and their track, 'My Ruin', was featured on the *Mortal Kombat* soundtrack. However, a band by the name of Crawlspace reportedly demanded money for the rights to the band name, and so Sevendust was born.

A self-titled debut album followed in 1997 via the label TVT, with the alternative metal anthems of 'Black' and 'Bitch' becoming popular early on. 'My Ruin' was also included on the album before Sevendust was welcomed onto the 1998 Ozzfest tour. Becoming known for their empowering bottom-heavy riffs and accessible melodies, which went well with Witherspoon's soulful vocals, Sevendust touched down in 1999 with their sophomore album, *Home*. Deftones' Chino Moreno guested on 'Bender', while Skunk Anansie singer, Skin, contributed on the single, 'Licking Cream'. Other powerhouse singles 'Denial' and 'Waffle' helped the record peak at 19 on the *Billboard* 200, showing Sevendust's momentum was quickly gathering.

1999 also saw the band appear at Woodstock before they went out on tour with Korn, Staind, Godsmack, Limp Bizkit and Disturbed, and before Sevendust returned to the studio to write and record *Animosity* for a 2001 release. Shooting to 28 on the album chart, *Animosity* included 'Angel's Son', which had originally featured on Snot's Lynn Strait tribute album, *Strait Up*. 'Praise' and 'Live Again' were other addictive singles, and *Animosity* was also the third straight album for which Sevendust received gold certification, but all momentum was lost when the band went on hiatus after Witherspoon's brother was tragically murdered in 2002.

A more determined Sevendust returned with their next album, *Seasons*, in October 2003, which was to be their final record with TVT. Debuting at 14 on the *Billboard* 200 and spawning the band's highest-charting single, 'Enemy', which reached number 10 on the Mainstream Rock Tracks chart, Sevendust's pace was picking back up when Lowery would then leave the band to join his brother in Dark New Day, who had just signed to Warner Bros. Sevendust then went and signed with WineDark Records and Sonny Mayo (Snot, Amen) took over the vacant guitar position, and the band's fifth album, *Next*, was released at the back end of 2005. The huge single 'Ugly' was a highlight and the following 'Pieces' made its way onto the *SAW II* movie soundtrack, but after the implosion of WineDark Records, the band considered themselves as bankrupt with an outstanding debt reportedly close to one million dollars. Eager to get themselves out of the hole that was made by others, Sevendust roared back in March 2007 with *Alpha* – their first record put out through Asylum, who was affiliated with Warner. Sevendust was also the first metal band to join the roster, as it had traditionally catered for rap and hip-hop artists at that point. *Alpha* debuted at 14 in the US and the single, 'Driven', hit the Mainstream Rock top 10.

Returning to the studio only a few months later, another album emerged just over a year after *Alpha* in the form of *Chapter VII: Hope & Sorrow*, which dropped in April 2008. Mark Tremonti from Creed guested on the track 'Hope', *American Idol* contestant-turned-rockstar, Chris Daughtry, featured on 'The Past', and Myles Kennedy from US hard rock sensations Alter Bridge turned up on 'Sorrow'. Looking like Sevendust was hitting their stride in the mainstream; Clint Lowery then returned to the band in time to lay down his guitar skills on *Cold Day Memory* – Sevendust's eighth record, which arrived in April 2010. Going straight to number 12 in the US, it became the band's highest-charting album and included the prominent singles, 'Unraveling', 'Forever' and 'Last Breath'. Huge tours alongside the likes of Chevelle, Puddle of Mudd, Ill Nino, Slayer, and the mighty Iron Maiden ensued, and they continued to consistently put out new music, with *Black Out the Sun* dropping in 2013, the acoustic album, *Time Travelers & Bonfires* coming soon after; and then the self-produced *Kill the Flaw* bringing another alternative metal onslaught upon its release in 2015. In 2017, Sevendust signed to the renowned Rise Records, with whom they have released their last two records, *All I See is War* in 2018, and *Blood & Stone* at the end of 2020 – both of which were met with critical acclaim.

A turbulent but action-packed career that keeps on motoring, Sevendust are one of the most hard-working bands in all of rock and metal. They are also one of the most popular bands from the nu metal era, with many newer bands citing the Georgia crew as a major influence, and if you listen to any of their albums, you will probably see why.

Killer Cuts – 'Black', 'Bitch'

Shuvel

Years Active: 1997-2011
Location: Wichita, Kansas, USA
Main era line-up: Jeff Hollinger (vocals), Isaac Ayala (vocals), Ryan Stuber (guitar), Carlos Sandoval (bass), Kyle Hollinger (drums)
Albums: Set It Off (2000), Return of the Fist (2006), As the World Burns (2009)

Shuvel made a slow start to their career until a move to California paid dividends. In a story which could have come straight out of Hollywood, and if it had not have happened in a suburb of Los Angeles, then no one would have believed it, Shuvel was reportedly put in contact with an artist relations agent for the mighty Interscope Records – by a stripper who saw the band perform at a house party. From there, Shuvel signed to Interscope and released their debut album, *Set It Off*, towards the end of 2000. The track 'Clean Slate' was already doing well, having been featured on the *Celebrity Deathmatch* soundtrack, while the 'Hit List' and title track singles continued to showcase the band's energetic rap metal formula. Tours with Crazy Town, Sevendust, Kittie, and a second stage stint on Ozzfest in 2000 gave Shuvel further exposure. However, a hoped elevation failed to materialise and the band parted ways with Interscope in 2001. Having always doubled up on the vocal front, Jeff Hollinger then quit, which allowed Isaac

Ayala to take the lead by himself, and although Shuvel pressed on and released *Return of the Fist* in 2006 and *As the World Burns* in 2009, there appeared to be very little interest in the band and so they officially dissolved in 2011.

Killer Cuts – 'Clean Slate', 'Hit List'

Simon Says

Years Active: 1992-2004
Location: Sacramento, California, USA
Main era line-up: Matt Franks (vocals), Zack Diebels (guitar), Mike Arrieta (bass), Mike Johnston (drums)
Albums: Little Boy (1997), Perfect Example (1997), Jump Start (1999), Shut Your Breath (2001)

A band put together by three high school friends who then added a fourth member a few years later, Simon Says released two independent albums before signing to Hollywood Records in 1998. The Sacramento alt metallers put out their major-label debut, *Jump Start,* a year later, and it included the singles 'Slider' and 'Sever' before another album followed in 2001 titled *Shut Your Breath.* Like the album which came before it, *Shut Your Breath* didn't get the credit it deserved, but songs such as 'Syphon', 'Silk Moth', and the sole single released, 'Blister', showed Simon Says to be a decent band capable of writing strong and diverse rock songs. Later in 2001, Simon Says left Hollywood Records due to promotional issues, and then they changed their name to Key To Arson; but after a 2004 self-released record titled *Light Em Up*, the band parted ways.

Killer Cuts – 'Slider', 'Blister (Nothing)'

Skindred

Years Active: 1998-
Location: Newport, Wales
Main era line-up: Benji Webbe (vocals), Michael 'Mikey Demus' Fry (guitar), Daniel Pugsley (bass), Arya Goggin (drums)
Albums: Babylon (2002), Roots Rock Riot (2007), Shark Bites and Dog Fights (2009), Union Black (2011), Kill the Power (2014), Volume (2015), Big Tings (2018)

Putting Wales on the map for nu metal, Skindred fused reggae with metal and later added elements of hardcore, ska, hip-hop and drum and bass into a cataclysmic wall of sound. Their 2002 debut, *Babylon* was reissued by RCA in 2003 and then re-released by Lava Records in 2004, and it produced the bouncing anthem 'Nobody' and the raucous 'Pressure'; while the album also introduced people to the enigmatic vocals of Benji Webbe.

After touring with Korn, Skindred continued their upswing with their second album, *Roots Rock Riot,* in 2007, and then a third effort in 2009 titled *Shark*

Bites and Dog Fights spawned the lead single and popular cover of Eddy Grant's 'Electric Avenue'. Papa Roach's Jacoby Shaddix guested on the 2011 single 'Warning', which preceded the album *Union Black* (released via BMG), and the fifth album, *Kill the Power,* followed in 2014. After leaving BMG and signing with Napalm Records, Skindred's first output on their new label was the 2015 album, *Volume*, and in 2018 the Brits brought more groovy chaos with the fully-functioning *Big Tings*. Led by the annoyingly catchy single, 'That's My Jam', which could easily be at home in nightclubs as well as metal festivals, Skindred continue to create music that is equally heavy and genre-bending. Known for their explosively energetic live show, which relies a lot on crowd participation and the 'Newport Helicopter', Skindred are one of the best-loved and most original acts to come out of the UK in the last two decades.

Killer Cuts – 'Nobody', 'Warning'

Skrape

Years Active: 1997-2004
Location: Orlando, Florida, USA
Main era line-up: Billy Keeton (vocals), Brian 'Brix' Milner/Mike Lynchard (guitar), Pete Sison (bass), Will Hunt (drums)
Albums: New Killer America (2001), Up the Dose (2004)

Starting out as Jojo in 1997, this Florida quintet changed their name to Skrape in 1999 and signed to RCA Records – quickly becoming one of the only major label rock and metal acts from the Orlando area at the time. Ulrich Wild produced their debut album, *New Killer America,* which was released in 2001, and the singles 'Waste' and 'Isolated' helped the record sell over 100,000 copies in the US, while further strong songs such as 'I Know' helped the band gain some strong exposure in Japan.

Returning with their second album, *'Up the Dose',* three years later, Skrape included some more feisty rap-tinged metal which was included on the standout tracks, 'Stand Up (Summer Song)' and the anthemic 'In the End', but two months after the record's release, the band would be dropped after RCA was taken over by J Records, and then Skrape called it a day soon after.

Killer Cuts – 'Waste', 'In the End'

Slaves on Dope

Years Active: 1994-2004, 2009-
Location: Montreal, Quebec, Canada
Main era line-up: Jason Rockman (vocals), Kevin Jardine (guitar), Frank Salvaggio (bass), Rob Urbani (drums)
Albums: One Good Turn Deserves Another (1997), Inches from the Mainline (2000), Metafour (2003), Over the Influence (2012), Horse (2016)

Starting out during the grunge explosion in 1993, a line-up change or two saw Slaves On Dope quickly move into alternative metal territory upon relocating to Los Angeles at the end of the 1990s. The independently released *One Good Turn Deserves Another* showed initial promise when the band was back home in Canada, but having caught the eye of Sharon Osbourne after a show with Papa Roach in Las Vegas, Slaves on Dope signed to Ozzy and Sharon's Divine Recordings and released *Inches from the Mainline* in 2000.

'Pushing Me' and 'Thanks for Nothing' were the standout moments as Slaves on Dope proved themselves popular courtesy of Jason Rockman's harsh screams on top of some fine and frenzied instrumentation, and joining the Ozzfest 2000 line-up to promote *Inches from the Mainline,* the band's stage show endeared themselves to the crowds so well that their major-label debut sold over 70,000 copies in America.

After various issues with their record label, Slaves on Dope decided to go elsewhere and eventually, they signed with Bieler Bros. ahead of releasing a hard rock/post-grunge-driven second album in the form of *Metafour* in 2003. Including the almost made-for-radio anthems of 'Go', 'September' and 'So Clear', Rockman's screams still shone through on some heavier songs, but during the shift in the music industry brought on by illegal downloading, as well as issues within the band, Rockman then announced his departure and Slaves On Dope called it a day.

A few years later, Rockman and fellow mainstay, Kevin Jardine, revived Slaves on Dope and returned to their heavier sound for the 2012 album, *Over the Influence,* and the bruising 2016 effort, *Horse,* and a lot of people were happy to see the band back on top form. A couple of small releases followed, and whether we hear any future new Slaves On Dope material remains to be seen, but at one stage, this mighty quartet was one of Canada's finest metal exports.

Killer Cuts – 'Pushing Me', 'Thanks for Nothing'

Kevin Jardine speaks:

Slaves on Dope started out in 1992 when we had our first rehearsal. Back then, we were influenced by Faith No More and Jane's Addiction, and alternative rock. Jason grew up listening to Depeche Mode and Tears for Fears and he wasn't a rock guy at all. I was the one who listened to the heavier stuff.

When we started developing the sound of the band, it took us years to get to where we found we didn't sound like anybody else, and once we got a deal in Canada, which was around 1996 and we put out *One Good Turn Deserves Another,* we wanted to be an alternative rock band. We didn't want to be metal or too heavy, but as we pushed through that record and came out the other side in 1998, we felt like the heavier stuff was getting better reactions live. This was back when video channels like *MTV* were super popular. They sort of drove record sales and drove band's careers. So, we didn't really want to be a heavy band, and we liked what we were writing, but we weren't getting any love at radio or video. All the heavy songs were what people wanted to hear live, so we wrote the *Klepto* EP and some heavy shit. We wrote ten songs and six made the EP, and that was when everybody was like, 'Whoa, this band is on to something!'

We moved from Montreal to Los Angeles in 1999. We had a record deal in Canada, but we couldn't get radio play and we couldn't get the things that most bands got, so when we moved, it was because that was where the scene was happening. When we actually sat down and decided to move, it was because LA was where the opportunity was and where we felt more people would hear our music, so we didn't have a lot to lose. If it didn't work out after three months, we would just move back to Canada.

As soon as we arrived in LA, everybody was like, 'Who is this fucking band?' We had done eight Canadian tours, two records, three videos and easily four or five hundred shows before people even knew who Slaves On Dope was in America. But as soon as we started playing live, people knew we had our shit together. We blew by all the LA bands because we were more proficient live, and we put on better shows. We were a solid unit and we had also developed the craft of songwriting. We weren't just playing the song we wrote the week before, we had been writing for well over a year and we had worked with real producers in Canada who had platinum records, so we had established ourselves a little bit more than the average LA rock band.

We liked being part of the nu metal movement because it was a cool movement, but we always felt we were on the outside of it. We were a little bit more eclectic than a lot of those bands and there was a lot more depth to our music. I think the kind of band we always wanted to be was the kind that didn't stick to a specific formula of writing songs. We didn't really care if it was heavy, or groovy, or funky; we didn't write straightforward and we were always pushing to be a little different. Those were our main goals. We liked the Korns and Deftones and the bands that started the movement in the mid-1990s, but that wasn't who we grew up on. We appreciated what they did, but we didn't really want to sound like them. We didn't use down-tuned guitars and we didn't do the breakdown riffy type stuff; we had a punk vibe and we were always a little more up-tempo. We were kind of all over the map and we always liked that. The bands we played with sounded more like each other than we sounded like them, but once you really dug into it, there was a lot more depth to the movement. There was a lot of great songs and great records to come out of that era, and there was an honesty and realness to the music, as well as an energy you don't really find these days.

LA is the land of opportunity. All you need to do is go out on a random night and you will run into somebody. The music business is so small that there is only so many clubs and bars, and everybody is always looking for new talent, new sounds and new looks. When we moved there, the first thing we did was get an agent and a manager. Our manager's best friend had signed Sepultura, Fear Factory and Coal Chamber to Roadrunner, and then Sharon Osbourne hired him. She was adamant she didn't want to sign a baby band – she wanted to pick up a band who has been recently dropped by a major record label, who had a fan base and could grow from something instead of starting fresh.

Scott Givens had seen us twelve times before he brought Sharon out. He was a friend of ours and we would go to his house and hang out, Burton from Fear Factory would be there and a couple of other band guys, and we would have a good time and form a friendly relationship. Eventually, Slaves On Dope was playing to two or three hundred people within three or four months, so Scott decided it was time to bring Sharon out to see us. We had got offered deals from Sony and Columbia at that point, but we really wanted to do Ozzfest, and we knew the only way that was guaranteed was if we went with Sharon. We could have signed to Sony or Columbia, but there was no guarantee, plus there was a huge buy in to be on those tours from the marketing departments. It wasn't that we were wary we wouldn't get it; we just knew if we went with Sharon, then it was a done deal. The show Sharon was supposed to come to she missed because she was sick, and then we played with Papa Roach in Las Vegas and she flew out to see us there, and we killed it. She sat us down and she said, 'I want to sign you; you'll be in the studio as soon as we can get studio time, you'll make the record, and you'll be on Ozzfest this summer.' I think that was in February or March 2000, and we were literally in the studio the whole month of May, and when we were done, the day we printed the last mix, we drove to Florida to start Ozzfest.

The first full tour of Ozzfest was in 1998 and we had gone to it in 1999 when we first moved to Los Angeles, and we actually played the outdoor stage for the campers the night before. Then we got passes for the weekend, so we saw what it was, and we saw the Slipknots and the System Of A Downs, who were nothing at that point. It was the festival which was breaking bands. The internet was so new and people couldn't find out about you and listen to you, and there wasn't hundreds or thousands of pictures, so people still went to see you. You saw the band, you liked the band, you bought the shirt and CD; it was all-encompassing. We knew if we got in front of them, they would love the band. It was just a matter of getting on the right tour, and we knew Ozzfest was the right tour. We did around thirty shows in America alone in two months, playing every second day. We were playing to arguably 10,000 people on the worst day and then the best day may have been 60,000, so we were reaching massive amounts of people very quickly. It was imperative we did that tour because we had been a band for around seven years at that point, and I don't want to say we were struggling, but if it was going to happen for us it was going to have to happen now. We didn't want to wait around and do a whole bunch of club tours – we wanted to do the right tour and play with the right bands and have people hear our music.

We knew beforehand who was on Ozzfest because we would go into Sharon's office and see the whiteboard with all the possible bands on it, and it was interesting because we loved all the bands on that tour. They were bands we had grown up listening to or had listened to for a long time and we appreciated their songwriting and creativity, so we were playing with all these bands we never thought we would play within our lifetime- all at the same show. The way the stages worked was you did eight or nine slots on the second stage and there was one slot on the main stage, so you would start with the first set at 11:30 in the morning, then you would do the 12:15 set, and so on. You moved your way up until you were right before Soulfly, and then you went up to the main stage before you went back round again.

The gates were stormed when they opened around 11 a.m. Everybody wanted to be there first so there would already be 20,000 or 30,000 people in the crowd. The main stage started later, and I think the first band on there was Queens Of The Stone Age, so the heavier stuff was on the second stage. It was cool because through the day you played to more people. You would play to people at the beginning, but you might only play to 2,000 or 3,000 people. We played early a few times and I remember a lot of people came specifically because they had heard about Slaves On Dope. I remember going up on stage one day and playing a song with Kittie, which was fun, and although I didn't particularly go up and play with Soulfly, all the other guys in the band did. You are waiting around all day to play, or you have already played, and then you have nothing to do, so you watch all the bands and hang out. And you wanted to watch all the bands because they were all really good. One of the bands I liked the most was Pitchshifter. I watched them every day and John (Clayden) became a really good buddy of mine. Pitchshifter were phenomenal.

Ozzfest was like a summer camp, just with a whole bunch of band dudes. I remember those moments of watching from the side of the stage and seeing all the bands I grew up listening to or knew. We were all together every day and everyone was doing the same thing. You're all trying to get people to listen to your music; you're all trying to present your band to the public the best you can and put on the best show, so we were all in the same boat.

It was clear as it started to move forward that Disturbed was pulling ahead of the pack, which was neat to see because they started at the same level as us. About halfway through the tour there was a lot of people going to see them and you kind of hoped your band was going to be next, because that was what Ozzfest was for – breaking bands. It's weird because unless you are on a club level, you don't really experience what that is like, but there was arguably twenty-five bands and when you are driving around the country with that many bands, it is very different.

I remember watching Vinnie Paul get a vitamin B12 shot in his butt, which was pretty funny. Nobody wants to get sick, so a lot of guys would get B12 shots. Vinnie and Dimebag were characters. One day, Dime and Zakk Wylde just destroyed a backstage room and I got so scared that I fucking ran because Zakk is a big boy. Dime wasn't very big and he wasn't intimidating at all, but Zakk is a big burly mountain guy and when he picks up a coffee table and throws it through the wall, you best get out of there. I used to go and sing 'This Love' with Pantera every night. I would do backups, one night, I would do Dime's side and another night, I would do it on Rex's side. I remember we was in Houston and we had to drive super far to Seattle, so we had to leave, and it was the one night I missed seeing Pantera. I remember showing up at The Gorge in Seattle and sitting there watching Ozzy, and Phil Anselmo came and sat beside me and said, 'Where the fuck were you the other night, you weren't on stage with us?' I told him, 'Dude, we had to fucking drive, like eighteen hours', and he was all, 'That's bullshit, next time you make sure you sing with us!' and that was trippy because I was just some dude, but Phil was always nice to us and very friendly. I never saw any other side of him than genuine. He had his demons, but a lot of guys did on Ozzfest. We were all musicians; we've had bouts with alcohol or drugs and whatever. Crazy Town almost got thrown off the tour because one of the guys got arrested one night. They had to cancel two shows and I think they begged for forgiveness, so Sharon put them back on the tour. I was sitting there like a little Canadian boy and I was like, 'How the fuck do you get arrested?' and then you meet the guys … they really partied.

There was all sorts of stuff going on, but for the most part, we kept our noses clean. None of us really drank and nobody did drugs – we were clean cut boys. Maybe it was because we had been touring for so long that we just never really did that. We traded all our beer away for bags of chips and stuff, and if anybody wanted beer, they would come to see us because they knew we had beer we wouldn't drink. It's funny because our name was Slaves On Dope and nobody did drugs, or drink, and that was why we named our band that because if you do drugs, you become a slave to them. It was a subtle message we had that wasn't really in our music.

Ozzfest was the last real touring festival. There hasn't really been a movement of music that big, which has needed a festival like that since. To try and do something now would be very difficult. Lollapalooza has a hard time doing a couple of shows and that was the first really big festival that toured. It was a different time then, there were street teams, and we did meet and greets, signing posters and baseball cards for hours on end; it was very different discovering music and getting into music. You left a club after seeing a band feeling very different than you do now.

You can't really discover bands these days because everybody is already out there. You can't discover a band the way you used to, and when you do, there is so much shit on the band out there that you don't really get the excitement of seeing something new. You can get your fill of a band in a month, whereas back then you saw the band, there was maybe one record and a couple of photos in a magazine, and that was it. You were almost starved of seeing that band again or get some new information or a see a new picture, and it made you hungry for more. It made you more of a lifelong fan because you felt connected.

We only did one show of Ozzfest 2001 and that was the Toronto show. When we did the show, we were trying to get out of our contract with Sharon because the relationship wasn't what we thought it was going to be. We were supported to do the whole tour, but she wanted us in the studio making a record. *Inches*

From the Mainline only came out in October 2000 and it wasn't even a year into the cycle yet. We wanted to do a full year, but Sharon wanted us in the studio in the summer, and that was one of the biggest sticking points. Another was that we never shot a video. We did videos ourselves before and shelled out $20,000 to make them, but with the biggest deal we never did a video, and that was really aggravating to us. We felt we didn't do everything we could for that record and it was pretty frustrating, but regardless, it was fun. And that is the inner politics of being on a record label. Once you hand that record over, it's not up to you anymore. You give it away to them and let them do whatever the hell they want and you end up hating everybody. That is the way it goes.

We recorded *Metafour* in 2002 and it came out in 2003, and there were no real signs that anything was changing, musically. The landscape was still solid, bands were still touring, people were still going to shows, but what you did see was file-sharing and record sales going down. Two weeks before *Metafour* came out, it was already online and people were downloading it. Our record deal wasn't as big as our last deal, but it was still almost a $100,000 deal. Our label was a subsidiary of MCA and they were losing record sales. They sent out a bunch of subpoenas to pull the record offline and when our record came out, it was already too late. MCA folded three weeks after because of the drop in sales. We were seeing it from a band our size, so imagine what MCA was seeing already on their first six months of the year. They had probably lost tens of hundreds of millions of dollars, and so they folded. There was no saving a label that had invested millions of dollars in artists and then lost millions of dollars, so we were in the position of 'What do we do?' The label pressed 30,000 copies of *Metafour* and we sold them all in the first two months. They were all gone, the label wasn't going to press anymore, MCA had folded, so our label said, 'We've gotta find another distributor and another label home', and by the time our record cycle was done, they still hadn't found a new home. It would take them almost two years to do so.

I was an early adopter of the internet. I got my first computer in 1996, so I knew what the power of it was. I remember doing interviews in 2000 and 2001, saying if everybody gets high-speed internet, then the music industry is screwed because once people can download a record in five minutes, it is game over. A buddy and I used to make music on our computers, a very early sort of music production, and we used to send MP3's to each other. When I sent one, it took almost a half-hour to send one song, so at the time, I said the technology was not there, but once everybody has high speed, it will be game over for music. From 2003 to 2004, we saw the music industry collapse within two years, and that is kind of what took the scene down just as much as every other music endeavor that was going on. It just so happened it coincided with nu metal going away and the metalcore thing starting.

Metalcore was never as big as the nu metal movement because of that, I think. If metalcore had come out and there was no problem with the internet, I think it would have thrived a lot more, and tours like Ozzfest would have continued to flourish. When labels lost their source of income though, the whole industry deflated. You lost a huge amount of money that was going into supporting bands and artists, and it just disappeared within two years. For me, two years is like overnight. That is fast to literally watch the music industry die, and it was eye-opening, to say the least.

I produce records now, so I deal with bands on the frontline all the time. There was a way the music industry functioned that worked before, they were almost the gatekeepers of bringing music to the masses and it worked. Did bands get their fair share – no, they did not. They never did and they never will. The bands and artists were always the ones to get the shitty end of the stick. The fact of the matter is it has only changed; it hasn't got better. Yes, you can spend $15 on Spotify and listen to all the music you want, and yes, you can get Instagram and Facebook to see all these bands, so there is a lot of benefit, but there are also a lot of drawbacks. It hasn't helped anybody or made the industry better, and it hasn't made it easier for bands. If anything, I think it is harder for bands now. Back in the day, we had our fair shot because we were better than anybody else, but now it is very hard to tell who is better because of making music on computers. Anybody can sound good and you can make a record for cheap, so you take a lot out of the equation that you didn't have when I made music – when you were only good if you were good. Good bands and great bands made records, and bad bands died in their garage. Back in my day, only the good bands toured and made records, so if you saw a band show up in your town, you knew they were good and there was no second-guessing it.

If I am listening to music on my own, still, one of my favourite bands is Deftones – as far as a band that has carried a sound and has always stayed true to themselves. I still listen to Korn, and while they have been around for a long time, they are still putting out quality music; that is impressive in this time and age. I will reference some Limp Bizkit because I love Wes Borland's guitar sound. One of my favourite sounding records is the first Limp Bizkit record, *Three Dollar Bill, Y'all.* Occasionally I'll throw on some Linkin Park, Papa Roach and Disturbed. They all did something unique, as did System of a Down. They wrote really interesting stuff and I am always intrigued to listen to them because they really stood out from the pack.

We toured with Hed PE and I still talk to all of the original guys. I am always in awe of that band because they were one of the first bands we got to play with when we moved to LA. I have always liked their stuff and always thought Jahred was a really cool frontman. They never tried to be anything they wasn't. I have always loved Incubus, and *S.C.I.E.N.C.E.* is still one of my favourite records. I don't even know what the hell they were doing, it was just whacky. Godsmack has always written great songs too. They are what they are, which is just a great rock band. I could go on for days; I just think it was a very interesting era for music because it was about the songs and emotion. It wasn't about the flashy playing, and I find that with metalcore and stuff like that, they just write the same songs, throw in a flashy guitar solo, and they think they are doing something cool. I think they missed the point of what being metal and edgy is all about. I find that nu metal was the last movement where the bands all strived to be different.

It was an honour and a blessing to have had the opportunity to be part of the nu metal movement. We worked our asses off to get to where we were. We did everything we could, and we wrote the best music we could. It was so cool and everybody was doing the same thing – trying to make a career and build something out of nothing. You sat in a rehearsal room and wrote all these songs, and then you went out on stage and hoped people like them. Making music is such a weird thing to do, but I feel blessed that I had the opportunity. We were four dudes from Montreal who were trying to be honest and bring music we thought was cool to the stage. I accomplished way more than I thought I would. We thought we would move to Los Angeles and we would be going home with our tails between our legs. We had $3,000 between the four of us, we had enough to pay rent which was about $600 a month, and we knew that was more than half of the money we had. The rest would go on food and gas, and we were like, 'If this is gonna happen, then it's gonna have to happen quick!' and we were lucky.

The music business is not like any other business. It is built on relationships and friendships, and you want your friends to succeed. We never wrote a 'Last Resort' or a 'One Step Closer', and I know why those kinds of bands are still around. They wrote radio poppy, rock tunes, and we never did that. That was never really our goal. We wanted to be the outside band, so we were heavy enough to have the mosh pits, but we were accessible enough that we wasn't too screamy like death metal. We wanted to bridge that gap and that is what we did. We toured with legends and I got to share stages with Ozzy, Black Sabbath, KISS, Pantera, Queens of the Stone Age; all these bands I grew up listening to. It was a weird time, but I wouldn't trade it for the world. For me, I have had an experience that maybe in all the Ozzfests, maybe a thousand people on the planet had the same experience; and that is unique to me. That for me is success. I got into the business to share art, music, feeling and experience, and everything else was just a bonus.

Slipknot

Years Active: 1995-

Location: Des Moines, Iowa, USA

Main era line-up: #0 Sid Wilson (turntables), #1 Joey Jordison (drums), #2 Paul Gray (bass), #3 Chris Fehn (percussion), #4 Jim Root (guitar), #5 Craig '133' Jones (keyboards, samples), #6 Shawn 'Clown' Crahan (percussion, backing vocals), #7 Mick Thomson (guitar), #8 Corey Taylor (lead vocals)

Albums: Mate.Feed.Kill.Repeat (1996), Slipknot (1999), Iowa (2001), Vol. 3: (The Subliminal Verses) (2004), All Hope is Gone (2008), .5: The Gray Chapter (2014), We Are Not Your Kind (2019)

Without doubt the most recognisable thing to ever come out of Des Moines, Iowa, it was impossible to predict from the beginning quite what a phenomenon Slipknot would become in the years which followed. Just another noisy and brash metal band, or so it appeared, Slipknot self-released their *Mate.Feed.Kill. Repeat* in 1996, which was limited to 1,000 copies. Later considered a demo by the official band line-up as the first incarnation only featured three of the nine members who would go on to be one of modern metal's leading forces, it was in 1999 when the nightmare became all too real, as nine jumpsuit and mask-wearing maniacs burst onto the scene with the support of Roadrunner Records.

Band members assigned themselves the numbers 0-8, reportedly as a way of stating they were a product, and with huge hype surrounding the nine-headed behemoth, Slipknot's monster of a debut album was released on 29 June 1999. Produced by Ross Robinson, this aggressive and anarchic self-titled barrage of venomous bile was led by the more radio-friendly singles of 'Wait and Bleed' and 'Spit It Out', and after America had the first taste of the band, the rest of the world was also sent into raptures. Tracks such as 'Surfacing' and 'Eyeless' contained elements of death, speed and thrash metal, while blast beats and turntable samples also forced their way into the craziness. Fronted by Corey Taylor – his maniacal vocal deliveries quickly elevated him to superstar status, as *Slipknot* went on to be certified double platinum in the US (at the time, a first for a Roadrunner Records album) and platinum in the UK.

After already proving to be a strong influence on the nu metal scene, the band's stock rose even higher with their sophomore album, *Iowa*, which was again produced by Robinson and hit the shelves in August 2001. Underlining their power to cause mainstream mayhem, *Iowa* debuted at number 1 in the UK and number 3 on the *Billboard* 200, and it showcased good progression from Slipknot's earlier abrasive release. Still containing death and thrash metal flurries and adding more melody to the likes of 'My Plague' and 'Left Behind', it was the likes of 'The Heretic Anthem' and the rebellious middle finger to the world statement of 'People=Shit', which became future Slipknot classics. *Iowa* would quickly go platinum in the US and Canada, and gold in the UK, as Slipknot became the poster boys for all of heavy metal for the next handful of years.

Due to some strife within the band and perhaps struggling with the pressures of fame, Slipknot announced a hiatus in 2002 after finishing up their world tour, and various members would go on to focus on side-projects which most notably saw Taylor and Jim Root reviving their original band, Stone Sour, and Joey Jordison forming the goth punk outfit, Murderdolls. Slipknot still managed to put out a live DVD titled *Disasterpieces* during this time, where the concert on show had been filmed at London's Dockland Arena nine months prior, and then came the news that fans were praying to hear – Slipknot's hiatus was coming to end.

Roaring back in 2004 with their third record, *Volume 3: The Subliminal Verses,* the Rick Rubin-produced effort continued the band's evolution by including some ballads for the first time ('Vermilion' and 'Vermilion Pt. 2'), as well as acoustic guitars and solos. Songs such as 'The Blister Exists' and 'Three Nil' were punishing heavy metal stomps, and explosive singles included 'Duality' and 'Before I Forget'; the latter of which won a Grammy Award for Best Metal Performance. *Volume 3* peaked at two on the *Billboard* 200 and 5 in the UK, later receiving platinum certificates in both countries, and in 2005 Slipknot put out their first live album, *9.0 Live.* Another hiatus came and went and in 2008, *All Hope is Gone* combined heavier death metal-influenced songs as well as sentimental ballads. Debuting at number 1 in America, the groove orientated singles of 'Psychosocial', 'Dead Memories' and 'Sulfur' went down a storm, as did and the hauntingly epic 'Snuff'.

During some more downtime for the band, Paul Gray was found dead in an Iowa hotel on 24 May 2010. The remaining eight members would quickly hold a press conference alongside Gray's widow and brother, with the band appearing unmasked and understandably shaken with grief – as was most of the heavy metal community. Unsure if the band would continue without one of their most vital members, it wasn't until 2011 when Slipknot returned to the stage and later, they confirmed a brand-new record was on the way. Before that, in June 2012, they released a greatest hits compilation titled *Antennas to Hell,* then they headlined their inaugural Knotfest in August, and with the Slipknot machine seemingly firing on all cylinders once again, a spanner was thrown in the works when it was announced that Joey Jordison had left the band, citing personal reasons. Jordison himself was quick to come out and say he hadn't quit the band at all, but regardless, Slipknot had now lost two core members in the space of a year-and-a-half.

On the first day of August in 2014, Slipknot released their first new song in over six years ('The Negative One') and later in the month, they put out a radio single titled 'The Devil in I'; as well as announcing *5: The Gray Chapter* as the name of the band's fifth record. With various rumours circulating about who would be the bassist and drummer on the new album, a photograph was apparently leaked which showed British-born Alessandro Venturella on bass and Jay Weinburg on drums, although other members of the band quickly refused to confirm that they were to become full-time members of Slipknot.

.5: The Gray Chapter was released in October 2014 and it went straight in at number one in the US and number two in the UK. The album title a tribute to the late Paul Gray, musically the songs contained all the elements which made Slipknot such a massive success in the first place. The brutally dark and heavy 'Custer', and softer numbers such as 'Killpop' and 'Goodbye', and the moody singles which had already been released – it was all still unashamedly Slipknot in its vitality. To support the album, the band went on a co-headline tour with Korn before performing at their annual Knotfest, and at Ozzfest 2016, Slipknot performed *Iowa* in its entirety. Another strong and well-received album followed in 2019, as *We Are Not Your Kind* kept the band in the public eye, and there is already talk of more new music coming from the heavy metal masters.

Being part of a controversial genre, it was inevitable that Slipknot themselves would be enveloped in hullabaloo during their colourful career. Two young killers blamed the lyrical content of 'Disasterpiece' in 2003, and in 2006, lyrics to 'Surfacing' were found at the scene of a grave robbing. A long-standing (and far less serious) feud began when fellow metal band, Mushroomhead, accused Slipknot of copying their image. Mushroomhead claimed to have had the idea of wearing masks and uniforms first, and Corey Taylor, while not denying the bands were similar, put their images purely down to coincidence. Fans of the bands became involved in the feud, but regardless of the arguments, Slipknot had the last laugh as they became, and still are today, one of the biggest metal acts the genre has ever seen.

Killer Cuts – 'Wait and Bleed', 'People=Shit'

Snot

Years Active: 1995-1998, 2008-2011, 2014-2017
Location: Santa Barbara, California, USA
Main era line-up: Lynn Strait (vocals), Mikey Doling (lead guitar), Sonny Mayo (rhythm guitar), John 'Tumor' Fahnestock (bass), Jamie Miller (drums)
Albums: Get Some (1997), Strait Up (2000)

Snot was founded by Mikey Doling and led by the enigmatic vocalist Lynn Strait, and the band built a strong early following from their live shows in and around the Los Angeles area. Signing to Geffen Records after catching various label attention due to their impact on the Sunset Strip, Snot released their debut album, *Get Some,* in May 1997. Although it wasn't commercially successful, Snot's combination of funk metal and hardcore punk was a refreshing inclusion to the rising nu metal scene, and the critically acclaimed album featured the highlights 'Stoopid', 'The Box' and 'I Jus' Lie'. A stint on 1998's Ozzfest also helped get Snot's name out further, especially when Strait stole people's eyes away from Limp Bizkit's set when he climbed their toilet bowl prop and proceeded to receive a sex act from a more than willing young female.

While the band was writing their second album and hype was growing around them due to their Ozzfest stunt, Strait and his dog, Dobbs (who was pictured on the *Get Some* album cover) were tragically killed in a road accident on 11 December 1998. The rest of Snot later decided to disband after refusing to go on without their lead singer, but in November 2000, the remaining members got together with a number of nu metal vocalists and friends of Strait to record the vocal parts to the already written music for an intended second album. Titled *Strait Up*, it acted as the perfect tribute to Strait, and amongst the contributors were Fred Durst on 'Forever', Jonathan Davis on 'Take It Back', Serj Tankian on 'Starlit Eyes'; and Corey Taylor on 'Requiem'. The songs combined punishing metal, hip-hop and melodic rock, and *Strait Up* reached 56 on the *Billboard* 200, which was a fitting way to say goodbye to a likeable and hugely popular musician who was taken way too soon.

The rest of Snot has since continued in various forms, but at their peak, the original incarnation gathered a cult following which remains dedicated to this very day. We will never know how big Snot could have become, but considering *Get Some* still gets mentioned amongst the best nu metal albums ever made, it is pretty clear the band, as well as Lynn Strait, will never be forgotten.

Killer Cuts – 'The Box', 'Stoopid'

Mikey Doling speaks:

Sometime in 1994, when I was just starting Snot, I heard Korn for the first time and I was blown away. I had never heard anything like it. I didn't really know about nu metal or anything like that, in fact, there wasn't even a name for it at the time, but Korn were ground-breaking when they first came out.

I started Snot myself and I was trying to figure out a sound. I was being influenced by Nirvana at that point, believe it or not. I was really into the Beastie Boys, and I was also a metalhead. Shortly after I first heard Korn, I got Lynn (Strait) into the band, and about three months later I went to Shannon Larkin, who was in Ugly Kid Joe and also based in Santa Barbara, and I said I was looking for a bass player, a drummer, and a guitarist. Shannon had three guys from another band he was in, based in Washington D.C. called the M.F. Pitbulls, and those three guys were John 'Tumor' Fahnestock, Sonny Mayo and Jamie Miller. Shannon basically handed me half of Snot, and one by one, they came out. 'Tumor' was first, then we got Sonny, then we got Jamie; and by late 1995 or just into 1996, we had completely formed Snot. By that time, I had heard of Deftones and Coal Chamber and a lot of various bands who were playing in LA, so we started going there to play too. We played down at the Roxy Theatre on Sunset Boulevard, and that is where I discovered a very young System of a Down, and they were opening for us, which was pretty awesome. We were this new thing down in LA and we would have an unsigned band night at the Roxy where it would be Snot, Coal Chamber, System of a Down, Incubus and maybe a couple of other bands.

Deftones and Korn were already starting to do it and so shortly after those guys put out their first records, we got signed, and then the label 'Nu Metal' came out. I was like, 'Alright, if you want to call us that…' because when we first started with the entire band, we weren't into that. We appreciated what Korn and those bands were doing, but I was into Suicidal Tendencies and Infectious Grooves, and if you listen to *Get Some*, you can hear we were super into James Brown for some reason. We really liked that funk aspect, so I kind of used what James Brown, Infectious Grooves and the Beastie Boys were doing, but with a heavy metal twist. Then, the other nu metal influences that were happening kind of leaked their way into it. There was one more band who was influencing us and that was Faith No More. Mike Patton would rap and scat, and I think Faith No More had a lot to do with the sound of nu metal all round. I think they started nu metal, and then you take a little Pantera and Anthrax when they started doing the hip-hop thing, and that leaked into it also.

I didn't understand the term 'nu metal'; I just thought we were all rock bands. For a long time, nu metal became a bad word, and although I didn't mind it so much, I didn't see Snot as a nu metal band. I always thought we were a funk, punk and metal band and I was always more comfortable with that. Metal was killed by grunge. Thrash metal and the bands I loved so much like Exodus and Testament, all those bands got smashed by grunge, and we were trying to play metal again – but a new kind of metal.

All of our bands were friends, and we were all playing the same clubs – the Roxy, the Whisky, The Viper Room, the Troubadour, even Coconut Teaszer and the Dragonfly. We were all doing this thing in LA and all the bands were selling out the clubs. It was a crazy movement, and it was before there was any kind of social media, so it was something that drove people to come out and socialise with each other and there was this music thing they all had in common that they loved; so every show was fucking packed. It was such a great era for music.

The way we got signed was anywhere we played there was a line down the street, and being that we were right there in Hollywood, the labels were literally right down the street. Geffen Records was three blocks away from the Roxy and we sold that place out twice a month for a year, and the labels had to drive down from leaving work and see a line outside and the band 'Snot' up there in lights; or System of a Down, Coal Chamber or Incubus, so they had to take notice. It was pretty awesome because we would be playing and every label we wished would come would be in the crowd. There would be Geffen, Sony, Atlantic – everybody would be in the crowd and it got to the point where they started taking us out to dinner, they would buy us drinks, literally even buying clothes for us. It was stupid.

The two biggest labels were Atlantic Records and Geffen Records, and we had our last meetings with them. The first of those meetings was with Atlantic and it was kind of like an episode right out of *Curb Your Enthusiasm*. The president of Atlantic offered us a $250,000 record deal and we were like, 'Deal! We're in, we're totally into it!' but we still had a meeting across the street at Geffen. We were so green at the time that we didn't really understand that when you say it's a deal – it's a deal. So, we hugged all the staff at Atlantic and we were like, 'Yeah, we're signing to Atlantic Records!' and then about an hour later, we were across the street with Geffen, and they offered us close to half a million dollars; so we said, 'Deal!' They had signed Nirvana, White Zombie and Guns N' Roses, and their vibe was really cool. Later, we were outside of Geffen and hugging their president, Ed Rosenblatt, and shaking hands with the staff, and I remember looking across the street and there was the president of Atlantic, who we made a deal with about two hours earlier, looking at us with his hands in the air going, 'What the fuck?!' We just got into our cars and drove away, but he was really pissed.

So, Snot signed with Geffen and I was blown away by how that could actually happen. Shortly after, we started touring with Machine Head, with Suicidal

Tendencies, we did some shows with Fishbone, which was weird, we did some shows with Deftones and Korn, and then we landed right on top of Ozzfest in 1998. We toured for sixteen months in a van around America and when we finally got to Ozzfest, our manager said, 'You guys have worked your asses off – here's a tour bus'.

There was a really good and competitive feeling to Ozzfest. System of a Down were fucking savages. They would murder everyone, especially Daron Malakian, and he wouldn't even associate with us. It was almost like he was there to kill everybody on stage. We got along really good with the System guys and Shavo (Odadjian) would literally ride on our bus almost every day. We were also really close with the Incubus guys, and they were super young. They didn't even have a bus, they just rode in a van, but they were kicking ass. By the end of the tour, the friendships were amazing. Every night we got to see Motörhead and we got to see a younger Lemmy when he was just on fire, and it was fantastic.

The story of Lynn getting arrested during Ozzfest has almost become legendary. We were in Great Woods in Boston and Limp Bizkit was killing it at the time. There was a girl at the festival who was hanging out with different bands almost every day, and she was bit of a slut. Limp Bizkit had this giant toilet prop on stage and Lynn wanted to get us some attention to try and make the band bigger, so he had this big idea to take this chick in full dominatrix outfit and with a leash around her neck up through the back of this toilet prop which was thirteen feet in the air. You would actually come up the stairs at the back and stand on the lid of the toilet. Fred Durst would take giant pictures of Britney Spears and Hanson and whoever else was big at the time and flush them down the toilet, and it was a big deal for the crowd to enjoy. So, Lynn said he was going to get up on that toilet when Limp Bizkit was playing with this chick, and as Limp Bizkit was going on Lynn stripped naked and went up on top of this toilet, and this chick blew him in front of 20,000 people. You could clearly see it from the crowd like it was live porn. Lynn also had a huge Snot sticker on his stomach which was pretty hilarious. It only lasted about a minute before security and police tried to get up there and get them, but Lynn ran down the back of the toilet, grabbed his clothes – which he had strategically hidden – and ran butt naked through the backstage area and into Ozzy Osbourne's dressing room. He was literally in Ozzy's dressing room, naked, and there was Ozzy's kids and wife in there. Lynn said, 'Sharon, I'm so sorry, the cops are coming after me,' so Sharon went and locked the door so the cops couldn't get in. Lynn got dressed and Sharon totally had his back. She said, 'You've gotta go out there but I'll make sure you're gonna be okay' so Lynn opened the door and the cops arrested him. They handcuffed him and took him to a makeshift onsite jail if you will. The people booking him didn't even know his name at this point, so they took the report and Lynn told the police his name was Dave Mustaine. Megadeth was on that tour too, and the police report went down as 'Dave Mustaine – indecent exposure'. They let Lynn out and he came back to the bus and said it was all good and that he was fine, so we continued the tour. The very next day after that incident, Snot was all over

MTV and it made our band kind of explode, so Lynn's stunt totally worked. A couple of days later though, Lynn got arrested again for giving the wrong name and it all came out, but still, we got to finish Ozzfest. Of course, Lynn never got to make it to court, but he was actually going to go to jail. They were going to give him a little bit of time, and we think he was probably going to do three to six months; but who knows.

When Lynn died, the label and everybody was asking what we wanted to do and if we were going to get a new singer, but we were so devastated that we just stopped. We couldn't really deal with it at the time because it was too much. Lynn was my best friend, we founded the band together, and when he died we were living together in the same place. I even had to collect his belongings and give them to his mother. It was so heavy that the music side of it really took a backseat to the emotional part of losing my best friend. Even to this day, it is hard, and even now, I am having a hard time talking about it. I miss Lynn a lot.

At the time, 'Tumor' and I were already starting to write stuff, not songs that would have necessarily made a record for Snot; we were just messing with some ideas. We were talking to Shannon Larkin one day and we were like, 'Snot's over man.' We were friends with a lot of the singers, and I don't know how it came up, but we decided to make a tribute album with all these singers, and it just snowballed and became a thing. I kind of regret it even though a lot of people liked the *Strait Up* record. It was really hard to put together and I'm not a big fan of those songs. Of course, the singers all kicked ass, but I feel like they sang to subpar music, personally. If I had the chance to do it again today, I wouldn't. We just weren't there anymore, and we weren't writing like Snot. It wasn't the whole band, we weren't excited, and it was sad. We were just trying to write these songs for people to sing on and when I listen back to it now, it isn't a fond memory.

Max and Gloria Cavalera were good friends of ours because Snot had opened a lot of shows for Soulfly. That was one of the bands we were touring with the most and even before Ozzfest, we were really close with those guys. When Lynn passed, it was pretty close to the same time Logan Mader was parting ways with Soulfly. I guess my name came up as a possible replacement for Logan, just for some touring because they had some dates booked with Korn and Marilyn Manson in New Zealand and Australia. They couldn't cancel the shows because it was just too huge, and then there was Japan right after, and so they called me. I was buried in sorrow and torn back, and I was sitting with 'Tumor' when they called, kind of bonding together through the loss of Lynn. The phone rang and it was Gloria, and she said something like, 'Hey man, how are you doing, I hope you're okay. We need a guitar player for this tour; we're going to Australia, New Zealand and Japan – can you do it?' At first, I told her I was still in way too much pain to go on any kind of tour, and 'Tumor', sitting next to me and listening in on the conversation, was like, 'Fucking do it.' I asked Gloria if I could think about it and call her back, and she said, 'Dude, you better call me back within thirty minutes because we don't have time. I love you, Mikey, but we need to know now.'

I hung up the phone and 'Tumor' was all, 'Dude, just go and fucking tour with Soulfly. You know those songs, you've been touring with them forever,' so I called Gloria back and said I appreciated the opportunity, and I would do it. Eight days later, we left for the tour. It was a really easy transition because I had probably played three months of shows with Soulfly. I came from a thrash metal background before Snot, not that Soulfly was thrash metal back then, but they had that metal twist. Not only that, but I was a huge fan of Max from his Sepultura days, and I just sat right in there and I ended up playing in Soulfly for five years. I played Ozzfest with them in 2001 and the one in the UK was amazing. We were backstage and the guys in Black Sabbath were all hanging out, the guys from Iron Maiden had come to hang out; there was Slipknot and Tool; it was insane. Not only that, Amen played on the second stage and that was half of Snot, so it was really awesome. We got on stage in front of 80,000 people in Milton Keynes and I remember I was walking up the ramp and I literally had to pass Tony Iommi and Adrian Smith and say, 'Excuse me,' and they both said, 'Have a good show, mate.' For me it was my sixteen-year-old self freaking out.

In the US we were headlining the second stage, but Pantera was on that tour. We actually ended up touring with them just after Ozzfest on their *Reinventing the Steel* tour, and I ended up being pretty damn good friends with those guys. I think I cherish that the most out of my entire career because I can say I was friends with Vinnie Paul and Dimebag Darrell, and my heart breaks into a thousand pieces when I think about Pantera. They were the greatest heavy metal band of all time and it was just the saddest outcome for all of those guys.

Pantera used to take their own bar on tour with them, so every single night, we would get off stage and Pantera would have a designated room for their bar, with the same rugs and the same posters on the walls. We got to drink with Vinnie Paul, Dime was the host, and it was just insane. One night we were backstage and it was towards the end of maybe seventy shows we had played with Pantera. I was with Dime, just talking, I had a bunch of drinks in me (of course), and I said, 'Hey man, I wanna play guitar with you, I wanna play 'Walk'', and he was like, 'Fuckin' aye dude, tomorrow night, you're on!' The next night I played 'Walk' on guitar with Pantera. There were two guitar players in the band for one song, and I did that for eleven nights all the way to the end of the tour. I think that is probably the greatest moment of my entire life, being on stage with Pantera and playing guitar with Dime.

I think nu metal was really good for heavy music – what else was there? There was no metal happening and we needed some loud guitars and big drums, and it is so weird that what we were doing has become this old school thing because it was so new at the time. It was the last great time in music.'

Soil

Years Active: 1997-

Location: Chicago, Illinois, USA

Main era line-up: Ryan McCombs (vocals), Adam Zadel (lead guitar), Shaun Glass

(rhythm guitar), Tim King (bass), Tom Schofield (drums)
Albums: Throttle Junkies (1999), Scars (2001), Redefine (2004), True Self (2006), Picture Perfect (2009), Whole (2013)

Soil announced themselves with their debut album, *Throttle Junkies,* through MIA Records in 1997, although the label was to fold not long after the album's release. Not letting this early setback defeat them, the quintet developed new demos, which led to Soil earning a major label deal with J Records – owned by Clive Davis, who had previously taken on the likes of Pink Floyd and Bruce Springsteen.

Soil's breakthrough sophomore album, *Scars,* became the first heavy metal album released on J Records, coming out on 11 September 2001. The outrageously groovy single 'Halo' launched the band into the mainstream, and led by the powerful vocals of Ryan McCombs, the chorus was to become a singalong anthem for metalheads all over. 'Unreal' was the ideal choice for the second single released from the record, this time showing off a dark and brooding number which helped *Scars* gain silver status in the UK in the years that followed.

With a solid foundation laid down thanks to relentless touring, Soil returned with *Redefine* in 2004 and it was another tasty slab of alternative metal. Driven by meaty hooks and catchy choruses, the album peaked at 78 on the *Billboard* 200, and powerful anthems like 'Remember' (a tribute to Drowning Pool's Dave Williams), 'Obsession' and 'Pride' found the band maturing and their songwriting strengthening.

Later dropped from J Records due to BMG and Sony merging, McCombs had also left the band to join Drowning Pool in 2005 before little known A.J. Cavalier would come in and vocal on Soil's fourth album, *True Self,* in 2006 and released through DRT Entertainment. Also sticking around for 2009 release *Picture Perfect*, Cavalier had left by the middle of 2010 and he was replaced by Jordan Lee who stood in for upcoming tour dates. McCombs then returned to Soil in 2011 to tour and celebrate the tenth anniversary of *Scars,* and soon after, it was confirmed that he had indeed returned to the band full-time. After a few more comings and goings, the band settled as a trio with original members Adam Zadel, Tim King and McCombs, and they brought back the classic sound of Soil's earlier albums on *Whole*, which was released in 2013 via Pavement Entertainment. The barnstorming lead single, 'Shine On', displayed crunching riffs and the familiar McCombs snarl, while 'The Hate Song' and 'Way Gone' added strength-in-depth to an impressive tracklist. Having recently announced they are working on a new album which will be the first in eight years, Soil continues to have an army of dedicated fans behind them; however, 'Halo' will forever be the band's signature song and their finest moment in the spotlight.

Killer Cuts – 'Halo', 'Unreal'

Shaun Glass speaks:

My roots always came from stuff like Metallica, Slayer, Kreator, Celtic Frost, Exodus and crossover thrash; so even when we formed Soil, we were all coming out of playing in death metal bands except for Ryan, and we were all kind of burned on it. I was in Broken Hope playing bass for a couple of albums, and Tim, Adam and Tom were in a death metal band called Oppressor. We were listening to Alice in Chains, Pantera and Black Label Society, but we were trying to do something more melodic and more accessible- to play something that could reach wider audiences. That was the Soil vision.

To be blunt, I never looked at Soil as being a nu metal band; it was just the timing of coming up, especially in Chicago when we got signed to a real label before *Scars* came out. We had so many bands around us like Disturbed, From Zero, No One and some other cool bands from our era who put out albums, but I really thought – especially when we were writing the songs that became famous, that they were just heavy rock and metal. The only thing that made us more nu metal was that we didn't have a lot of guitar solos on the early albums, and that was largely due to our producer at the time.

Johnny K was going with the times and he was telling us we didn't need that many leads, so we never really included those on the popular Soil albums. We should have had that element to make us a little more different and separate from the rest of the bunch, and I don't think with Ryan's voice and image that he was a nu metal-looking frontman at all. I thought he was more of an iconic rock singer or heavy metal frontman because he never really got into the whole make-up and dreads or nail polish look, that really wasn't our thing; so for me to say Soil was nu metal ... okay I guess. I grew up on KISS, Mötorhead, Sabbath, early Van Halen, and I loved Thin Lizzy, UFO and shit like that, so I really wasn't raised on nu metal, although I wasn't ashamed of the tag.

I hate our album, *Throttle Junkies*. The production is awful and when we recorded it, I didn't want to work with the producer, Steve Albini. The rest of the band all thought we should go to Steve because he was in Chicago and he was a popular producer, but I said, 'Guys, he's not a producer for the right kind of sound we want to go for.' At the time, I wanted to make our album with a *Load*, *Reload*, or The Black Album (*Metallica*) vibe, and I had a different producer in line who was willing to do the album, which would have been perfect – I thought, but I was outvoted. I was on tour with a different band at the time filling in playing bass, and when I got back from the tour, the guys said we were going into the studio in two weeks to record *Throttle Junkies* with Steve Albini. I like Steve and he was a really nice guy, but he told me, 'What you want this album to sound like – I am not the guy (to do it). I am an engineer and not a producer', and there's a huge difference between an engineer and a producer. What my vision was for that record is nothing how it came out, so I can honestly tell you I never listen to that record. I fucking hate it.

I was at a party at Johnny K's studio for Disturbed, who just finished recording *The Sickness*, and he had kind of heard of Soil because we started to build a little buzz in Chicago. We were playing out and building a fan base and I said to Johnny K that we wanted to record some new music, and Johnny was like, 'Hey, this is what I'll charge you to do two or three new songs' and I told him the new stuff was really different. We were going a little heavier, a little more modern, we were getting rid of the Southern shitkicker sound of *Throttle Junkies*, and then Johnny heard some demos and made some notes, gave us some constructive criticism, and we went back to the drawing board and worked on the songs.

One of the songs was called 'God of the Day', which later became 'Halo'. We recorded the demos and then I helped build a website with a friend of mine, and we put the three songs on the internet as a free download. Then we made about a thousand sampler CDs in Chicago and we just hit the streets and started giving them out. I really championed 'Halo' and I wanted it as the first song on the CD, but the guys said it was too heavy. Then all of a sudden, we put the demo on the street, got it on the website, and all these people were praising 'Halo'; and then it got in the hands of a guy at Atlantic Records who lived in Florida. He put the song on a radio station in Orlando as a test song and it just blew up. The website kept crashing from downloads as more and more people just grabbed the songs, and then the labels started calling. Every record deal you sign is a risk because the labels come at you with open arms, and you have to make sure they don't have a knife in their hand after a six-month relationship and they stab you in the back. We started getting flown to New York at weekends to do shows, we had a showcase in Chicago playing for a bunch of labels – one of which was Atlantic Records – and at the same show, there was about two or three other A&R guys ready to basically offer us money and beg us to sign for their label. The real truth we signed to J Records was because they offered the most money. Clive Davis, the biggest cheque, a new label through BMG, we were the only rock/metal band being signed at that point to the label, there was no competition on the roster to compete with; we knew we would get all the attention and they offered us the most money. It was a no-brainer at the time for us. Elektra made a really nice offer, Atlantic came in with a decent deal, and should we have gone to Atlantic or Elektra – I don't know. Maybe, but I will tell you this, I think those labels would have understood and been able to work the band to radio a little better than a label that didn't have any other bands like us. That is the one thing looking back, in my opinion, that maybe it would have been smarter to sign to a label that had a little more on the roster that was aligned to what Soil was.

'Halo' was our signature song. It had huge groove and a great production. When I came up with the verse riff, I was jamming it with the guys at practice and I remember I felt like it had a Pantera, 'Walk' stomp. Adam and Ryan started working on vocal ideas for it and once we heard the chorus and the 'I will stone you, stone you…', that chorus was on a different song that we demoed and put on the backburner. Then when we were working on the original version of 'God of the Day', Adam asked Ryan to try singing the old chorus for 'Halo' that we had, which we thought was kind of Rob Zombie-ish at first. Ryan had to change the timing a little bit, so when he started singing that over the chorus riff we had, it became 'Halo' because the word was in the title. If we never had that chorus on it, I don't think the song would have ever been as good.

From my memory, the song was basically about Ryan's love/hate relationship with the music industry. 'I will stone you, stone you...' as in 'I hate you, but I'll wrap my arms around you, because I love music, yet I hate this fucking industry'. We were going through hell and back after *Throttle Junkies* and trying to get on a real label. We were on some shitty label that couldn't give a damn about us, and then we did the demo with Johnny K and all of a sudden, that song reacted. When we wrote it, we didn't know it was going to be our trademark song, but to me, when I hear the song today, I think it still sounds modern.

Scars came out on 11 September 2001, and that day was one of the worst days in the history of our country. It hurt momentum (for the band), it hurt morale; I think the horrible event that took place that day sent tremors to everything. Aside from my life and our music business, it hurt the entire world. 9/11 definitely hurt Soil. Stations started pulling songs like Saliva's 'Click Click Boom' and Drowning Pool's 'Bodies', and that hurt those bands' momentum because they were riding high on those singles. I don't think 'Halo' got injured by the song title so much as 'Click Click Boom' or 'Bodies', but it hurt the industry and I think that a lot has changed since then, dramatically. The only thing that benefitted us was that we already had momentum with the song before we got signed. We were already on tour at the time, and we had the major label machine and money behind the band.

After we released *Redefine*, Ryan quit and told us he was done with the music business. The label let us go and we were like, 'Okay, we just toured the world and we have millions of fans right now, and our record label let us go and our singer quit- so what do we do?' The four of us at the time said, 'Fuck it, let's find a new singer, write some new music, and just do what we do.' Pat from Damageplan and Wayne Static both suggested checking out A.J. Cavalier, and then we demoed some songs, gave them to a couple of labels, and Derek Shulman, who was the man who signed Pantera to Atco for *Cowboys from Hell,* had a new upstart label called DRT. He had American Head Charge and a couple other bands on the label, and he offered us a pretty decent deal. We got A.J. in and then we made *True Self*. We did some huge tours for that record, including almost all of the US and Europe with Staind. We had some amazing shows, and I know we did pretty damn good in the UK still. The 'Give It Up' video was still getting played everywhere, and I knew that nobody was done with the band yet. *True Self* seemed to at least stabilise the band, but then nearer the end of that tour cycle, I started seeing some issues with other members re-occurring, and it was just an uncomfortable home for me to be in after touring hard. I thought at first when we put out *True Self* that it had great momentum and it was a different era of Soil but it still sounded like Soil, and I'm proud of that record.

Leaving Soil was tough. It was a large part of frustration with business stuff going on with the band that I wasn't agreeing with, and my musical tastes were going more into metal again. I wanted to play stuff more in the Trivium, Killswitch Engage, Slayer, Hatebreed style. I was already writing demos for my Dirge Within project, but to be brutally honest, I really wasn't happy living with alcoholics. It was really frustrating for me to be on tour when I was on a bus full of a majority of people who were non-stop drunks. I was the guy that wasn't really getting drunk every day. I had beers of course and there were nights where I partied, living the dream and doing stupid stuff, but my eye was always on making sure I was sober and clean for the next day on stage and making sure I played my guitar to the best of my abilities. My work ethic was totally different to theirs.

My favourite nu metal band, if you want to call them nu metal, was Static-X. I grew up with Wayne Static in Chicago and I knew he had moved to LA, but I didn't really know what he was doing. Then, all of a sudden, my buddy asked me if I'd heard Wayne's new band. There were sampler cassettes at record stores where record companies would place them for people to take, and I think Adam and I were at a record store putting flyers out to promote a Soil gig and we listened to Wayne's band and were like, 'Holy fuck! This production, this guitar tone… this is amazing!' and then I was like, 'Wait a minute, that's Wayne – I know who he is, he used to live in Chicago!' Once Soil got signed to a real label, we toured so much together that a lot of Static's *Machine* and *Shadow Zone* records are a part of the soundtrack to my life, because I was around those albums and tour cycles, so much. I loved Static-X and I think they are one of the best ever nu metal bands. I thought they were so much better than a lot of bands because they were so original, so heavy, so catchy, and so groovy. It is a tragic story, what happened with Wayne and his passing.

Soulfly

Years Active: 1997-

Location: Los Angeles, California, USA

Main era line-up: Max Cavalera (vocals, rhythm guitar), Jackson Bandeira/Mikey Doling (lead guitar), Marcelo Dias (bass), Joe Nunez/Roy Mayorga (drums)

Albums: Soulfly (1998), Primitive (2000), 3 (2002), Prophecy (2004), Dark Ages (2005), Conquer (2008), Omen (2010), Enslaved (2012), Savages (2013), Archangel (2015), Ritual (2018)

After his bitter split from Sepultura, Max Cavalera returned with Soulfly in 1997. Basing themselves in Los Angeles and playing heavy, thrash-influenced metal which also incorporated Brazilian tribal and world music elements (much like Sepultura did during their flirtation with nu metal), the band signed to Roadrunner Records- ironically the same label that Sepultura was on, and brought Ross Robinson on board to produce their self-titled debut, which came out in 1998.

As nu metal began to make strong waves, a handful of artists from the scene's up-and-coming bands featured on the record, including Limp Bizkit's Fred Durst and DJ Lethal on 'Bleed', Fear Factory's Dino Cazares and Burton C. Bell on 'Eye for an Eye'; and Deftones vocalist Chino Moreno, on 'First Commandment'. *Soulfly* quickly reached gold status and later in 1998, the band played Ozzfest alongside the likes of Ozzy Osbourne, Megadeth and Tool, before playing smaller club tours with System of a Down and Snot.

Primitive followed in September 2000 and featured a similar thrash and alternative metal formula. Mikey Doling, formerly of Snot, took over guitar duties and once again, the album featured guests aplenty. Slipknot's Corey Taylor stole the show on the live favourite, 'Jumpdafuckup', while Slayer's Tom Araya and the returning Chino Moreno lent their talents to 'Terrorist' and 'Pain', respectively. Reaching 32 on the *Billboard* 200, *Primitive* earned Soulfly their highest chart position and strong tours followed along with Ozzfest once again, plus a worldwide trip with groove metal legends Pantera. Less than two years later, Cavalera and company were ready to assault eardrums again with *3*. 'Seek 'n' Strike' and 'Downstroy' were popular singles, and Ill Nino's Christian Machado vocal-led on 'One', but a year later, turmoil would strike the band. Marcelo Dias was fired, and then Doling and Roy Mayorga also quit, and so Joe Nunez returned, having played drums on *Primitive*, while ex-Ill Nino guitarist, Marc Rizzo, came in along with ex-Primer 55 bassist Bobby Burns.

Soulfly was once again a powerhouse quartet, and when they released the storming fourth album, *Prophecy,* in 2004, it included a lot more tribal and world music elements, along with a much heavier emphasis on a thrash sound. The title track remains one of Soulfly's best ever songs, and the album also featured a good cover of Helmet's 'In the Meantime', but it was clear by now that Cavalera was taking his band into much heavier waters as death metal also began to seep into his band's music. The next chapter would spur Cavalera to write some of the darkest and most ferocious material of his career. Close friend, Dimebag Darrell, was shot dead while playing on stage with his Damageplan band in 2004, and then Max's grandson, Moses, heartbreakingly passed away. Soulfly's fifth album, *Dark Ages* (released in 2005), focused on aggression and darker themes influenced by the year or so leading up to its creation. Recorded in five different countries, the album included 'Frontlines' (featuring Slayer's Kerry King) and 'Riotstarter', with the bass work being covered by Megadeth's Dave Ellefson.

Undoubtedly a bad period for Max Cavalera and his family, it would soon be 2006 and the tenth annual D-Low Memorial Show. Originally set up to honour Max's stepson, Dana, who had died in a car accident back in 1996, the anniversary show would see Max's brother, Igor, (and co-founder of Sepultura) reunite on stage to perform the classic Sepultura songs, 'Roots Bloody Roots' and 'Attitude'; helping to rebuild the foundations for the siblings to become close once again.

As nu metal faded out of the limelight, Soulfly moved on to become one of the most popular thrash and death metal bands of the next decade, with more pummeling album releases in the forms of *Conquer* (2008), *Omen* (2010), *Enslaved* (2012), *Savages* (2013), *Archangel* (2015); and *Ritual* (2018).

Killer Cuts – 'Back to the Primitive', 'Jumpdafuckup'

Spineshank

Years Active: 1996-2004, 2008-2016
Location: Los Angeles, California, USA
Main era line-up: Jonny Santos (vocals), Mike Sarkisyan (guitar), Rob Garcia (bass), Tommy Decker (drums)
Albums: Strictly Diesel (1998), The Height of Callousness (2000), Self-Destructive Pattern (2003), Anger Denial Acceptance (2012)

From the outset, Spineshank cited Fear Factory as a huge influence on their industrial metal sound, and the band's very first live show would be opening for Fear Factory at the Whisky Au Go Go in LA in 1996 after becoming friends with Dino Cazares. Further support slots with the likes of Coal Chamber, Snot and Soulfly helped spread Spineshank's name around Los Angeles, which was becoming a hotbed for new musical talent, and their reward was penning a deal with Roadrunner Records.

Spineshank released their debut album, *Strictly Diesel,* in 1998. Featuring Orgy's Amir Derakh as a special guest on The Beatles cover, 'While My Guitar Gently Weeps', who also co-produced the album with Jay Baumgardner, the album sold around 75,000 copies on the back of some coarse industrial metal where the likes of 'Shinebox' and 'Intake' stood out. A decent beginning, if not quite the success Roadrunner thought the band would be, it wasn't until Spineshank's sophomore release, *The Height of Callousness,* where the quartet really broke through at the turn of the new millennium. Videos for the popular singles 'New Disease' and 'Synthetic' received strong airplay, and a stint on Ozzfest ultimately helped the album – whose title came from a phrase in the movie, *A Clockwork Orange* shift over 150,000 units.

In September 2003, Spineshank released their third long-player, *Self-Destructive Pattern,* and it reached 89 on the *Billboard* 200. The lead-off single, 'Smothered', had more of a straightforward hard rock feel and it was nominated for a Grammy in the category of Best Metal Performance in 2004, while the pulsating opener of 'Violent Mood Swings' was as good as anything Spineshank had ever written.

Jonny Santos left the band in 2004 and quickly formed a new and heavier group called Silent Civilian, while the remaining members decided to carry on with a new lead singer; however, no new music was ever released and Spineshank decided to call it a day. Four years later, Santos returned to the fold with the rest of the original line-up, and they set to work on writing and recording their fourth studio album, which finally arrived in 2014, titled *Anger Denial Acceptance.* Released through Century Media and welcoming back the original Spineshank

sound, standout moments on the record came on 'Nothing Left for Me', 'I Want You to Know', and the furious 'Murder Suicide'. A timely reminder of how good the band still was, it proved to be Spineshank's final release, but at least they went out on a high.

Killer Cuts – 'New Disease', 'Synthetic'

Mike Sarkisyan speaks:

Before Spineshank formed, three out of the four of us were part of a band called Basic Enigma. We were just kids playing music rather than getting into other kinds of trouble. I would go out and play shows, come home at one or two in the morning, and then I would go to school the next day; but at some point, Basic Enigma had run its course. A few months later, we were all making music and then Tommy (Decker) started putting it all together. At the time, we had two guitar players and when we needed someone to sing, Jonny (Santos) would come down and balance vocal ideas. It was non-committal and just demo stuff, but after a few months went by, we realised all this could be part of one thing – and so Spineshank was born.

We didn't play shows; we just wrote songs. We made an eight-song demo and then we took three of those songs and made a cassette, and we would pass them out at any and every show in LA. I was a huge fan of Fear Factory and our tape got into the hands of Dino Cazares. I had given a tape to 'Meegs' from Coal Chamber and he and Dino were neighbours. A week later, I went to a Sick Of It All show and I ran into Dino, and he said he had heard of Spineshank. Fear Factory had a show coming up at The Whisky, and when I met Dino, I simply asked if we could play with them, and he said yes. So, there we were – a band who had eight songs, a three-song demo, we had never played a show before, and our first show was opening up for Fear Factory at The Whisky Au Go Go, and it just took off from there. Within a year, we would have a record deal.

There was a resurgence of heavy music at the time, but it was before record labels figured out there was a commercial value to it. There was Machine Head, a band called Misery Loves Company, and those bands were heavy influences on Spineshank, as were Korn and Pantera. It was cool to be part of that scene, but it was also not cool being left out of it at the same time. I feel like there were bands that came after us who got to be a lot more successful who didn't deserve it – that is just my opinion. Did we have our part to play in the nu metal movement – I'm sure we did, but it's kind of like being in the right place at the right time.

When we came out, there was no such thing as 'Nu Metal', and it didn't really start until halfway into the cycle of our second record, *The Height of Callousness*. It used to be called 'LA Metal' because of Korn, Coal Chamber, Fear Factory and System of a Down etc. but when Slipknot and Limp Bizkit came out, you couldn't call it 'LA Metal' anymore because those bands weren't from LA. If I am not mistaken, all of this started with *Kerrang!* so it started in the UK. America isn't really obsessed with labels like the way the UK is, so they called it 'Nu Metal' and we were like, 'Nu Metal – what the fuck is that?!' It was all happening as we were doing our thing, so there was a lot of stuff we didn't notice and then it kind of caught up with us.

Later on, you've got Limp Bizkit and Spineshank, who sound nothing alike, but they're both the same genre of music, and that was weird. As a musician and somebody who went through it, are there similarities between all those bands – if I want to play devil's advocate, then sure, because it was all about vocal hooks, whether it be rapping or singing. So, if you really want to break it down, there were definitely similarities between a lot of those bands. I still don't like the nu metal tag, though. When our last record came out (*Anger Denial Acceptance*), I don't know if this worked in our favour or not, but they stopped calling Spineshank nu metal and started calling us alternative metal – but what were we alternative to? In 2009, we did the Music As A Weapon tour with Disturbed. One of the bands on the second stage with us was Suicide Silence, and I found out that their guitar player, Chris Garza, was a huge fan of Spineshank. He told me, 'Dude, I grew up on you guys,' and it made me feel really old. He came out on stage every day and played 'The Height of Callousness' with us, but when you listen to *Suicide Silence* I don't really hear us in their sound. I guess one way or another, we influenced another generation of bands.

We signed for Roadrunner Records at a very transitional time for them, and when we signed, they only had one type of record deal. Us, Coal Chamber; Fear Factory were way before us, Machine Head, Vision of Disorder – we all got the same seven-album deal. I think we got $30,000 for the first album, and then it went up in increments of $5,000 and $10,000 for every album after. However, just because you have signed a certain deal, it doesn't really mean anything – that I know. *Strictly Diesel* cost over $100,000 to make. Roadrunner were obliged to give us $30,000, but they actually gave us more than $100,000, and the option was on them to do it.

After all of this, that is when the majors really jumped on bands like us. There was only two major label deals for nu metal bands at the time. One was System of a Down (American Recordings) but Rick Rubin had been courting them for forever, and the other one was Snot, who signed with Geffen. I remember talking to Lynn Strait and Mikey Doling about this at the time and I thought they were the new Guns N' Roses – that is who they kind of reminded me of. I think they would have been insanely huge. As punk rock as they were, they had a commercial appeal and I think they would have been one of those bands to break down the barriers, and they would have done amazing on huge festivals. You could put them in front of fifty people in a club and they would light up the room, or you could put them in front of 50,000 people and they would just kill it. They were good everywhere and it really sucks what happened to Snot.

Spineshank didn't really catch that wave of having major label offers, but we did get two offers. One was from Noise Records, who were a little indie label, but it wasn't really a formal offer, more like, 'Yeah, we wanna sign you guys, we'll give you this much, if you're interested then let's continue the talks,' and the other offer we received was from Earache, which wasn't a formal offer either. It was, 'Hey, we're definitely interested in signing you guys, who is your manager?' We didn't have a manager though, and we didn't even have a lawyer – it was just the four of us. Four knuckleheads trying to navigate through the dog-eat-dog world of the music business. The only guy we knew who we could ask things to was Dino Cazares because we were really close with him.

Kevin Estrada was coming to all of our shows and he was basically the West Coast A&R of Roadrunner. Obviously, he would get Monte Connor's okay before signing anyone, but Kevin was coming to our shows and we were getting close to him, and then he took us out to lunch. At the time, Roadrunner had offices in Santa Monica, so we went to this little Mexican restaurant over there. We thought Roadrunner was going to offer us a demo deal, as in they would pay for us to do a demo and if the demo came out good, they would sign us. Coal Chamber was doing pretty well back then, so this demo deal was going to be with the same group of people who did Coal Chamber's record – Amir Derakh, Jay Gordon and Jay Baumgardner. They had also just done System of a Down's demo before they got signed. So that was what we were thinking, and then Kevin says, 'You know what, I was thinking of giving you guys a demo deal but screw that, I just wanna offer you a record deal.' I remember that was one of the happiest days of my life.

Every band I loved was on Roadrunner. In England, it was a little different because they were a major label, but in the US, it wasn't really like that, but to be signed to that label was insane. I was eighteen years old when this happened, and I didn't know anything about anything, and I didn't care. I was like, 'Okay cool, where do I sign?' and they said, 'Well, you guys need a lawyer because we need to send you a contract, and you need to look it over.' We didn't know we even needed an entertainment attorney specifically, so Dino referred us to Fear Factory's attorney and he was the one who sorted our contract.

In all honesty, I think Roadrunner was expecting for us to sell 30,000 or 40,000 copies of *Strictly Diesel* in the US and another 10,000 in the UK, and that would have been perfect. That was all they wanted, but because of the strength of what Coal Chamber ended up doing, Roadrunner were more open to marketing other bands. Coal Chamber had just sold 300,000 copies of their debut album when they were only expecting 30,000, so all these other bands were worked too, but I don't think *Strictly Diesel* was given a fair shot. A bunch of bullshit happened on the tour cycle of it, so we didn't really tour for that long, and then we went home and wrote *The Height of Callousness* and looking back, that was the best thing that ever happened to us. We had considered *Strictly Diesel* a failure and so did Roadrunner, but they gave us a shot to do another record and that was a whole other story. We locked ourselves in a room and wrote until we were 100% happy with what we had. It was a very focused record and I look at *The Height of Callousness* as our real debut. *Strictly Diesel* was kind of like a glorified demo.

A lot of people say Ozzfest 2001 was the best-ever line-up, and I don't really think there was anybody missing from it. Perhaps the one band who should have done it was System of a Down and then it would have been the be all and end all of that entire era. It was weird because 2001 was the only year where the second stage was done and then the main stage would open. I think the second stage went until 5 p.m. or so, and then the main stage would open up. It was kind of cool because for certain shows we would play to 15,000 or 20,000 people, as opposed to maybe 7,000 to 10,000. The second stage was rotating also, meaning there was a band on and then a band behind it would set up, and as soon as one band was done, the stage would just turn and there would only be about a five-minute changeover. What sucked about it was how many times my guitar tech would just roll onto the bus and say, 'Shark, you've got ten minutes until you go on stage,' and I was like, 'Fuck!' Normally, you would have at least an hour of stretching and this or that to get ready for the show, but on Ozzfest, you would get out of bed and you would have just minutes before you hit the stage.

Every band who was part of that particular Ozzfest killed it. There was a really cool camaraderie between the bands, even with the main stage bands. We were really good friends with Disturbed and the Slipknot guys, and there wasn't this whole main stage versus second stage thing, even though within the second stage we were all pretty much on the same level back then. We would go on around 12:30 and we only had a 25-minute set. All the second stage bands had the same except Mudvayne, who were sort of the de facto headliners, and I think they got about 35 minutes. Right after we played there was an FYE tent which was kind of like a music store, and we would do a signing in there, then we would do a Jägermeister signing, and then we were done doing whatever we were doing by half-two tops; and we would just be drinking ourselves into a stupor every day. There was free Jäger and at the time, Grey Goose vodka came out. This was when Grey Goose was really good. We got all this free booze and it was just insanity. I was twenty-four years old and they just threw this idiot on tour with a bunch of other idiots, and that's what ends up happening – idiot stuff. It was like summer camp with a bunch of dudes, and then you get to play a rock show.

If I'm not mistaken, we were in Columbus, Ohio, and the whole show was done. Black Sabbath had already left, and for whatever reason, our bus driver was stuck somewhere and he couldn't come back to pick us up. We found this golf cart (this was at around three in the morning) and we decided to set one of those foldable tables on fire; then Tommy and I were going to drive the golf cart through the table. The cart wasn't really that fast, so we kept driving it into this table, but it would only move a little. We thought it was going to be fun but it wasn't really that much fun. Then we started doing donuts and Tommy and I began fighting over the steering wheel, and somewhere in the process of this we were thrown out of the cart and it flipped on us. We were just lying on the ground and laughing our asses off and we couldn't get out. Someone came and got the cart off us and then we got caught by security. They were like, 'Who the fuck are you guys?', so we told them we were Papa Roach. Any kind of misbehaviour was getting reported to Sharon Osbourne, and I don't know if Papa Roach ever got in trouble but it was stupid shit like that we did. We flipped porta potties in the hope that all the shit would come out of them, and that was our thing. We were complete fucking idiots, but that is what happens when you throw a bunch of kids in a tube and say, 'Go and do whatever the fuck you want.'

Those who didn't really hang out were the Black Sabbath dudes because they were old men, and they didn't want to hang out with knuckleheads like us. Marilyn Manson didn't really hang out either, I only saw him one time, at catering, and he was wearing a G-string. Other than that, it was a free-for-all. I remember me and Shawn 'Clown' Crahan from Slipknot would get drunk and just punch each other in the face for fun. One day we ended up in a trash can and we just talked about life. We had this really deep conversation, but I don't think either of us made any sense. You play a show, do whatever obligations you had, then the main stage would open, and you would just be everywhere finding trouble here and there. Then you would hide from Sharon Osbourne because she knows everything and you don't want her to bust you, and it was definitely an exciting time.

Because Ozzfest played every other day, a lot of the time, we ended up doing a tour that kind of went along with it called 'Off-fest'. It was Slipknot headlining for the most part, and then Linkin Park, Papa Roach, Spineshank, Mudvayne and Hatebreed. I was actually at the first Ozzfest and we were trying to get on Ozzfest 1999, which would have been in support of *Strictly Diesel*. We didn't get on it, and I guess we aspired to be on it, but I don't want to say it was a dream of mine. In 2000, we were supposed to do the Tattoo The Earth tour and I still don't know what really happened. Our booking agent told us we were on the tour, but we weren't. We ended up following it for four or five shows and played only one of them, and then the year after that, we did Ozzfest, and it did a lot for our career. It opened up so many opportunities for us and it solidified us as a different type of act, and that pretty much happened with every band on that tour. You would play a show and on the next week's Soundscan, you would see your stats go up. Later on, when we played all the towns that we did with Ozzfest, people were saying, 'The first time I heard of you guys was on Ozzfest. I saw you and you were amazing. I became a fan and I went and bought the record' so the tour in itself did wonders for every band that was on it, and for the entire scene. We have Sharon and Ozzy to thank for all of that.

I have so many memories that I could just sit for days and talk about. There are definitely things I don't remember, but that comes with the territory. I think the best thing that happened was the friendships I made. Me and 'Meegs' still hang out, me and B.C. from Hed PE still hang out. You get a group of people that for one reason or another kind of grow up together and even though we were all in our different camps and doing different things, we would all cross paths every now and then. To me, that is probably the most valuable thing to happen out of it all. Even me and Tommy and Rob, we're still close friends, and it's all that matters. We did some cool shit, made some cool music, played some cool shows, but all that is over now. There are still the friendships and the fact you can count on each other for other things.

All the bands that came out back then were very lucky to experience the music business the way it was – the way it was meant to be. We experienced the real music business when bands were selling records and people were buying records. There were budgets and you could actually think of things creatively and bring ideas to fruition. We had a lot of fun and all the rock and roll clichés were true.

Staind

Years Active: 1995-2012, 2019-
Location: Springfield, Massachusetts, USA
Main era line-up: Aaron Lewis (vocals, rhythm guitar), Mike Mushok (lead guitar), Johnny April (bass), Jon Wysocki (drums)
Albums: Tormented (1996), Dysfunction (1999), Break the Cycle (2001), 14 Shades of Grey (2003), Chapter V (2005), The Illusion of Progress (2008), Staind (2011)

Staind was another band who could never have foreseen the storm they would create in the future, upon their emergence out of Massachusetts in 1996. A self-released debut album (*Tormented)* was limited to 4,000 copies and distributed locally, where the raw alternative metal on show resonated with the younger generation, and after playing a successful show with Limp Bizkit, in which Fred Durst initially tried to get Staind taken off the bill because of their 'satanic' looking album cover for *Tormented,* Staind won Durst over with their live performance and he helped sign them to Jordan Schur's Flip Records.

Releasing their major label debut in 1999, *Dysfunction* was produced by the in-demand Terry Date, and after a slow start, the second single released to promote the album found 'Mudshovel' send Staind to the next level. Still their most popular song, the accessible alternative metal on show and its relatable lyrical content drove people to check what else Staind had to offer, and six months after its original release *Dysfunction* went to number 1 on *Billboard*'s Heatseeker. Becoming known for the dark and moody themes penned by Aaron Lewis, Staind explored depression, relationships, substance abuse and death on a record which drew in new fans and set the four-piece up for their next big release.

Staind's quest for superstardom ultimately circulated around their third album, *Break the Cycle,* which dropped in 2001 and featured the same tried and tested formula as on their previous release, but more commonly, the band made a calculated move into post-grunge territory. Thanks in part to the massive singles 'It's Been Awhile' and 'Outside', *Break the Cycle* surged to number 1 on the *Billboard* 200 by selling a massive 716,000 copies in its very first week. With American success being less of a surprise due to nu metal's relentless momentum, it was more of a shock that the UK also grasped what Staind was doing (and saying), as *Break the Cycle* went straight to number 1 on the national album chart. By the end of 2001, the album had sold over four million copies worldwide, as later singles 'Fade', 'For You', and the absorbing 'Epiphany' continued to propel the band and their album to even greater heights.

In 2003, *14 Shades of Grey* debuted at number one in America and although it would later go platinum, the album was unable to reach the success of its predecessor due to illegal downloading. Less heavy and featuring a more melodic edge, the singles 'Price to Play' and 'So Far Away' were still strong tracks to add to Staind's back catalogue, while further fan favourites such as 'Yesterday' and 'Fill Me Up' also deserve a special mention. In 2005, *Chapter V* followed Staind's previous two albums in debuting at number 1 in the US, with 'Right Here' and 'Falling' getting heavy rotation over the airwaves. Another platinum-certified record, Staind would then go out on tour with P.O.D., Taproot and Flyleaf, before embarking on a solo European tour and, later, a debut trek to Australia. At the end of 2006, the band put out a 'best of' compilation before returning with a brand-new album in 2008, titled *The Illusion of Progress*.

Big tours with Nickelback and Creed took place in front of thousands of fans, and during the recording process of Staind's 2011 self-titled effort, Jon Wysocki announced his departure from the band due to issues occurring in the studio. Heavier, darker and raw, *Staind* included bruising numbers such as 'Not Again', 'Eyes Wide Open' and 'Now', which were put out as singles, while hip-hop superstar Snoop Dogg guested on the excellently tongue-in-cheek album track, 'Wannabe'. By this time, Lewis had been doing some solo work on a country rock project and Staind would announce a hiatus in 2012. Lewis released his debut full-length, *The Road*, later in the year and since then, he has remained active in the country music scene. A few reunion shows have occurred over the years, and Staind's latest return was announced in 2020, with tour dates due to take place later in 2021, along with the release of a new live album.

One of the most successful nu metal bands of the whole movement, Staind obliterated mainstream charts with emotive and moody metal, which was loved by millions, and 'It's Been Awhile' and 'Outside' especially, continue to promote the original movement's finest moments.

Killer Cuts – 'Mudshovel', 'It's Been Awhile'

Jon Wysocki speaks:

> Staind started out as a cover band, but we were able to throw in original songs here and there, to the point where when we played live, people started asking for more original stuff because they had developed a liking for it. We started playing shows in the Boston and Rhode Island areas, and we were playing all original songs. We have always been lucky as far as having a good fan base who would follow us around, so at that time, we were swapping shows with Godsmack,

who were from Boston. If they sold a place out, we would open for them, and in places where we were a little more popular, Godsmack would open for us. After that came the show where we opened for Limp Bizkit and Fred Durst came out and saw us play. He tried to have us removed from the bill because he hated the cover art for our first album, *Tormented*. I think he thought we were more like a satanic black metal band or whatever, so I can understand how he felt. I didn't really care for the *Tormented* artwork either, but Mike (Mushok) got into one of his twisted little moments and came up with that cover and I was like, 'Dude, are you alright man, do you need some therapy or something?'

Fred came out to watch us that night and he was probably ready to kill us at that point, but he listened to us and he liked us. He asked if we had anything new and that night, we ended up on his bus, playing him some new songs – and he loved them. He took us right under his wing and maybe a month later, we were in LA doing our first demo at Sound City Studios. Signing to Flip Records was the beginning of everything.

The label actually wanted to buy and release *Tormented,* but we never wanted to do that. I think we wanted to separate that from what was to come because that was just the beginning for us. It was very raw, which is good in a lot of ways, but it wasn't as mature. If you listen to 'Mudshovel' on there and then the version on *Dysfunction*, you'll hear how much that song progressed. *Tormented* was only sold locally and it was also made available on our website at the time when bands were only just starting to use the internet to promote themselves.

With *Dysfunction*, I thought we were doing something a little different melodically because Deftones and Limp Bizkit was doing the rap metal thing, Korn was out, and we were right in the nestle of those guys. It was pretty amazing to work with Terry Date who is a brand name producer, and a guy who just knew how to produce and also engineer properly. We pretty much lived in the studio all day long and other than that, we would just go back to our condo and drink beer. I think we had one or two days off a week, but we didn't really want any days off. We were there to work and to create the best product we could or that we knew how to do. We had that fire. It was a pretty spiritual type of thing when you're in the moment and you're really trying to focus and create the best part that you can because you have to remember, it's going to be on tape forever, so you want to be at your best.

Management picked 'Just Go' to be the lead single and we made a cool video for it, but I think as far as the band goes, we were all shooting for 'Mudshovel' to be released first. They were like, 'We'll get there, but let's see what kind of momentum 'Just Go' gets for us', and it really didn't do much. Then we released 'Mudshovel' and that really took off for us on some level. I hear all the time from hardcore fans that *Dysfunction* was so rocking and heavy and raw, and it was. That was how it was produced, and it was how we wanted it to be. I thought we had a shot at making it big and the songs we were writing were heavy. We had 'Home', which is a more melodic rock ballad, but we thought we had all the parts. It was just hard to believe it was going to be as big as it was.

Some of us kept our jobs even when we were doing pretty good on the bar scene. We were still making decent money because we were able to call our own shots and we were selling out every place (sometimes there were lines all the way around the building), so we knew we wanted to make a career out of being in a band from the beginning. I think it took Johnny (April) the longest to adapt because he would say they could pull the rug out from underneath us at any time, but it all seemed pretty legit to the rest of us. When you sign a record contract, it doesn't mean you can just lay back and do whatever. You have to work harder and I knew the work ethic of everyone in the band was great because we all had the same vision.

We didn't have the option of working with Terry Date on *Break the Cycle*. Josh Abraham was brought in through management, and when we got together, everything fitted. Terry was the one who created a lot of the sound on *Dysfunction* and gave us that signature dark sound. He was more of an engineer type and he would let us do our own thing, but obviously, he would have his input as well; whereas Josh was a little more hands-on from the bass tracks to guitar tracks, to layering and vocal melodies, and so on.

When we started work on *Break the Cycle*, it wasn't a conscious effort to change our sound. Aaron and I played in a band before Staind with two other guys and we had done 'It's Been Awhile' and 'Outside', but when Aaron performed 'Outside' with Fred on the Family Values tour, that kind of carried us through our off time from *Dysfunction* and into *Break the Cycle*. When our producer heard those two songs, he said we had to track them, so we did, but we had no idea they were going to be as big as they were. I don't think you ever know it's going to be big, but they took us from one level to a greater level, and *Break the Cycle* was the big one for Staind. We were actually fighting ourselves on the charts because 'Outside' was being drilled to death the whole time of us being off and then we re-tracked it and put it out, and then 'It's Been Awhile' came along and they were fighting each other to number 1. If we could hit the rewind button, we probably should have thrown a different song between those, but 'It's Been Awhile' and 'Outside' were what really brought it home for us.

The day the first week sales for *Break the Cycle* were announced, I remember Aaron and I were on a golf course and our manager called us. He had already talked to Mike and Johnny, and he said,' Are you guys sitting down right now?' I was like, 'No, we're playing golf, what's up?' He said maybe we should sit down and then he said, 'You guys just sold 716,000 units in one week'. By the halfway point of the second week, *Break the Cycle* had already gone platinum and it was crazy times. We enjoyed hearing those numbers, but at the same time, we were working, so it was business as usual for us. It was an awesome feeling to have a platinum record, but we were so involved with what we were doing that we had to keep the ball rolling. It was definitely a little bit of a life changer, though. We were pretty serious, and we really adored our fans, so we just wanted to try and always do our best for them. A lot of people would ask us if it was how we really were and it was true – we weren't trying to do something just to do it. You could take certain bands who would do something just because it was popular at the time, but that wasn't us and we always busted our butts to do the best we could.

Our success, like a lot of other bands at the time, showed nu metal's mainstream appeal. When the grunge era happened, Nirvana, Soundgarden, Pearl Jam and Alice in Chains all came out and took over, and then nu metal hit with Korn, Limp Bizkit, us, Linkin Park; and our genre lasted longer than I ever expected, to be honest. After that came Puddle of Mudd, Saliva, Seether and Shinedown, but we kind of hung in there for a good amount of time with no complaints.

When grunge came out I was still into Skid Row and some other bands, and I wasn't ready for something new, but when I opened my mind to it, there was some good stuff. Alice in Chains and Soundgarden blew me away, and I am sure there were plenty of people who weren't ready to hear the nu metal scene. Some jumped on board and some didn't, but everyone is entitled to like what they want to like. There was a lot of crossovers in nu metal, too, so you would get some rap, you would get some metal, and you would also get some melody, but I don't think people really knew what to make of it. It was the era that we came up in and we were just trying to be us. If you listen to *Tormented*, we were metal, but we kind of developed into Staind once we got a producer and we started writing more. We are all super grateful for being able to come up in that time and play with some great bands. We were very lucky to be in the situation that we were under the same management as Korn, Limp Bizkit, Godsmack, and so on. They had some clout, so they got us on some really good tours.

It took us a while to write *14 Shades of Grey,* but we got it done, and people wanted to hear another 'It's Been Awhile'. We did 'So Far Away' to cater for that vibe, but that album is super deep if you really listen to how it is musically structured. We put a lot of time into that album and I don't know why that one sticks out to me, but it's probably my favourite album that we made. Maybe it is because I know all the fighting and the blood, sweat and tears that went into it.

In the beginning, we really suffered from illegal downloading. *14 Shades of Grey* had just come out and we were ready to go on this big world tour and we had all this great stage stuff ready, and then we had to downsize. The downloading thing certainly had an effect on every band and anyone in the music business, really, because no one was buying CDs and all the record stores were shutting down. It was tough and it jammed us up for a minute, so it really did have an effect on a lot of things. To me, it always felt like the music business got harder. In order to stay on top, you had to work harder, but I don't think any of us had that problem. However, the music downloading thing was pushing against us and then there was another group of bands coming up with Slipknot at the forefront, followed by all these metalcore bands such as Lamb of God and Killswitch Engage. Things were constantly changing, and the nu metal movement as a whole seemed to be dying out.

For *Chapter V* we worked with David Bottrill and he was a great guy. He definitely deserves to be up there a bit higher as far as a name people know and from the records he has done. David knows his way around a studio and he came in with a sound engineer who set up the microphones and the placements of them, and so on, while David stuck more to thinking about the parts. 'This works with this, let's try this; instead of going here with it, let's go here', and he was awesome to work with. We had our own way of writing songs together as a band – just the four of us and our sound guy, who was involved with everything. We would all be in a room and work the parts out. I think we all understood what we had at the time, and we were all one-fourth of the band and it is like your baby, but when it came to the last record, it wasn't like that at all.

We ended up working with Johnny K, who also did *The Illusion of Progress*, and I never got along with him. He is an excellent engineer, and he has a great ear for sound, but he's a terrible producer. Nick Raskulinecz had just come off of Green Day's *American Idiot* and he came up and pulled each one of us aside to see what we were looking to do for the self-titled record. He was really cool and I couldn't wait to work with him, and then out of the blue, Johnny K was producing the record and I was like, 'Man, all I do is fight with that guy all day'. I think also, we all had our own things going on. I had just had a child with my wife at the time, Mike had his twins, Aaron had his solo career going and Johnny was just Johnny; so, I think there were a lot of distractions on that last album and there were a lot of cameras in our faces. It just wasn't really our way of doing things and I was very frustrated with it all, so I said to the guys, 'I can't deal with this anymore. As much as I love this band and I love you guys, I gotta go. This is not the Staind we started out being.' It was sad and unfortunate, but I couldn't personally do it anymore. I didn't want to leave, but I didn't like the direction it was going. That last album also felt very rushed because we waited until the last minute to record everything and we had to have it turned in by a certain time. The label gives you a time limit to turn a record in else you're in breach of contract, and we had never had a problem with that before because we were always way ahead of the curve, but with *Staind* it was a rush job. I think some songs came out pretty good, but there's other stuff I listen to now that I know we would have done certain parts differently. To me, it didn't seem as well rounded as all the others. After I left Staind, I joined Soil when Ryan McCombs was coming back after fronting Drowning Pool. They were heading over to Europe and they asked me to do it and I did it, and I ended up staying with them for a little over a year. After that, I moved to LA real quick, and then I moved to Nashville and I've been here ever since.

With Staind, we drew off all our influences and tried to make the best music we could whilst doing it the way we wanted to do it. Most of the albums were based on life experiences and things of that nature, and if any of the songs on any of the records got people through tough times or helped them understand those tough times, that is always one of the biggest compliments a band can ever have.

Static-X

Years Active: 1994-2010, 2018-

Location: Los Angeles, California, USA

Main era line-up: Wayne Static (vocals, rhythm guitar), Koichi Fukuda (lead guitar), Tony Campos (bass), Ken Jay (drums)

Albums: Wisconsin Death Trip (1999), Machine (2001), Shadow Zone (2003), Start a War (2005), Cannibal (2007), Cult of Static (2009), Project: Regeneration Vol. 1 (2020)

After Wayne Static relocated to Los Angeles and met Koichi Fukuda, Tony Campos and Ken Jay, Static-X was formed, and in 1998, they signed with Warner Bros. Records. *Wisconsin Death Trip* followed in 1999 – introducing the world to a punishing onslaught of industrial metal which, to those who knew Static previously, may have raised an eyebrow due to the fact that his previous band, Deep Blue Dream, performed melodic pop rock and also featured future Smashing Pumpkins hero, Billy Corgan, in its line-up.

'Push It', 'I'm With Stupid' and 'Bled for Days' helped to propel the album to platinum status, and a stint on Ozzfest didn't do the quartet any harm either, but with Static feeling pressured to produce a successful follow-up record, he reportedly wrote the whole of the album by himself, which led to some strife within the band that ultimately saw Fukuda leave Static-X. Recording the album as a trio, *Machine* dropped in May 2001 and the sophomore effort reached 11 on the *Billboard* 200. The groovy 'Black and White' became a nu metal gem and 'Cold' was a popular addition that featured on the *Queen of the Damned* movie soundtrack. *Machine* has sold over 500,000 copies in the US and it has often been regarded as Static-X's heaviest album, but the band had never received so much exposure and Wayne himself quickly became a prominent figure in nu metal, and he became renowned for having his hair styled in a vertical position and his beard fashioned into what was named a 'chintail'.

If *Machine* was considered the heaviest Static-X record, then *Shadow Zone* was undoubtedly their most melodic. Tripp Eisen was now a full-time member (replacing Fukuda), Josh Freese stood in as a session drummer due to Jay leaving the band, and coming out in October 2003, *Shadow Zone* debuted at 20 in the US and 'The Only' proved to be the spearhead for the band's catchier side, with an extremely addictive radio chorus and featuring cleaner singing vocals throughout; as did further album highlights 'All in Wait', 'Kill Your Idols', and the stunning rock ballad, 'So'. A rarities and demos collection materialised in 2004 and was titled *Beneath...Between...Beyond,* before the band toured with fellow industrialists Fear Factory ahead of starting work on a fourth studio album. In February 2005, Eisen was fired for reasons better left unsaid in this book, and Fukuda returned to the band before *Start a War* announced itself in June. Heavier and more aggressive than *Shadow Zone*, scream vocals were more prominent and two singles were released in the form of 'I'm the One' and 'Dirthouse'. *Cannibal* (2007) and *Cult of Static* (2009) sustained the band's movement into groove metal territory, but then Static-X would enter a hiatus to allow Wayne to focus on his Pighammer solo project – which didn't sound massively different to his full-time band.

Static-X officially broke up in June 2013 and Wayne sadly passed away on the first day of November in 2014 at the age of 48. In tribute, Fukuda, Campos and Jay revived Static-X to honour Wayne's legacy, taking on the masked vocalist, Xero, who has never been officially unveiled (we all know who it is, though, don't we?). Touring the world with a visually spectacular stage show dedicated to their former singer, Static-X then put together *Project Regeneration, Vol 1* in 2020, which featured some of Wayne's final recordings. A triumphant release that confirms Wayne Static as one of nu metal's greatest frontmen, his distinctive vocal style and even more distinctive appearance made him loved and admired by all who knew him.

Killer Cuts – 'Push It', 'Black and White'

Stereomud

Years Active: 1999-2003
Location: New York City, New York, Atlanta, Georgia, USA
Main era line-up: Erik Rogers (vocals), Joey Zampella (guitar), John Fattoruso (guitar), Corey Lowery (bass), Dan Richardson (drums)
Albums: Perfect Self (2001), Every Given Moment (2003)

Forming from the ashes of Life of Agony, Joey Zampella and Dan Richardson started Stereomud and the quintet released their debut album, *Perfect Self,* through Loud/Columbia Records. Going straight to number one on *Billboard*'s Heatseekers Chart, thanks in part to *MTV* strongly rotating the lead single, 'Pain', which reached a highly respectable eight on the Mainstream Rock Chart, and second single, 'Steppin Away' – a largely hard rock sounding record was well-received by fans and critics alike. Emphasising Erik Rogers' hugely impressive vocal range, *Every Given Moment* packed more marauding anthems in 2003 when the likes of 'Breathing', 'My Addiction' and 'Control Freak' showcased a slightly more active rock sound. Again, the album hit the top spot of the Heatseekers Chart and then Stereomud joined Hed PE, Saliva, Systematic and Breaking Benjamin on the Jägermeister Music Tour. After Loud Records dissolved, Stereomud was dropped by Columbia just three months after the release of *Every Given Moment*, leading to the band calling it a day after a brief but fairly successful career.

Killer Cuts – 'Pain', 'Control Freak'

SugarComa

Years Active: 1999-2004, 2013
Location: Romford, London, England
Main era line-up: Jessica Mayers (vocals), Claire Simson (guitar), Heidi Fisk (bass),

James Cuthbert (drums)
Albums: Never Born (2001), Becoming Something Else (2002)

Possibly the closest thing you could get to a British (or any) version of Kittie, SugarComa was a quartet where three out of the four members were females. Best known for their cover of Britney Spears' '(You Drive Me) Crazy', which featured on their 2001 album, *Becoming Something Else*, the band played groovy metal with delicious pop melodies. 'Zero Star' and 'What Goes Around' had catchy choruses which brought some minor success, while the deep growls of Jessica Mayers drew the Kittie comparisons by many. Earning tour slots with Machine Head and Fear Factory, SugarComa earned a small buzz around them in the UK, and then they repackaged and uploaded their debut album, *Never Born,* to iTunes under the title of *Life Before Colin.* Not long after, SugarComa parted ways. However, a few reunion shows took place some years later as an anniversary celebration.

Killer Cuts – 'Zero Star', '(You Drive Me) Crazy'

Sunk Loto

Years Active: 1997-2007
Location: Gold Coast, Queensland, Australia
Main era line-up: Jason Brown (vocals), Luke McDonald (guitar), Sean Van Gennip (bass), Dane Brown (drums)
Albums: Big Picture Lies (2000), Between Birth and Death (2003)

Sunk Loto was a popular band in the few years they were around, after coming up in 1997 under their original name of Messiah. The Australian quartet signed to Sony Music in 1999 when the band's drummer, Dane Brown, was only thirteen years old, and bassist, Sean Van Gennip, was the oldest member at seventeen. However, the quartet effortlessly fused rap metal with alternative and hard rock like seasoned professionals. After releasing a successful EP which was titled *Society Anxiety* and featured the excellent track 'Lift', the band's debut album, *Big Picture Lies,* landed in 2000 and included 'Make You Feel' and 'Sunken Eyes' – both of which received plenty of airplay in Australia.

It was Sunk Loto's sophomore album that really broke them into the public eye, though, when *Between Birth and Death* was released in 2003. Showing every intention of trying to expose themselves to a much wider audience, the band chose the explosive 'Everything, Everyway' and the moody 'Starved' to show what they were truly capable of, and national chart success unsurprisingly followed. A heavier and more complex record, *Between Birth and Death,* would later be called one of the most influential Australian heavy metal releases, and it was hard to disagree with such a statement as Sunk Loto finally started to reap the rewards of their hard work.

Unfortunately, the band announced their split in December 2007 and although new projects were worked on by various members, the four-piece proved in their short career as Sunk Loto just how much star quality the band had – with musical talent way beyond their very young years.

Killer Cuts – 'Sunken Eyes', 'Everything, Everyway'

Superheist

Years Active: 1993-2004, 2016-
Location: Melbourne, Victoria, Australia
Main era line-up: Rod McLeod/Joey Biro (vocals), DW Norton (guitar), Drew Dedman (bass), Sean Pentecost (drums), Fetah Sabawi (keyboards)
Albums: The Prize Recruit (2001), Identical Remote Controlled Reactions (2002), Ghosts of the Social Dead (2016), Sidewinder (2019), MMXX (2021)

Possibly the most popular Aussie nu metal band, Superheist originally started out as a grindcore act in the early 1990s and earned quite a name for themselves in the Melbourne area. As the new millennium approached, DW Norton decided the band should head in the nu metal direction, and Superheist reinvented themselves with rap vocals and a punishing display of heavy rock. An EP titled *8 Miles High* was released in 1998 before the band would earn support slots alongside Fear Factory and Sepultura when the American heavyweights ventured onto Australian soil.

Independent label Shock Records would then take the band under their wing, releasing the debut album, *The Prize Recruit,* in 2001. Two strong singles bothered the Aussie charts ('Crank the System' and 'Bullet') before Superheist's notoriety was boosted through two live show support slots for hip-hop sensation Eminem, in the cities of Sydney and Melbourne. Enlisting Joey Biro as their new vocalist for their second album, *Identical Remote Controlled Reactions,* Superheist went next level upon the release at the end of 2002. '7 Years' was a good choice of lead single, and it was followed by the ballad-of-sorts, 'A Dignified Rage', which encapsulated much of what the nu metal movement was coming out with at the time. As popular as they were in their homeland, Superheist was looking to broaden their horizons and they were close to securing a record deal in the US before the 9/11 terrorist attacks occurred. Trying again in 2003, this time there were no takers, and so Superheist decided to call it quits at the beginning of 2004. As a goodbye to their fans, they released the two-disc compilation, *New, Rare, Live* later in the same year, and although there were various attempts at reformations, it wasn't until 2016 when Superheist officially announced their return – this time led by the vocalist Ezekiel Ox.

A new album full of fiery rap-tinged metal was unleashed in the form of *Ghosts of the Social Dead* and it was spearheaded by the singles, 'Hands Up High' and 'Fearing Nothing', before the impressive 'Raise Hell' was released in 2017. Backed up by the impressive B-sides of 'Got the Bounce' and 'Fully

Loaded', it could be argued that the new version of Superheist was on the form of their lives; and backing up that statement with the explosive long player, *Sidewinder* in 2019, Superheist was the pride of Australia once again. Sadly, Ox quit the band in 2020 out of nowhere, but Superheist are pressing on with Norton stepping up to the vocal plate, and a new album is due to drop in 2021.

Killer Cuts – 'Bullet', 'A Dignified Rage'

Switched

Years Active: 1999-2010
Location: Cleveland, Ohio, USA
Main era line-up: Ben Schigel (vocals), B.C. Kochmit (lead guitar), Joe Schigel (rhythm guitar), Shawn May (bass), Chad Szeliga (drums)
Albums: Subject to Change (2002), Ghosts in the Machine (2006)

Sometimes stylised as 'Sw1tched', this underrated but popular band soon signed to Immortal/Virgin Records and released their debut album in the first quarter of 2002. Titled *Subject to Change,* the main single to promote the album was the roof-raising 'Inside', while 'Walk Away' and '10 Dead Fingers' also became fan favourites. A stint on Ozzfest in the same year was important in getting the band's name out further, and *Subject to Change* went on to sell over 100,000 copies worldwide. In mid-2003, the band would leave Immortal and also part ways with their management team, and after Stereomud called it a day, Corey Lowery joined Switched just in time for a planned reincarnation under the new name, Sky Fall Down; but instead, the band would enter a hiatus which would last for over two years.

Reforming with the Schigel brothers, Kochmit, Lowery and Szeliga, Switched released a second album titled *Ghosts in the Machine* in 2006, with one disc containing eleven new songs at their demo phase and a second disc of tracks from the band's first album, plus the B-side, 'She Blinded Me with Science'. Proving to be Switched's last release, it was a decent way to bow out but *Subject to Change* perfectly showed what the band had to offer, even though they perhaps didn't reach the heights their music deserved.

Killer Cuts – 'Inside', 'Walk Away'

System of a Down

Years Active: 1994-2006, 2010-
Location: Glendale, California, USA
Main era line-up: Serj Tankian (vocals, rhythm guitar), Daron Malakian (lead guitar), Shavo Odadjian (bass), John Dolmayan (drums)
Albums: System of a Down (1998), Toxicity (2001), Steal This Album! (2002), Mezmerize (2005), Hypnotize (2005)

Armenian/American nutters System of a Down caused a huge stir in the LA area in their early days, so much so that Rick Rubin headhunted the band and signed them to his American/Columbia Records label in 1997. Releasing their self-titled debut in June 1998 and introducing the world to one of the most original bands in all of heavy metal, the singles 'Sugar' and 'Spiders' showed different sides to this chaotic and almost schizophrenic quartet. 'Sugar' was rough and ragged and featured frequent changes in pace, while the crazy vocals of Serj Tankian and backing vocalist/guitarist Daron Malakian, literally left people stunned. Shavo Odadjian (bass) and John Dolmayan (drums) completed System's line-up, and together they made 'Spiders' sound eerie and almost progressive, which was slower in pace and at times saw Tankian's vocals verge on hypnotic. At the time, *System of a Down* only gained moderate success, but the singles were radio favourites and *MTV* played the hell out of their accompanying promo videos, ultimately leading to the record reaching gold certification around two years after its original release. Opening for the likes of Slayer and Metallica led to a slot on the second stage of Ozzfest in 2000, before 2001 came round and *Toxicity* propelled System of a Down to megastardom.

Released on 4 September, the album went straight to number 1 on the *Billboard* 200 courtesy of the fan-favourite lead single, 'Chop Suey!'. Another radical slab of melody-tinged metal mayhem, the song featured an irresistible singalong chorus, and it remains a hotly played song on Radio and TV today. *Toxicity* would go on to be certified triple platinum, and the record has sold well over twelve million copies worldwide. Featuring elements of thrash metal, hard rock, progressive metal and Middle Eastern music, *Toxicity* simply threw out the heavy metal rulebook upon its release. Lyrical themes focused on drug addiction, the overpopulation of prisons, group sex, Charles Manson's beliefs on the environment (yep, you read it right), and the protests surrounding the 2000 Democratic National Convention; all of which further proved that System of a Down was a truly original commodity with incredible vision and artistry.

Looking for more success, System's third album was released in November 2002 and reached 15 in America. Originally, medium quality mp3's had been leaked online under the name *Toxicity II*, and the band expressed their disappointment that fans were able to hear unfinished material. Producing better quality versions and repackaging the album, the band ironically titled it *Steal This Album!*, with the front cover designed like that of a bootleg CD. With text styled as if written in black marker pen, in a response to those who had previously leaked the tracks, *Steal This Album!* would go platinum in the US and spawned the popular single 'Innervision', as well as other favourites such as 'Mr. Jack' and 'I-E-A-I-A-I-O'.

Underlining their lack of desire in following formulas and sticking to the norm, System embarked on a project in 2005 that saw them release two albums within the space of six months. *Mezmerize* arrived in May and was led by the crushing single, 'B.Y.O.B.' (Bring Your Own Bombs), and it was followed by *Hypnotize* in November which included the strangely normal rock number of 'Lonely Day' – where Malakian took on lead vocal duty. Both albums reached number one on the *Billboard* 200 – helping System join an elite group of artists to have released two number one selling records in the same year.

After many years of inactivity save for a few live shows here and there, System of a Down announced in 2016 that they were working on new music and a brand-new record was due sometime in the future. A headline slot at the UK's Download Festival also went down a treat, and while no new album has ever surfaced, System of a Down released their first new material in almost fifteen years at the back end of 2020 with two new songs, 'Protect the Land' and 'Genocidal Humanoidz'. Just as bonkers as ever but still with an important message to distribute to the masses, System remain one of the most intriguingly original bands in modern metal history.

Killer Cuts – 'Sugar', 'Chop Suey!'

Taproot

Years Active: 1997-
Location: Ann Arbor, Michigan, USA
Main era line-up: Stephen Richards (vocals, rhythm guitar), Mike DeWolf (lead guitar), Phil Lipscomb (bass), Jarrod Montague (drums)
Albums: Gift (2000), Welcome (2002), Blue-Sky Research (2005), Our Long Road Home (2008), Plead the Fifth (2010), The Episodes (2012)

In 1997, Taproot sent a demo to Limp Bizkit's Fred Durst in order to try to gain a foot up in the scene. Shortly afterwards, Durst offered the band a recording contract through his Flip imprint of Interscope Records. However, Taproot turned the offer down and instead landed a lucrative deal with Atlantic Records. Leading to the rather infamous voicemail message left by Durst on the phone of lead singer Stephen Richards, Taproot became known for giving Durst the proverbial middle finger, which, if anything, earned the quartet more respect by peers and music fans alike despite Limp's flourishing success.

The band's debut single, 'Again & Again', gained heavy exposure on *MTV2*, before the accompanying album, *Gift,* was released in June 2000. A solid rap metal record in which Richards showed great diversity of singing, rapping, screaming and deep growling, *Gift* underlined that Taproot were the new kids on the block whose guitar sound was so abrasive, that no one else sounded quite like they did. Selling over 250,000 copies, the record helped Taproot land a spot on the Ozzfest tours of both 2000 and 2001, and after a full-on touring schedule was completed, the quartet returned to the studio.

Backing up their early promise, *Welcome* followed and became Taproot's most successful album to date – debuting at 17 on the *Billboard* 200 in October 2002. Lead single, 'Poem', went straight to number 5 on the Mainstream Rock chart, while the rest of the tracklisting showed a more melodic progression as well as containing less emphasis on rap vocals. 'Mine' was chosen as the album's second single; however, the general feel amongst Taproot's dedicated fan base was that

Welcome failed to reach the heights of the band's impressive and refreshing debut album. Narrowly missing out on a gold record, *Welcome* sold close to 475,000 copies in America altogether.

A third album titled *Blue-Sky Research* dropped in August 2005 and it saw Taproot moving further into hard rock territory. Still featuring some pummeling alternative metal on occasion ('I Will Not Fall for You' and 'Facepeeler'), tracks such as the lead single, 'Calling', showed cleaner vocals and stronger melodic hooks. Smashing Pumpkins hero Billy Corgan, co-wrote three tracks on the album, and with Atlantic hoping *Blue-Sky Research* would be the one to finally see Taproot hit gold (at least), it only peaked at 33 on the *Billboard* 200 with sales of around 140,000.

After Taproot hit the road with the Staind and P.O.D., the band left Atlantic Records due to failing to live up to the label's expectations, and so they chose to remain an independent artist. In September 2008, *Our Long Road Home* was released and contained the stirring singles of 'Wherever I Stand' and 'Path Less Taken', indicating a return to a heavier alternative metal sound. It would be the last record to feature original drummer Jarrod Montague, with Nick Fredell taking over in time for Taproot's next album, *Plead the Fifth,* in 2010. By now, the band was signed to Victory Records and their debut release on the label went back to Taproot's nu metal origins. 'Fractured (Everything I Said was True)' and the emphatic closer of 'Stares' sounded like classic Taproot, and although *Plead the Fifth* only peaked at 107 on the *Billboard* 200, hardcore fans of the band were undoubtedly pleased with the direction of the record. In April 2012, *The Episodes* featured the brilliant single, 'Never Surrender', before Mike DeWolf decided to down guitar and quit under somewhat of a dark cloud.

Montague has since played a handful of reunion shows with the band- including an anniversary gig in May 2017 to mark fifteen years since *Welcome* was released, and in 2018, Taproot released the treasure-chest boxset, *Besides,* which contained eight discs of unreleased material from across the band's whole career.

Killer Cuts – 'Again & Again', 'Poem'

Jarrod Montague speaks:

> Taproot came together after Steve (as I call him) and Mike had grown up together, and then I met them when I was at the University of Michigan in my freshman year when I lived with Steve's cousin. Steve was always the drummer in various bands he had been in and Mike was usually the guitar player, so Mike would bring me tapes over of their bands. He was into fast metal and was influenced by bands like Pantera, and I remember we were all listening to the first Korn album and it was crazy because it felt like a new twist on metal with the dark chords and down-tuning.
>
> Steve and Mike used to be in a band called Skumbag, and they really sounded

like Korn. They wrote maybe four or five songs and then they decided they wanted to move in a different direction with some more melody added to it, so they asked my then-roommate, Phil, who was a bass player, to join the band in about 1995. In our sophomore year, we lived in this house with nine guys in seven bedrooms, and Phil was one of my roommates. We turned our dining room into a jam room and I had my drums in there. People would come in and out and just jam and Steve and Mike came over a couple of times because of the connection with his cousin Mark who lived with us. Fast forward to 1997 and Steve and Mike had formed the first incarnation of Taproot, but they decided they didn't want a drummer. They wanted to be way out leftfield, only using drum machines. Their first show was in Jackson, Michigan, and me and a group of friends went to it and the show was a complete disaster. The drum machine was pushing too much bass and it shorted the power from the bass drum and blew up all the amps, so Steve and Mike came over to the house a couple of days later and asked me if I would play drums in the band.

We would get together and jam and we would listen to whatever had just come out. We had heard that Limp Bizkit was coming out although they hadn't put out their record yet, and we were listening to the first Hed PE record, Far, Incubus's *S.C.I.E.N.C.E.* record. Steve and Mike were always the primary songwriters so our sound stemmed from trying to put our own unique stamp on the general sound that was developing at the time, and then when Steve found a promo copy of *Three Dollar Bill, Y'all* at a used CD store, in the CD it said 'Send me your demos...' and Fred Durst had an address in there. At that point we already had a handful of songs we had recorded in this studio close to Detroit. We were going in there for eight hours and recording six songs the best we could, just to knock them out, so the songs sounded really raw. We sent a demo to Fred and within a couple of weeks, he called back and said he really liked what we were doing, and that he was playing near us in Pontiac, as Limp Bizkit was touring with Sevendust. Fred had such an aggressive scream and combine that with the rapping – it was a really cool sound. It seemed like that was what was coming next, and we didn't make a conscious effort to sound like Limp Bizkit, but the sound was what we were really feeling at the time. Around 1997, 1998, 1999, Limp Bizkit was coming to town and we were going to hang out with them, and then they did some guerrilla shows around the country; they had just come from Boston (I think) and they were going to do one near Detroit, at Royal Oak. The guys came to our house where we jammed at the day before they were going to do the show at Royal Oak, and Fred was telling us how he had just been on *The Howard Stern Show* and he had hooked up with Carmen Electra, and we thought this was fucking crazy. He invited us down to the guerrilla show and we went on their bus and heard the entire *Significant Other* record which was about to be released. They were super cool and it really felt like we were on to something really big, especially having their support behind us.

Fred had this label called Flip and after he came and hung out at our house, within a month or so we got sent this really long contract. It was a production deal and basically what it said was 'You will record three songs for Flip/Interscope and if we like them, then there is a chance we will sign you to a deal, but if we don't like them, then we get to keep the rights to those songs and you can't use them…' and that just seemed really fishy to us. At the same time, we were pretty active online. There were all these message boards, we had an Angelfire.com website, and it seemed like us and the band Juice, who later became Adema, were the only bands that were really out there doing a good job of promoting themselves online.

Mike Jakubiak was part of this streetwise street teaming company based in Los Angeles, and those guys asked Mike if there were any cool bands in Michigan. He got them to check out Taproot and they hooked us up with a show opening for System of a Down in Grand Rapids, Michigan, which was about two hours from our home base. Mark Wakefield, who became our manager, was the old singer for Linkin Park when they were called Xero, and he ended up leaving to form this management company called Velvet Hammer, with David Benveniste (known as 'Beno'). Mark came to the show where we opened for System and it was an awesome crowd, and before we knew it, we were on the phone to Mark and 'Beno' when they got back to LA. They said they were really interested in us and they arranged for us to fly to LA to meet Rick Rubin. We played three or four songs for Rick and it was super-nervy watching him nodding his head to our songs, and once Fred had heard that we were in LA showcasing for Rick Rubin, that is when he called Steve and left the infamous voicemail message basically saying, 'Fuck you, you guys are done…'. I think Fred got his feelings hurt that we were in LA and didn't hook up with him, and of course, he knew if we had showcased for Rick Rubin, then we had already made some connections on our own. We were flying back and forth between New York and LA, showcasing for all the major record labels like Elektra, DreamWorks and Columbia, but the Atlantic guys seemed like they were going to make us a priority. We were offered a seven-record deal and we thought it was legit, and that was the way we wanted to go.

So, *Gift* came out and we did the first Ozzfest where we ended up meeting Jack and Sharon Osbourne. We hung out with Jack and he promoted us, but it was obvious when we got on Ozzfest and played with these other bands that were in the same boat that we were, I could see why we were all signed. There was Papa Roach, Nonpoint; Kittie had their own thing going on, Pitchshifter was on the first Ozzfest, and what all these bands had in common was melodic hard rock with hip-hop elements.

With *Welcome,* our producer, Toby Wright, had this reputation for taking bands to the next level, and when we decided to work with him, he beat the shit out of us. He told us we couldn't play; he told us to watch each other playing so we could be more in sync because apparently, we weren't in sync. He made us play along to a click to make sure we could be on time if we needed to, and then once you learn how to play to a click, you can start fluctuating if you are going to be ahead of the click for a more aggressive song, or behind the click for more of a laid-back feel.

Welcome was more melodic and 'Poem' did really well, but I think it had enough of the key sound that kept a lot of our fans who came to us because of *Gift* happy; but we also heard a lot too that some people didn't like that album and *Gift* was still their favoured record. We continued into more melody for our third record, *Blue-Sky Research*, but I guess I always kind of wonder the fact that although we saw ourselves continuing to grow, we also saw our audience diminish because they still wanted the *Gift* sound. Maybe it was conscious and maybe it wasn't, but we didn't want to be part of a dying scene and so we felt like we wanted to evolve. Funnily enough, when *Gift* first came out, Rolling Stone magazine actually named us one of the potential heirs to the nu metal crown.

With our third record – here came the pressure. I think we sold almost 475,000 copies of *Welcome,* so we didn't quite make gold, but the label always felt we were one hit away from being a massive band. We always joked that a lot of bands who we started out with on the same level, such as Linkin Park, Disturbed, Alien Ant Farm and Chevelle, we were all on the same playing field at one point, but these bands took off and the label always felt if we had the right record, we would be up there with those guys selling two to four million records.

After *Welcome* we spent a bunch of time at home to recharge our batteries and then we started writing again. We started with a bunch of different producers and then we met with Michael Beinhorn, who famously did Soundgarden's *Superunknown*, and we started working with him, but he wasn't pushing us nowhere as hard as Toby Wright was; so the songs weren't evolving as fast. Our manager and label felt we didn't have the right material for the album that was supposed to push us over a million records, so we felt we were in a rut and banging our heads against the wall. The label suggested possibly writing with other people, but we were against that because we had never done it before. We ended up agreeing to put a shortlist together and Billy Corgan was on that list, so our label made it happen. I think they paid him about $30,000 to write with us for a week, plus his writing credit on the record, so it was a pretty good deal for Billy.

We were only with him for a week, but I'll never forget it, because Billy just oozes music. We met him at a bar in Chicago on the Sunday night before we were going to start writing with him, and he told us he had listened to *Gift* and *Welcome*. We asked him what he thought and he said, 'I think you guys rely too much on dynamics to move your songs along, so you will typically have a soft verse, then go into a heavy chorus, then another soft verse, then a heavy chorus...' He kind of unmasked our formula tore apart the songs, and gave us challenges, and if the songs sucked, he would tell us they sucked. On the Friday we were going to leave, he told us we had inspired him to pick up a guitar and write a song for us. He played the skeleton of 'Lost in the Woods' and it had a rough vocal melody over the top. He said our homework was to take that song back to LA and make it a Taproot song, so Steve changed the lyrics and we made it heavier. It was just awesome spending time and working with Billy Corgan.

We got re-energised when we got back to LA and parted ways with Michael

Beinhorn because we still didn't feel we were getting that progress. We had Toby come back and then he's kicking our asses again, but we felt that was what we needed, and we finally felt like we had the right material. We probably spent almost two years on that record, and then it came out. We didn't think 'Calling' was necessarily going to be the right lead single, but we really liked it, but it just didn't light up the phone lines on the radio like 'Poem' did. Then we did a soft release for 'Birthday', which didn't have a video for it, and it just seemed like the whole thing started stalling out. We sold about 130,000 copies of *Blue-Sky Research*, so I don't really know what happened. I don't know if people thought 'Calling' was too poppy with the 'C-C-C-Calling' thing, or if it just wasn't heavy or fast enough, but that is what happened.

One facet I don't think people talk a lot about is around that same time, I think kids started to have their own computers that could burn CDs quicker. We would be doing signings at record stores and probably half the kids that would come in had a burned CD, and they would ask us to sign it. We were always cordial about it, but we were like, 'What the fuck is this? That shows some balls coming to an artist asking them to sign a CD you burned – that you haven't even bought'. I did the maths and we basically made about $15 an hour. We made enough money to pay the bills, but I was broke at the end of 2005 and I had just got done playing in front of 55,000 people in Syracuse, New York, with Staind, Papa Roach and some other bands. I went to my ATM and I was broke because we spent nearly three years doing *Blue-Sky Research*, and we got our advance for that, which was about $60,000 – but that money has to last you three years. I was renting a house and driving a five or ten-year-old car, I was married, and I was broke, and that is when I started looking elsewhere for work.

By that time, my first kid was on the way and we had parted ways with Atlantic because of disappointing record sales, and I knew being in a band was not going to work to support a family. If people don't think that paying $9.99 for a record is worth it, then it's not worth that anymore. A lot of people like to blame the labels, but it is the people who aren't voting with their dollars for music anymore. They are not putting the monetary value on it that they once did because they would rather listen to their subscription of Spotify or whatever. The revenue isn't there in the music industry anymore and it's not the record label's fault.

When I left Taproot in 2008, right after we had recorded our fourth record, *Our Long Road Home*, it felt like it was all done and nobody cared. I don't know exactly how many copies of that album we sold, but it was probably around 30,000 or 40,000. I know we sold 7,000 in the first week, but *Welcome* sold 51,000. Because we never even had a gold record, I never had a good sense of how well-known the Taproot name was, but now I've been out of that world for a while, most people have at least heard of Taproot and that surprises me, and it tells me there was a lot of downloading and burning going on so the sales did not necessarily reflect the size of the bands back then. People from our label have said if *Gift*, *Welcome*, or any of them had come out five or ten years earlier, we could've been two or three-times platinum, easy.

Dave Grohl (Nirvana, Foo Fighters) gave a great interview where they asked him what it takes to have a successful band, and he said as long as you have great songs and a kickass live show, people are going to hear about you, and I think that is still true. You see little videos go viral all the time, and then I think about Evanescence and how their song, 'Bring Me to Life', started playing at one radio station in Florida when it came out and then it caught on fire. Everyone wanted to hear that song. I really think that even though the revenue might not be there anymore if something comes out and strikes the right chord with enough people, it is still going to spread like wildfire.

We got to do two Ozzfests, in 2000 and 2001. Everyone says it is like a summer camp for hard rock, so just being able to wake up every day and you're parked right next to stage, you're hearing hard rock music start to play, and you crawl out of your bed and go and stand at the side of the stage and watch the likes of Pitchshifter or Soulfly – and you get to know these guys. One of my favourite memories is that sense of community. We were all away from our friends and family, and for us, we just drank a lot and had fun. We didn't know that some of these bands would still have a career today, but back then, we were all just a bunch of kids in our twenties and we had a blast playing music to a bunch of hot, sweaty, sunburned people, every day. Steve used to jump off balconies and jump into pits and from a member's perspective, it was always a blast for me to watch that. I would lose concentration because I was always looking at what was going on in the pit. We watched Black Sabbath, Pantera, Marilyn Manson – all those main stage bands from the side of the stage. Dimebag, Vinnie and Phil were always running around playing pranks, and the only time I've ever cried when a celebrity died was when Dimebag Darrell passed. That was really tough. I remember going to a strip club in Tennessee and we had been on Ozzfest for about a week, and I met Vinnie and told him he was one of my favourite drummers. I told him I was the drummer for Taproot and he said, 'I heard you guys were the best band on the second stage; I'm gonna come and check y'all out' and sure enough, he checked us out. Every time I saw him after that, he would nod and say hi, and that was awesome.

I think us, Incubus, a couple of the Osbournes and a couple of other bands got together and pulled some money together at the first Ozzfest for a guy on the tour. I think he sold merch or something, but we came up with $900 to get him to eat a piece of Ozzy's dog's shit. I have a video of it somewhere and he's chewing it, he has it all stuck in his teeth and he's gagging like crazy, and then he throws up everywhere. That is what being on tour is all about, just doing stupid shit, hanging out and having fun. We stole golf carts and drove them around, jumping them like they did on *Jackass*; people would pass out and we would draw on them with sharpies – it was so much fun. We were all doing the same thing and it was a really great time because we all got to hear our songs on the radio, we all had videos on *MTV*, we all got to sign autographs and we got to play music every night. We all have the same fond memories of that period of time.

Getting to tour with Deftones was a 'Holy shit!' moment because they were a big influence of ours, and after Ozzfest 2000, we went out on the *Back to School* tour with them and Incubus, and then we went over to Europe with them and Linkin Park. We went to nine or ten countries throughout Europe for what was my first time over there. I loved getting to meet people and hear all the different accents. One of the first stops was in Scotland and we were sitting there for a signing at a record store and I could not understand a fucking word these guys were saying. It took me about three or four hours until my ears adjusted and then I started to understand what they were saying.

If I had to choose one album which epitomized nu metal, it has to be the first Korn album. I remember going to see them in 1994 when I was a senior in high school and Jonathan Davis came out with bagpipes and he was wearing a skirt. 'Fieldy' had all the baggy Adidas gear on, as did 'Head' and 'Munky', and David just looked like a model with his bleach blonde hair and no shirt on. It was just one of those moments. If I had heard that album when I was in seventh grade, it probably would have had the same impact as hearing Metallica's *...and Justice for All* or *Smells like Teen Spirit* when Nirvana first released that. It felt like that same moment, as in, 'Wow, this is something new'.

Tool

Years Active: 1990-
Location: Los Angeles, California, USA
Main era line-up: Maynard James Keenan (vocals), Adam Jones (guitar), Justin Chancellor (bass), Danny Carey (drums)
Albums: Undertow (1993), Ænima (1996), Lateralus (2001), 10,000 Days (2006), Fear Inoculum (2019)

Tool has often been described as a love them or hate them kind of band, and very rarely are people in between on how they feel about them. Maybe it is because this quartet has a sound that is complex and ever-evolving, coming across cerebral, visceral and heavy, but also melodic, tender and yet thoroughly abrasive. Either way, Tool are an enigma and simply put – one of the most diverse bands of the last two decades.

After Maynard James Keenan met Adam Jones at the end of the '80s, having moved to LA due to the endless possibilities the city seemed to possess, Jones would be introduced to future drummer Danny Carey, courtesy of Rage Against the Machine's Tom Morello and the trio would form a band which would be completed by Paul D'Amour. From there, Tool soon began to play shows around the Los Angeles area and Keenan especially caught people's attention due to his incredible stage presence. Two years went by before Zoo Entertainment came calling, and a debut EP titled *Opiate* would surface in 1992. The tracks boasted a more straightforward alternative metal sound as opposed to their later progressive/art metal. However, the EP strengthened Tool's foundations. 'Hush' was released as a single and an accompanying promo video for the song gave the band some small exposure, and as their stock rose at an exponential rate, *Opiate* would go on to sell over one million copies in the US.

Tours with Rollins Band and Rage Against the Machine boosted Tool's increasing notoriety before their debut full-length, *Undertow,* put the four-piece firmly on the heavy metal scope. Released in April 1993, the album saw Keenan & Co. venture into progressive metal territory with the standout tracks of 'Sober' and 'Prison Sex'. The latter song included lyrical themes of child abuse and its accompanying music video was refused airtime by *MTV* due to its graphic and obscene content. However, this helped rather than hinder the band and regardless of any controversy, *Undertow* has sold just under three million copies to this very day – quite a result for a debut record. It would also be the final release that featured D'Amour, who would leave the band in 1995 and was replaced on bass guitar by Justin Chancellor.

Tool's sophomore album, *Ænima,* went straight in at two on the *Billboard* 200 upon its release in 1996, in part due to the explosive single, 'Stinkfist'. Later singles 'H.', 'Forty Six & 2' and 'Ænema'- which would go on to win a Grammy for Best Metal Performance in 1998, helped to keep the album selling, and by the end of 2003, the record had reached triple platinum status. Volcano Entertainment then took over the defunct Zoo label and in 2001, they put out Tool's third studio album, *Lateralus*. Rocketing straight to number 1 on the *Billboard* 200, the release added some art rock and math rock structures to the already complex Tool formula, and from the very first listen it was clear that Tool had made the best record of their career. The mesmerising singles 'Schism' (known for its uncommon time structures), 'Parabola', and the incredible title track helped *Lateralus* go double platinum within two years of its release, while the booklet for the album was almost as artistic as the music, where each turn of a page translucently revealed another layer of the human body. Music videos for 'Schism' and 'Parabola' showed Tool's desire to use vivid imagery, and they would win their second Grammy in the Best Metal Performance category in 2002 for 'Schism'.

It would take five long years for the band's next album, and *10,000 Days* finally got its release in May 2006. Following in the footsteps of *Lateralus* by going straight to number 1, first week sales of over 550,000 confirmed Tool's ever-increasing popularity, and even more surprisingly it also crept into the top five in the UK's Album chart. 'Vicarious', 'The Pot' and 'Jambi' were chosen as singles, and Tool would win yet another Grammy – this time for Best Recording Package in 2006.

Various tours and a hiatus later occurred, where Keenan most notably remained busy with his various side projects, which included the art rock band A Perfect Circle and the trippy alt rock Puscifer, and then after years of media talk regarding a possible new Tool album, the band returned in 2019, thirteen years since their previous release, with the epic *Fear Inoculum*. Almost 90 minutes in length and with the average song length approaching the twelve-minute mark, fans could not accuse Tool of coming back half-arsed. The stunning 'Pneuma' and '7empest' highlighted the album's standout moments, as 'Pneuma' especially has shown up in discussions regarding Tool's best-ever songs in the years since its release.

Trailblazing, one of a kind, true artists in every way; Tool has become one of the most fascinating metal bands in history. By listening to any of their studio albums, you will find that the technicality in the musicianship verges on genius. Love them or hate them, Tool are and will always be incredibly popular; just look at the record sales and the Grammy Awards to prove it.

Killer Cuts – 'Stinkfist', 'Schism'

Trust Company

Years Active: 1997-2005, 2007-2011
Location: Prattville, Alabama, USA
Main era line-up: Kevin Palmer (vocals, rhythm guitar), James Fukai (lead guitar), Josh Moates (bass), Jason Singleton (drums)
Albums: The Lonely Position to Neutral (2002), True Parallels (2005), Dreaming in Black and White (2011)

This quartet originally started out under the name of 41 Down in 1997, but after signing to Geffen Records, they interestingly changed their name to Trust Company to avoid any confusion with the well-known Canadian punk rockers, Sum 41, who were also coming up at the time.

Trust Company's debut album, *The Lonely Position of Neutral,* emerged in July 2002 and it was promoted by the storming single, 'Downfall'. One of the many bands to come out on the back of Linkin Park's explosive rise to fame, Trust Company was clearly influenced by the *Hybrid Theory* heroes as their punchy record peaked at 11 on the *Billboard* 200, and later it would receive gold certification by the RIAA. To continue promoting themselves and their album, Trust Company would go out on tour with high profile bands such as Papa Roach, Korn and Disturbed.

Originally scheduled for a 2004 release but finally coming out in March 2005, sophomore album, *True Parallels* reached 32 on the *Billboard* 200 with sales of over 200,000 copies. The lead single 'Stronger' was used by *WWE* like 'Downfall' previously had been, before Trust Company went on hiatus so band members could focus on various side-projects. Reconvening in 2007, the band posted two new tracks ('Waking Up' and 'Stumbling') on their official MySpace page, and then after some line-up changes and a small US tour, Trust Company finally released their third album, *Dreaming in Black and White* in 2011. 'Heart in My Hands' was a great returning single, and the record contained twelve post-grunge hard rockers which more than convinced listeners that Trust Company was still capable of writing catchy melodies and stadium-sized choruses. Sadly, album number three would be the last, but *The Lonely Position of Neutral* still deserves frequent spins as it contains a consistent set of songs which are as good as anything released during nu metal's heyday.

Killer Cuts – 'Downfall', 'Figure 8'

Twisted Method

Years Active: 1998-2005, 2014
Location: Cape Coral, Florida, USA
Main era line-up: Derrick 'Tripp' Tribbett (vocals), Andrew Howard (guitar), Derek DeSantis (bass), Ben Goins (drums)
Albums: Escape from Cape Coma (2003)

Four years after their original inception, Twisted Method signed a multi-million-dollar deal with MCA Records, and their first, and what would prove to be only studio album followed in 2003. *Escape from Camp Coma,* of which the title paid homage to the band's hometown that – in their words – portrayed a town with an ageing population, featured the songs 'Reach' and 'Inside Out', ultimately helping to get Twisted Method's various points across. A second stage stint on Ozzfest not long after the album's release helped to gain further exposure, and 2004's high point came when the four-piece joined Motograter and Dope on the latter's *American Apathy* Tour. Thrown into turmoil when guitarist Andrew Howard and drummer Ben Goins quit, it led to Twisted Method going on an indefinite hiatus. In mid-September 2005, Howard was tragically found dead (no cause has ever been determined), before remaining members, Derek Tribbett and Derek DeSantis, formed a new band called MakeShift Romeo, which also included Dope frontman, Edsel, on drums, and then fellow Doper, Virus, on guitar.

Killer Cuts – 'Reach', 'Inside Out'

Ultraspank

Years Active: 1996-2001
Location: Santa Barbara, California, USA
Main era line-up: Pete Murray (vocals), Neil Godfrey (lead guitar), Jerry Oliveira (rhythm guitar), Dan Ogden (bass), Tyler Clark/James Carroll (drums)
Albums: Ultraspank (1998), Progress (2000)

Immensely popular for the short time they were in the spotlight, Ultraspank formed from the wreckage of Indica – a band which included Tyler Clark, Dan Ogden and Pete Murray, who would become three-fifths of Ultraspank's line-up. Rounded off by Neil Godfrey and Jerry Oliveira, the band signed to Epic Records in 1997 and released their self-titled debut a year later. Containing a strong industrial metal sound, the album failed to receive the support it needed from the band's record label, and after poor sales, it was regarded as a failure. When the non-album track, 'Five', found its way onto the Playstation game *3Xtreme*, Ultraspank earned some strong exposure which made Epic sit up and take notice, and with hopes high for the sophomore album, *Progress,* which came out in 2000, Ultraspank was ready to take the next step.

A more melody-driven record which featured Snot drummer, James 'Fed' Carroll, who had since replaced Clark, once again and almost shamefully,

Epic Records put little effort into fighting Ultraspank's corner and so *Progress* bombed, before Epic cut the band from their roster. Ironically, *Progress* received near-universal critical acclaim, and various sources even called it one of the best nu metal albums ever to be released; so had Epic done their job properly and given Ultraspank the help and promotion they needed, then this vibrant band would have gone on to much bigger and better things, instead of calling it a day not long after being dropped by their record label.

Killer Cuts – 'Slip', 'Push'

The Union Underground

Years Active: 1996-2002, 2020-
Location: San Antonio, Texas
Main era line-up: Brian Scott (vocals, rhythm guitar), Patrick Kennison (lead guitar), John Moyer (bass), Josh Memelo (drums)
Albums: ...An Education in Rebellion (2000)

The Union Underground rose to fame with *...An Education in Rebellion* in 2000. A major-label debut record distributed via Columbia Records, grunge elements were combined with some pounding alternative metal overtones, which endeared the band to Americans all over. Going on to be a cult classic amongst nu metal fans, album sales of around 400,000 were in part due to the hard-rocking single, 'Turn Me on Mr. Deadman', which stayed on the Mainstream Rock charts for well over six months. *...An Education in Rebellion* peaked at 130 on the *Billboard* 200 and, to promote the album, The Union Underground toured with the likes of Linkin Park and Marilyn Manson, as well as performing on the incredible line-up of Ozzfest in 2001.

Later releasing a new track titled 'Across the Nation', which was featured on WWE's *Forceable Entry* compilation album, and then a selection of live tracks under the *Live... One Nation Underground* title, The Union Underground would call it quits before a new full-length album was ever produced, with Moyer most notably of the band members going on to join Disturbed.

Brian Scott announced the revival of the band in early 2020, but no new material has emerged thus far, however, in the short time The Union Underground was around during the first movement, they showed just how well thought of they were with an album which still gets regularly discussed on forums all over the internet today.

Killer Cuts – 'Turn Me on Mr. Deadman', 'Killing the Fly'

Ünloco

Years Active: 2000-2003, 2014-
Location: Austin, Texas, USA
Main era line-up: Joey Duenas (vocals), Marc Serrano (guitar), Victor Escareno (bass),

Pete Navarette (drums)
Albums: Healing (2001), Becoming I (2003)

Ünloco was formed at the start of the new millennium by lead singer Joey Duenas, and their heavy but accessible alternative metal caught many an eye straight away. Releasing a six-track EP titled *Useless* via Captiva Records, Ünloco then went on to sign with Madonna's Maverick Records in 2001, where their debut album *Healing* came a few months later. Failing to gather significant mainstream attention, Ünloco was given another chance and in 2003, *Becoming I* followed and featured a heavier emphasis on melody and acoustics. 'Failure' was released as a single, before Ünloco appeared at Ozzfest 2003 and on the Music as a Weapon III tour with Disturbed, Taproot and Chevelle; as well as going out on tour with Korn. The album track, 'Hands and Knees', was a popular addition, while the punishing 'Bruises' was included on *The Matrix Reloaded* movie soundtrack and earned the band their biggest exposure.

Unfortunately, *Becoming I* failed to meet commercial expectations, and although Ünloco toured with a plethora of nu metal bands at the height of their careers such as Saliva, Drowning Pool, Trust Company, Taproot, Ill Nino and those mentioned above, inner turmoil led to the band's split at the end of 2003.

Killer Cuts – 'Failure', 'Bruises'

Vacant Stare

Years Active: 2001-2003
Location: London, England
Main era line-up: James Manning (vocals), Liam Williams (guitar), Nick Brown (guitar), James Norris (bass), Jay Micciche (drums), Ross Stone (turntables)
Albums: Vindication (2002)

Vacant Stare was another strong addition to the British nu metal scene. However, the sextet was another blink and you will miss them kind of band. A little bit of everything went into their one and only album, *Vindication*, which came out in 2002 via Copro Records. For the most part, catchy alternative metal with flourishes of rap vocals was the order of the day, and songs such as 'A Head Start' and 'Where I Stand' showed the band's true potential. Turntable scratching and a combination of clean and scream vocals made *Vindication* an enticing prospect, but by 2003, Vacant Stare had vacated the music scene and they never returned again.

Killer Cuts – 'A Head Start', 'Where I Stand'

Videodrone

Years Active: 1988-2000
Location: Bakersfield, California, USA
Main era line-up: Ty Elam (vocals), David File (guitar), 'Mavis' (bass), Kris Kohls (drums),

Rohan Cowden (keyboards, samples)
Albums: Videodrone (1999)

After having a fairly successful decade as Cradle of Thorns, Videodrone was born in 1998 as the line-up went from their early gothic rock sound to rap metal, and then finally industrial and electronic rock. Their self-titled debut was released via Korn's Elementree label in 1999, and Korn had plenty of say on the record. 'Fieldy' produced the whole thing, 'Head' played guitar on 'Power Tools for Girls', and Jonathan Davis provided guest vocals on the lead single, 'Ty Jonathan Down'. Limp Bizkit duo Fred Durst and DJ Lethal turned up on 'Human Piñata', and with some good contacts within the scene, Videodrone then went out on various tours with Korn, Orgy and Machine Head.

Unfortunately, Videodrone had a lack of support from the Reprise side of their record deal and they soon decided to split, which paved the way for drummer Kris Kohls, to join fellow Bakersfield upstarts, Adema. Lead singer Ty Elam reformed Cradle of Thorns with new members in 2006.

Killer Cuts – 'Ty Jonathan Down', 'Human Piñata'

3RD Strike

Years Active: 1995-2004, 2007-2010
Location: Los Angeles, California, USA
Main era line-up: Jim Korthe (vocals), Todd Deguchi (guitar), Erik Carlsson (guitar), PJ McMullan (bass), Gabe Hammersmith (drums)
Albums: Lost Angel (2002)

A Californian quintet that originally went by the name of Dimestore Hoods and brought some meaty rap metal to the table, the band was led by Jim Korthe, who had previously been affiliated with LA gang culture. Using his love of music to focus on powerful songs which documented gang life and the horrors surrounding it, Dimestore Hoods released a solitary album in 1996 before Korthe and Todd Deguchi formed 3rd Strike a couple of years later. Korthe laid his soul bare on the band's 2002 debut, *Lost Angel,* which was put out through Hollywood Records. The excellent singles 'No Light' and 'Redemption' brought new fans into 3rd Strike's family, while a cover of Black Sabbath's 'Paranoid' made for an interesting listen due to the addition of an added rap verse.

Later releasing a Japan-only EP titled *The Barrio Raid,* which featured the *Lara Croft Tomb Raider: The Cradle of Life Soundtrack* song, 'Into Hell Again' and B-sides which failed to make the *Lost Angel* album, 3rd Strike disbanded before returning in 2007, where they debuted some new songs and looked like they were close to releasing a new album. Things well silent shortly after that, and in 2010, Korthe sadly passed away from natural causes.

Killer Cuts – 'No Light', 'Redemption'

40 Below Summer

Years Active: 1998-2005, 2011-
Location: New Jersey, USA
Main era line-up: Max Illidge (vocals), Jordan Plingos (lead guitar), Joey D'Amico (rhythm guitar), Hector Graziani (bass), Carlos Aguilar (drums)
Albums: Side Show Freaks (1999), Invitation to the Dance (2001), The Mourning After (2003), The Last Dance (2006), Fire at Zero Gravity (2013), Transmission Infrared (2015)

40 Below Summer brought something a little different when they combined elements of New Jersey hardcore, hip-hop, jazz and hard rock with down-tuned guitars upon their rise in 1998. After a self-released album (*Side Show Freaks*), the five-piece signed with Warner's London-Sire to put out their major-label debut, *Invitation to the Dance,* in 2001. Max Illidge's vocals stood out from the crowd as he put on stellar performances on tracks such as 'Rope', 'Wither Away', and the excellent 'Falling Down'; however, the band would have to start all over again within a couple of months of the album's release, when London-Sire folded and Warner Bros. Records took the band under their wing.

Invitation... later got a reissue but by the end of 2002, 40 Below Summer had left Warner, but things started to look up when tour slots with Drowning Pool, Coal Chamber and Ill Nino took place, and then a deal was signed with Razor & Tie Records. A long-awaited sophomore album finally appeared in October 2003, where *The Mourning After* was promoted by the singles 'Self-Medicate' and 'Taxi Cab Confession'; but in 2004, 40 Below Summer was let out of their record contract and they announced their split a year later.

Demo albums and EPs would be re-released over the next few years before the band returned in 2013 with the album *Fire at Zero Gravity* and then *Transmission Infrared* in 2015. Both releases showcased a heavier alternative metal direction and while their momentum had stalled various times over the years, it was good to see 40 Below Summer back. *Invitation to the Dance* remains the quintet's defining moment in the nu metal spotlight, though, where despite its popularity amongst hardcore fans, it can perhaps still be considered one of the movement's most underrated album releases...

Killer Cuts – 'Rope', 'Falling Down'

Behind Every Great Album is a Great Producer

Ross Robinson

Often described as the man who shaped nu metal, Ross Robinson will forever be one of the most important soldiers in the nu metal army. Known for being an eccentric record producer due to his often extreme and antagonistic approaches in the studio, Robinson used Fear Factory's *Concrete* album to showcase his talents in 1991, and what came next remains the stuff of legend. Coming across a band who would later be known as Korn, Ross produced the Bakersfield quintet's ground-breaking debut in 1994, as well as their sophomore record, *Life Is Peachy,* in 1996 – earning a name for both the band and himself as nu metal would soon become a worldwide phenomenon.

He helped make Sepultura's *Roots* album the success it was (also in 1996), then he launched Limp Bizkit's attack on an unsuspecting world in 1997 with their *Three Dollar Bill, Y'all* album; and in 1998, he worked on the cult introductions from both Human Waste Project and Cold. A mixed bag of albums in 1999 saw the man with the seemingly golden touch work with Vanilla Ice, as the joke-rapper went serious (and heavy) for *Hard to Swallow,* then the fan-dividing Machine Head epic, *The Burning Red,* which saw the Bay Area band ditching their thrash metal sound for a good ol' slab of rap metal. And then came the earth-shattering introduction to Slipknot, as Robinson made their debut album sound so good that it wasn't long before the nine masked beasts became megastars. Also re-enlisted for Slipknot's second album, *Iowa*, Ross went on to produce critically-acclaimed records for post-hardcore bands such as At the Drive-In, the genre-bending Glassjaw, From First to Last and Norma Jean; before returning to work with Limp Bizkit and Korn later in the first decade of the 2000s. Having recently worked with a lot of indie rock bands, Ross was also able to put his mark on Suicide Silence's self-titled album at the beginning of 2017, as the band departed from their traditional deathcore sound in favour of a nu metal-influenced assault on the eardrums.

Undoubtedly doing as much for nu metal as Korn did (maybe not quite as much, but very close), we shall always be indebted to Ross Robinson for helping make the movement bold, brash and absolutely imperative listening.

Ross Robinson Nu Metal Production Discography

Korn – *Korn* (1994)
Korn – *Life Is Peachy* (1996)
Sepultura – *Roots* (1996)
Limp Bizkit – *Three Dollar Bill, Y'all* (1997)
Soulfly – *Soulfly* (1998)
Human Waste Project – *E-Lux* (1998)
Cold – *Cold* (1998)
Vanilla Ice – *Hard to Swallow* (1999)
Machine Head – *The Burning Red* (1999)
Slipknot – *Slipknot* (1999)

Amen – *Amen* (1999)
Glassjaw – *Everything You Ever Wanted to Know About Silence* (2000)
At the Drive-In – *Relationship of Command* (2000)
Amen – *We Have Come for Your Parents* (2000)
Slipknot – *Iowa* (2001)
Glassjaw – *Worship and Tribute* (2002)
Limp Bizkit – *The Unquestionable Truth (Part 1)* (2005)
Korn – *Korn III: Remember Who You Are* (2010)

Ross Robinson Speaks:

As a guitar player, it was instrumental in knowing what it was like to not know what is going to happen, that adolescent fear of 'How am I going to live, am I doing the right thing, is this what I should be doing?', and for some reason, producing was something I couldn't squash inside my heart.

You see a guitar player like James (Shaffer) from Korn or Wes (Borland) or any of those players in Limp Bizkit, and they have a timeclock inside of them that is extremely rare. It makes them extraordinary musicians and that internal timeclock – I didn't have that and I knew it, but I could hear it and I could feel it. I knew the difference between the backbeat of a pocket or pushing, and I have favourite drummers that know how to play around with a swing; so I didn't have the ambition of being a musician once I fell in love with the studio. It was so easy to drop the guitar and just drop the thought of becoming some popular rock star in an awful thrash metal band. It was like, 'Okay, I love this more than anything in the world, and I don't have to be locked into one band' because at the time, people only played in one band and that was it.

The *Concrete* (Fear Factory record) thing was a friend of mine who had invested in the recording of it, and I was friends with Dino Cazares and the guys, but then they got a manager and went on to do the deal and cut me out of it. I didn't have them sign anything at all before we recorded, so they just went on, and I learned a lesson from that.

The next thing I found was this band Creep, formally L.A.P.D., and I really liked the guitar player. For five minutes, we sat on the stage at soundcheck, just hanging out and something happened to me and I just fell in love with this guy. He was just so dang cool. I was basically doing nothing and I looked in the *LA Weekly* and saw Creep was playing, and the friend who invested in the Fear Factory thing – he was held up by some Crips because he sold weed. They broke into his apartment and put a gun to his throat and tied him up execution-style, but anyway, he told me he wanted to start a label. I found what turned into Korn a year-and-a-half after that, and I dedicated that full-on attitude of 'They're the ones, let's do it!' and they signed a little paragraph (thanks to my lesson learned with Fear Factory), and all we wanted to do in the recording was show it off to our friends. It had nothing to do with the world hearing it or getting record sales, and that was our pot of gold. There was a camaraderie, a pirate ship of extremely dedicated soldiers, and I learned so much. When you just know something and you know what you are, it cannot be denied. It isn't to impress anybody outside of you, it isn't to get something, and that was just our natural theme. A sell-out attitude was impossible because it had no influence in our realm to exist.

With Korn, I thought we would make records together forever but unfortunately, it wasn't to be. We're not here to keep repeating the past; it's our job to expand into whatever it is we're supposed to expand into. *Life Is Peachy* was like, 'Let's do it again, we're so badass, we can just write a record in less than a month and record it real fast!', and that was what we did. It is just absolute pure raw, destroyer energy, and it's a snapshot of the dudes at that moment – unleashing, and it reveals personality and no mask. I love it.

For me and from my personal experience, before the first Korn record, I was in a twelve-step program for an eating disorder, and my mom started coming up as a self-realisation sort of rock star and I was working on her early workshops with her. The intensity of people revealing their deepest, darkest, revealing and healing moments was my norm, so when Jonathan Davis was doing that through his lyrics, for me to be there was 'Oh yeah, this is normal'; to be so into the lyrics that the guitars and the drums and the bass and everything supported the lyrics.

If you were to take these subject matters and just put a shitty track of people playing correct, it wouldn't have had the same impact. You feel the breath in just one hit of the guitar; everything had that air of healing and revealing, gratitude, love, understanding; all of these things was the air of the room and the massive comfort of 'You're not stupid for feeling this way, don't hide, we love it when you let us know where you're at; and I understand' – that is what happened. There was such a beautiful place of safety on that mountain, and that right there is the core of that genre, and nobody else in the whole genre was able to fall into that level. I have never topped it since and I cannot try to, because it is its own universe and it is so beautiful.

In regards to choosing which records I worked on, I just had a sense of 'If this is real, I wanna do it'. If it is at that level of authenticity; it is everything to me. It still is and it always has been. It is really important for me to work with people who are authentic and want to give, and not just get something. It's unbelievable to get to be in that time period of music where there was a machine that supported the bands and that all of those bands (of that era) are still headlining because the machine was so good.

In the aftermath of Machine Head's *The Burning Red* record, my ego got in the way back in the day. I did some interviews because people did not like that Machine Head did rap, and I was afraid of not looking cool or something and some of the things I said hurt Robb's (Flynn) feelings. I broke a trust with him and I learned a huge lesson. But the bottom line is the dude is incredibly talented, he is incredibly passionate, and he likes that kind of stuff. He loved doing it and he is good at it. He is one of my favourite thrash guitar players from when he was in Vio-lence, and I think he is incredible. If someone decides to do something to be a creative artist because it is their passion, what people think is none of our business. We're here to do, to create and to give, and some will either take it or not, buy it or not, listen to it or not. My happiness, Robb's happiness, all the band's happiness – it has nothing to do with our happiness what people think of our stuff. It'll start editing our brains and it'll start making us make shit. The band was so willing and open and professional, and we just showed up and made a record; that was it.

Working with Slipknot came about because their manager at the time knew one person in LA, who happened to be my manager, and she made the one phone call to find out how to find this producer, Ross Robinson. For me, I was instantly in without even hearing the music- it was just too bizarre. So, we went over there and connected; again it was that first Korn sort of thing where we were in there to absolutely unleash everything to the absolute core. Unleash, impulse, be together and slam, and also destroy the commercialism of corporate Adidas Rock. It was a huge 'Fuck You' to how it was becoming, so washy and awful, in my opinion, and Slipknot was the perfect weapon. They brought it back and it was such a cool opposite of everything that was going on. I think about Corey (Taylor), how the dude was so raw, so willing, and he had the instrument in his throat to match like nobody I had ever seen in my life.

I produced the first two Korn records and the first two Slipknot records, and you get so close to people that it's an impossible thought that you wouldn't be working together again in the future, and when you find out you're not, it's crushing. Whatever happened with me mixed into those bands could never be reproduced. I think in order to grow it is good for people to move on and switch it up like that. I think it is what we're supposed to do now, but in the early stage of my career it was crushing; like during Soulfly – getting a phone call from Korn's managers saying I'm not doing the third record – my whole identity fell apart and it brought me to my knees. Because I loved the guys it felt like a horrific break-up. I felt the same way with Slipknot and it was kind of mind-boggling to me, and Limp Bizkit too – that was bizarre, but I understand now.

I'm a different thing to a normal producer.Who wants to go into a room with a guy that is just wanting to bleed? Who wants to go do that when you can just go in and record and do a great job because you are talented dudes? It's awful for somebody who just wants to sing about something and play it and be done, and I totally understand that now.

I teamed back up with Korn for their *Remember Who You Are* record, and it was good to be with the dudes again, but David (Silveria) wasn't there, Brian (Welch) wasn't there, and my knowing of what Korn is, was completely different to where they were at that point. They all had kids and families; Regi (Arvizu) would show up at the studio for an hour and then he had to go; it was stuff like that where my version of the band was like 'You live it, you be it, you're on the pirate ship, this is us!' and it didn't make sense because I wanted so badly for them to be the band that I knew from the past, and it wasn't fair. I think the performances are obviously not as authentic as on the first two records because my idea and what their ideas were aren't together anymore. My vision of what it was was way off, and it was not cool for me to go in there with that expectation, and I learned a lot from that experience.

On reflection, my favourite moment is where we (an artist and I) hike in the morning and exercise at Indigo Ranch, and just being in contact with nature and turning it into music, and I knew at the time it was special and beautiful; not having a world outside of us or an expectation. There are moments where I feel the slam, standing in the control room and being overwhelmed in tears and I cannot stop it, like a breathless thing- and I can't tell you exactly what moment that was, but each band that you know and have gone on and continued – that overwhelming tear-filled love that happens; and it just blows me away. It's a moment that won't ever stop being now.

Ross Robinson may well be considered 'The Godfather of Nu Metal', but there are plenty more who have stamped their own style and authority on some of nu metal's finest album releases. Whether it was producing, mixing or engineering – here are some other guys who deserve to be mentioned, with a list of their best moments which earned them widespread recognition.

Brendan O'Brien

Rage Against the Machine – *Evil Empire* (1996), *The Battle of Los Angeles* (1999), *Renegades* (2000)
Korn – *Issues* (1999)
Papa Roach – *Lovehatetragedy* (2002)
Incubus – *A Crow Left of the Murder* (2004)

Don Gilmore

Linkin Park – *Hybrid Theory* (2000), *Meteora* (2003)
The Union Underground – *An Education in Rebellion* (2000)
Trust Company – *The Lonely Position of Neutral* (2002), *True Parallels* (2005)

GGGarth (Garth Richardson)

Rage Against the Machine – *Rage Against the Machine* (1992)
Kittie – *Spit* (2000), *Oracle* (2001)
Spineshank – *The Height of Callousness* (2000), *Self-Destructive Pattern* (2003)
40 Below Summer – *Invitation to the Dance* (2001)
Downthesun – *Downthesun* (2002)
Chevelle – *Wonder What's Next* (2002)

Howard Benson

P.O.D. – *The Fundamental Elements of Southtown* (1999), *Satellite* (2001)
Reveille – *Bleed the Sky* (2001)
Crazy Town – *Dark Horse* (2002)
Cold – *Year of the Spider* (2003)

Adema – *Unstable* (2003)
Hoobastank – *The Reason* (2003)
Papa Roach – *Getting Away with Murder* (2004)

Jay Baumgardner

Coal Chamber – *Coal Chamber* (1997), *Chamber Music* (1999)
Spineshank – *Strictly Diesel* (1998)
Dope – *Felons and Revolutionaries* (1999), *Group Therapy* (2003)
Papa Roach – *Infest* (2000)
Drowning Pool – *Sinner* (2001)
Hoobastank – *Hoobastank* (2001)
Alien Ant Farm – *ANThology* (2001)

Johnny K

Disturbed – *The Sickness* (2000), *Believe* (2002), *Ten Thousand Fists* (2005)
Ünloco – *Healing* (2001)
No One – *No One* (2001)
Soil – *Scars* (2001), *Redefine* (2004), *Picture Perfect* (2009)
Machine Head – *Supercharger* (2001)
Drowning Pool – *Desensitized* (2004)
Earshot – *Two* (2004)

Josh Abraham

Orgy – *Candyass* (1998), *Vapor Transmission* (2000)
Crazy Town – *The Gift of Game* (1999)
Limp Bizkit- *The Chocolate Starfish and the Hot Dog Flavored Water* (2000)
Staind – *Break the Cycle* (2001), *14 Shades of Grey* (2003)
Dope – *Life* (2001)
Static-X – *Shadow Zone* (2003)

Rick Rubin

System of a Down – *System of a Down* (1998), *Toxicity* (2001), *Steal This Album!* (2002)
Rage Against the Machine – *Renegades* (2000)
American Head Charge – *The War of Art* (2001)
Limp Bizkit – *Results May Vary* (2003)
Slipknot – *Vol 3: The Subliminal Verses* (2004)
Linkin Park – *Minutes to Midnight* (2007)

Terry Date

Deftones – *Adrenaline* (1995), *Around the Fur* (1997), *White Pony* (2000), *Deftones* (2003)
Incubus – *S.C.I.E.N.C.E.* (1997)
Staind – *Dysfunction* (1999)

Limp Bizkit – *Significant Other* (1999), *Chocolate Starfish and the Hot Dog Flavored Water* (2000), *Results May Vary* (2003)
Otep – *Sevas Tra* (2002)

Toby Wright

Korn – *Follow the Leader* (1998)
Sevendust – *Home* (1999)
Soulfly – *Primitive* (2000)
Taproot – *Welcome* (2002), *Blue-Sky Research* (2005)

Ulrich Wild

Incubus – *S.C.I.E.N.C.E.* (1997)
Powerman 5000 – *Tonight the Stars Revolt!* (1999)
Static- X – *Wisconsin Death Trip* (1999), *Machine* (2001), *Shadow Zone* (2003)
Apartment 26 – *Hallucinating* (2000)
The Union Underground – *An Education in Rebellion* (2000)
Taproot – *Gift* (2000)
Skrape – *New Killer America* (2001)
Soil – *True Self* (2006)

When Worlds Collide: Rockers vs. Rappers

With nu metal being heavily influenced by hip-hop, it was inevitable that those two worlds would come together for some interesting and fairly outstanding collaborations.

The foundations were firmly put in place at the end of the 1980s when classic rockers Aerosmith combined with the immensely popular Run-D.M.C. – a trio who are widely regarded as one of the most influential acts in hip-hop culture. Originally written by Aerosmith and featuring on their 1975 album, *Toys in the Attic*, 'Walk This Way' was re-recorded and released by the two acts in 1986, with an accompanying promo video that is still played on TV today. 'Walk This Way' broke hip-hop into the pop mainstream and it became the first hip-hop song to make the top 5 on the *Billboard* Hot 100. The track also provided a major comeback for Aerosmith, who had been languishing in the doldrums for most of the decade. However, later releases sparked huge sales and put the band back in classic rock's major leagues.

For a few years after, it seemed that the Aerosmith and Run-D.M.C. duet was going to be a one-off, until in 1991, thrash metal titans Anthrax teamed up with Public Enemy to release an updated version of the hip-hop duo's 'Bring the Noise', which also featured on the *Less Than Zero* movie soundtrack in 1987. The new rendition was included on the Anthrax B-sides album, *Attack of the Killer B's* and on Public Enemy's *Apocalypse 91...The Enemy Strikes Back*, and the two bands then headed out on a joint tour. Sometimes spelt 'Bring tha Noise' or 'Bring tha Noize', the track's best chart position was in the UK where it reached a decent number 14.

In 1993, action movie, *Judgement Night* (starring Emilio Estevez, Stephen Dorff and Cuba Gooding Jr.) incorporated a soundtrack full of rock, metal and rap collaborations. The album saw the likes of Helmet, Biohazard, Slayer and Therapy? merge with House of Pain, Onyx, Ice-T and Fatal, respectively. Genre-hopping geniuses Faith No More were joined by Boo-Yaa T.R.I.B.E. for the song 'Another Body Murdered', while rap heroes Cypress Hill had two songs on the soundtrack – 'I Love You Mary Jane' with Sonic Youth and 'Real Thing' with grunge icons Pearl Jam.

The merging of rock and hip-hop would begin to take full effect in 1998, with rappers featuring on rock albums and vice versa. Combinations that never seemed possible were starting to become more likely, underlined by rapper DMX, who called on shock rocker Marilyn Manson to guest on the track 'The Omen' on his *Flesh of My Flesh, Blood of My Blood* record. In the same year, Kid Rock's mega-selling album, *Devil Without a Cause,* saw new rap sensation Eminem feature on the track 'Fuck Off', before nu metal godfathers Korn and N.W.A. legend Ice Cube helped each other out; firstly with Cube guesting on 'Children of the Korn' off the nu metal classic *Follow the Leader* record, before Korn returned the favour by turning up on 'Fuck Dying', which was found on Cube's critically acclaimed *War and Peace (Part 1)*. Also, on Korn's third album, Tre Hardson from The Pharcyde lent his vocal talents to the song 'Cameltosis', paving the way for many more examples of genre rule-bending between rock and hip-hop.

Limp Bizkit called upon Wu-Tang Clan member Method Man for the popular single 'N 2 Gether Now', as well as Eminem on 'Turn Me Loose'; however, only the Method Man guest spot made the final cut of Limp's explosive sophomore album, *Significant Other*. Fred Durst himself would later appear on various hip-hop albums, starting with Methods of Mayhem's self-titled debut in 1999. A side-project from Mötley Crüe's Tommy Lee, Durst sang on the single 'Get Naked', while Kid Rock also appeared- on the album track 'New Skin'. Limp Bizkit's ground-breaking third album, *Chocolate Starfish and the Hot Dog Flavored Water* had Xzibit on 'Getcha Groove On', plus the all-star cast of DMX, Method Man and Redman for the 'Urban Assault Vehicle' remix of 'Rollin''.

Let's face it, pretty much everyone has heard that terrible song, 'Ice Ice Baby', released in 1991 by white rapper Vanilla Ice. Well, he would go up in many rock fans' estimations when he returned from a hiatus in 1998 and packed a rap metal punch with *Hard to Swallow*. Produced by Ross Robinson, Ice's third album featured Korn on the song 'Prozac' and Amen's Casey Chaos on 'Fuck Me' and 'A.D.D.'. Released via Republic, the backing band included Snot and Amen duo Sonny Mayo (guitar) and Shannon Larkin (drums), before the following record, *Bi-Polar*, continued in the same nu metal direction with one half containing heavy rap metal and the second half leaning towards Vanilla Ice's customary hip-hop focus.

Cypress Hill released *Skin & Bones* in 2000 – a double album containing one disc of hip-hop and one of rock songs, where '(Rap) Superstar' featured Eminem and '(Rock) Superstar' had Deftones' vocalist Chino Moreno contribute. Also released in 2000 was a compilation titled *Loud Rocks*, which saw rock bands and rap artists collaborate to re-record the rappers' original tracks. 'Shame' was performed by System of a Down and the track's writers Wu-Tang Clan, 'Hip-Hop' was done by Static-X and Dead Prez, while Incubus and Big Punisher reworked his own track, 'Still Not a Player'. As the year progressed, the songs kept coming, and whilst annoying many metal fans in the process, the accessibility of rock and rap was helping to spawn a new generation of nu metal listeners.

Run-D.M.C. released *Crown Royal* in 2001 with Fred Durst guesting on 'Them Girls', Kid Rock on 'The School of Old', and Stephan Jenkins of Third Eye Blind on 'Rock Show'. Industrial metal outfit Fear Factory called on Cypress Hill's B-Real for the song 'Back the Fuck Up', which was included on the LA quartet's *Digimortal* release, and Body Count rap star turned heavy metal icon, Ice-T, guested on death metal band Six Feet Under's 'One Bullet Left'; which was arguably one of the most surprising and diverse collaborations of the era.

Linkin Park was already known for their rap rock stylings, and some of their members would guest on X-Ecutioners' single 'It's Goin' Down' in 2002, while in 2003, Korn brought along Nas on 'Play Me', which featured on their *Take a Look in the Mirror* record. In the same year, Papa Roach raised a few eyebrows when they performed on the Black-Eyed Peas album track, 'Anxiety', before the biggest rap rock project of the nu metal era pitched Linkin Park and Jay-Z together to release the *Collision Course* EP in 2004. Mashing together songs from each artist's back catalogue, the standout track was 'Numb/Encore' which won a Grammy Award for 'Best Rap/Sung Collaboration'. The EP itself would go on to sell over seven million copies, unsurprisingly making it the most successful EP in music history.

Stepping out of their comfort zones, each artist involved in these collaborations dared to bring something new to the table. While bands such as Limp Bizkit and Linkin Park already had a hip-hop background, the likes of Korn and Fear Factory, plus the brutality of Six Feet Under, broke all the rules to produce songs that should never have worked, but they did, and with largely glorious results.

Nu Metal in the Movies

Especially at the start of the new millennium, hit movies started to be accompanied by nu metal dominated soundtracks. Most of these movies fitted into the horror genre, as heavy music seemed to suit dark and often sadistic scenes, while also adding intensity and intrigue to what was being witnessed on screen.
Here are just a handful of movies and the tracklistings for officially released soundtracks:

Judgement Night (September 1993), Immortal, Epic

Helmet/House of Pain – 'Just Another Victim'
Teenage Fan Club/De La Soul – 'Fallin''
Living Colour/Run-D.M.C. – 'Me, Myself & My Microphone'
Biohazard/Onyx – 'Judgement Night'
Slayer/Ice-T – 'Disorder'
Faith No More/Boo-Yaa T.R.I.B.E. – 'Another Body Murdered'
Sonic Youth/Cypress Hill – 'I Love You Mary Jane'
Mudhoney/Sir Mix-A-Lot – 'Freak Momma'
Dinosaur Jr./Del the Funky Homosapien – 'Missing Link'
Therapy?/Fatal – 'Come & Die'
Pearl Jam/Cypress Hill – 'Real Thing'

Strangeland (September 1998), TVT Soundtrax

Dee Snider – 'Inconclusion'
Sevendust – 'Breathe'
Megadeth – 'A Secret Place'
Pantera – 'Where You Come From'
Anthrax – 'P&V'
Snot – 'Absent'
Dayinthelife – 'Street Justice'
Coal Chamber – 'Not Living'
Bile – 'In League'
Marilyn Manson – 'Sweet Tooth'
Soulfly – 'Eye for an Eye'
Hed PE – 'Serpent Boy'
Kid Rock – 'Fuck Off'
The Clay People – 'Awake'
System of a Down – 'Marmalade'
Nashville Pussy – 'I'm the Man'
Crisis- 'Captain Howdy'
Twisted Sister – 'Heroes Are Hard to Find'

The Matrix (March 1999), Warner Bros., Maverick

Marilyn Manson – 'Rock Is Dead'
Propellerheads – 'Spybreak!'

Ministry – 'Bad Blood'
Rob D – 'Clubbed to Death'
Meat Beat Manifesto – 'Prime Audio Soup'
Lunatic Calm – 'Leave You Far Behind'
The Prodigy – 'Mindfields'
Rob Zombie – 'Dragula'
Deftones – 'My Own Summer (Shove It)'
Hive – 'Ultrasonic Sound'
Monster Magnet – 'Look to Your Orb for the Warning'
Rammstein – 'Du hast'
Rage Against the Machine – 'Wake Up'

Dracula 2000 (December 2000), Sony

Powerman 5000 – Ultra Mega
Disturbed – 'A Welcome Burden'
Slayer – 'Bloodline'
System of a Down – 'Metro'
Monster Magnet – 'Heads Explode'
Godhead – 'Break You Down'
Linkin Park – 'One Step Closer'
Pantera – 'Avoid the Light'
Static-X – 'Ostego Undead'
Hed PE – 'Swan Dive'
Taproot – 'Day by Day'
Endo – 'Malice'
Flybanger – 'Blind World'
Halfcocked – 'Sober'
Saliva – 'Your Disease'

Valentine (January 2001), Warner Bros.

Rob Zombie – 'Superbeast'
Disturbed – 'God of the Mind'
Static-X – 'Love Dump'
Linkin Park – 'Pushing Me Away'
Deftones – 'RX Queen'
Orgy – 'Opticon'
Marilyn Manson – 'Valentine's Day'
Amanda Ghost – 'Filthy Mind'
Professional Murder Music – 'Fall Again'
BT – 'Smartbomb'
Soulfly – 'Son Song'
Filter – 'Take a Picture'
Snake River Conspiracy – 'Breed'
Beautiful Creatures – 1 A.M.

The Scorpion King (March 2002), Universal

Godsmack – 'I Stand Alone
P.O.D. – 'Set It Off'
Drowning Pool – 'Break You'
System of a Down – 'Streamline'
Creed – 'To Whom It May Concern'
Nickelback – 'Yanking Out My Heart'
Hoobastank – 'Losing My Grip'
Flaw – 'Only the Strong'
Rob Zombie feat. Ozzy Osbourne – 'Iron Head'
12 Stones – 'My Life'
Mushroomhead – 'Along the Way'
Lifer – 'Breathless'
Sevendust – 'Corrected'
Injected – 'Burn It Black'
Breaking Point – '27'
Coal Chamber – 'Glow'

Queen of the Damned (March 2002), Warner Music Group

David Draiman – 'Forsaken'
Chester Bennington – 'System'
Deftones – 'Change (In the House of Flies)'
Marilyn Manson – 'Redeemer'
Wayne Static – 'Not Meant for Me'
Papa Roach – 'Dead Cell'
Godhead – 'Penetrate'
Jay Gordon – 'Slept So Long'
Disturbed – 'Down with the Sickness'
Static-X – 'Cold'
Earshot – 'Headstrong'
Dry Cell – 'Body Crumbles'
Tricky – 'Excess'
Kidneythieves – 'Before I'm Dead'

Resident Evil (March 2002), Roadrunner

Slipknot – 'My Plague'
Marilyn Manson – 'The Fight Song'
Coal Chamber – 'Something Told Me'
The Crystal Method – 'Name of the Game (Clean Name)
Adema – 'Everyone'
Fear Factory – 'Invisible Wounds'
Static-X – 'Anything But This'
Rammstein – 'Halleluja'
Depeche Mode – 'Dirt'

Ill Nino – 'What Comes Around'
Mudvayne – 'Dig'
Method Man – 'Release Yo' Delf'
Saliva – '800'
Five Pointe O – 'The Infinity'
Marilyn Manson – 'Resident Evil Main Title Theme'
Marilyn Manson – 'Seizure of Power'
Marilyn Manson – 'Reunion'
Marilyn Manson – 'Cleansing'

XXX (August 2002), Universal

Heavy Metal Side:
Rammstein – 'Feuer frei!'
Drowning Pool – 'Bodies'
Hatebreed – 'I Will Be Heard'
Queens of the Stone Age – 'Millionaire'
Mushroomhead – 'Before I Die'
Flaw – 'Get Up Again'
Moby – 'Landing'
Gavin Rossdale – 'Adrenaline'
Fermin IV – '004'
Orbital – 'Technologicque Park'

The Matrix Reloaded (April 2003), Warner Bros., Maverick

Linkin Park – 'Session'
Marilyn Manson – 'This Is the New Shit'
Rob Zombie – 'Reload'
Rob D – 'Furious Angels'
Deftones – 'Lucky You'
Team Sleep – 'The Passportal'
P.O.D. – 'Sleeping Awake'
Ünloco – 'Bruises'
Rage Against the Machine – 'Calm Like a Bomb'
Oakenfold – 'Dread Rock'
Fluke – 'Zion'
Dave Matthews Band – 'When the World Ends'

Freddy vs. Jason (August 2003), Roadrunner

Ill Nino – How Can I Live
Killswitch Engage – 'When Darkness Falls'
Spineshank – 'Beginning of the End'
Mushroomhead – 'Sun Doesn't Rise'
Hatebreed – 'Condemned Until Rebirth'
Slipknot – 'Snap' ('97 Demo)

Chimaira – 'Army of Me'
From Autumn to Ashes – 'The After Dinner Payback'
Sevendust – 'Leech'
Powerman 5000 – 'Bombshell'
Murderdolls – 'Welcome to the Strange'
Seether – 'Out of My Way'
Stone Sour – 'Inside the Cynic'
DevilDriver – 'Swinging the Dead'
Sepultura feat. Mike Patton – 'The Waste'
The Blank Theory – 'Middle of Nowhere'
Nothingface – 'Ether'
In Flames – 'Trigger'
Lamb of God – '11th Hour'
Type O Negative – '(We Were) Electrocute'

The Texas Chainsaw Massacre (November 2003), Bulletproof/La-La Land

Pantera – 'Immortally Insane'
Hatebreed – 'Below the Bottom'
Soil – 'Pride'
Static-X – 'Deliver Me'
Mushroomhead – '43'
Seether – 'Pig'
Nothingface – 'Down in Flames'
40 Below Summer – 'Self Medicate'
Motograter – 'Suffocate'
Shadows Fall – 'Destroyer of Senses'
Meshuggah – 'Rational Gaze'
Fear Factory – 'Archetype'
Morbid Angel – 'Enshrined by Grace'
Index Case – 'Listen'
Finger Eleven – 'Stay in Shadow'
Lamb of God – 'Ruin'
Sworn Enemy – 'As Real as It Gets'
Core-Tez – 'Five Months'

The Punisher (March 2004), Wind-Up

Drowning Pool – 'Step Up'
Puddle of Mudd – 'Bleed'
Nickelback – 'Slow Motion'
Queens of the Stone Age – 'Never Say Never'
Seether feat. Amy Lee – 'Broken'
Smile Empty Soul – 'Finding Myself'
Trapt – 'Lost in a Portrait'

Chevelle – 'Still Running'
Damageplan – 'Ashes to Ashes'
Seether – 'Sold Me'
Edgewater – 'Eyes Wired Shut'
Finger Eleven – 'Slow Chemical'
Ben Moody – 'The End Has Come'
Strata – 'Piece by Piece'
Hatebreed – 'Bound to Violence'
Fallzone – 'Sick'
Submersed – 'Complicated'
Atomship – 'Time for People'
Mark Collie – 'In Time'

The Nu Metal Revival

The second half of the twenty-teens have seen many bands coming up who are influenced by the original nu metal movement. Easily heard in their sound, many of these musicians are at an age where nu metal was likely to be their introduction to heavy music, and having been inspired by the likes of Korn, Limp Bizkit, Linkin Park and Slipknot to create their own art, here are some of the Nu Breed who are helping to create somewhat of a nu metal revival.

Add1ction

Coming out of Brownsville, Texas, Add1ction bring back the glory days of witnessing Linkin Park in their prime with a delicious slice of rap rock, containing electronic undertones and arena-sized choruses, as well as a dual vocal combination that perfectly go back and forth with rapping and clean singing. Having released two stellar EPs (*Add1ction Nation* in 2016 and *Point of No Return* in 2017) to national acclaim, the quintet followed up with a stunning debut full-length in 2020, titled *Leave It All Behind*. Across Add1ction's three releases thus far is a plethora of quality music that harks back to nu metal's original movement, with the likes of 'Nothing Left to Lose', 'I Won't Give In' and 'Down' being ideal starting points for new listeners.

www.facebook.com/add1ction

Afterlife

From West Palm Beach, Florida, Afterlife put out their debut EP, *Vicious Cycle*, at the start of 2017, which was distributed through Stay Sick Recordings. A band that create raw, catchy and aggressive music which often gets thrown into the nu-metalcore category, Afterlife also includes rap sections, thunderous screaming, down-tuned guitars and subtle scratch effects into an uncompromising palette. Having penned a deal with Hopeless Records and released their debut album, *Breaking Point*, in 2019, a trip over to Europe saw Afterlife transfix new audiences, and with raging numbers like 'Pain & Pleasure' and the abrasive salvo of 'Throat' and 'PSA' amongst the band's already impressive discography, you can expect to hear a lot more from this Florida foursome in the years to come.

www.afterlifeofficial.com

Amerakin Overdose

Amerakin Overdose are another scary ensemble that rose out of Portland, Oregon in 2010. A groove orientated band that blend modern pop vocal melodies and integrated keyboards with aggressive industrial metal, the four-piece released a self-titled debut album not long after their inception and then played live anywhere and everywhere that would have them. A tour with Mushroomhead in 2015 didn't do the band any harm, and in 2016 they released their second record, *The Great Amerakin Dream.* With a production credit for ex-Machine

Head and Ill Nino guitarist Ahrue Luster, visceral but accessible songs such as 'Letting Go' and 'I, Alone' were great examples of how melody and aggression can often go hand-in-hand. In late-2017, the quartet released their own version of the Katy Perry hit, 'E.T.', which needs to be heard to be believed, and although their face-painted and mask-wielding members might be capable of giving you nightmares, Amerakin Overdose certainly deserve your time and attention.

www.amerakinoverdose.com

Bison

Coming out of Melbourne, Australia, Bison made early waves with their debut EP, *Within Earshot*, in 1999. Produced by Superheist's DW Norton, the release oozed nu metal swagger with an energetic flow of rap-tinged metal which was led by the bouncing single, 'Hard to Take', and the funk laden but raucous 'Brainsnap'. Signing to Faultline Records, Bison received decent exposure down under by having their music included on various TV shows which focused on skateboarding, surfing and snowboarding, and the quintet's momentum continued with their second EP, *Architect of Sound*, in 2002. Bringing more rap metal to the table with catchy numbers such as 'Mind State', and the hugely anthemic 'Looks Could Kill', Bison looked set to go to the next level. Sharing stages with the likes of Hed PE, Hoobastank and The White Stripes; as well as the finest talent Australia possessed such as Superheist, Sunk Loto, The Butterfly Effect and Karnivool, Bison expanded their horizons with a third EP, *DEMO*, however the band would call it quits in 2005 and the limited release of *DEMO* has seen it become a highly sought-after CD.

Inspired by bands like Korn, Helmet and Incubus, Bison's original line-up reformed almost fifteen years later with reinvigorated passion and feeling that there was some unfinished business to attend to, and *Perfect Mistakes*, which was released in May 2021, reminded everyone of just how talented and explosive this five-piece can be. With the six tracks becoming the best material the band has written to date, hopefully there is plenty more to come from Bison as they continue to make up for lost time. Feeling like a fresh start for the band, Bison's inclusion in the revival section of this book is completely justified.

www.facebook.com/Bison.aus

Blood Youth

Originally starting out as a melodic hardcore band who also threw in some pop hooks, Blood Youth dramatically changed their sound ahead of their 2019 album, *Starve*, where they elected for a dark and twisted dive down the rabbit hole. From Harrogate in the UK, Blood Youth had already put themselves on people's nu metal scope with a strong cover of Slipknot's '(sic)', but when they let the world check out the visceral 'Cut Me Open', 'Spineless', and the spotlight-stealing title track, the quartet entwined those classic '90s riffs with a contemporary yet primaeval metallic approach. With some Americanised flourishes filtering through, it looks like nu-influenced metal is the way forward for Blood Youth, who are signed to Rude Records, as they have seen their stock rise dramatically since debuting this effective and popular new sound.

www.facebook.com/bloodyouth

Cane Hill

Reportedly named after a psychiatric hospital in the UK, Cane Hill formed in New Orleans in 2011 and got straight to work on delivering some hellacious and brash alternative metal. Signing to Rise Records in 2014 and releasing their self-titled debut EP towards the end of 2015, Cane Hill showed a nod in the direction of Korn on the pulsating 'Gemini'. Always mixing it up and going from obliteratingly heavy to calm and hallucinogenic in the next breath, their albums *Smile* (2016) and *Too Far Gone* (2018) have earned the four-piece a legion of admiring fans in the years that have followed. Whether you listen to 'Time Bomb', 'You're So Wonderful', 'Erased' or 'It Follows', Cane Hill creates something for everyone across the heavy metal scope and without doubt, they have been one of the biggest success stories of the last decade.

www.wearecanehill.com

Cold Sin

Initially starting out as a solo project in early 2020, brainchild Riley Kirkpatrick then joined forces with HeadTrip Trauma guitarist, Jason Harris, to form Cold Sin, after Harris had shown interest in laying down some vocals on the then-instrumental track, 'Letting Go'. From there, the North Carolina duo went from strength to strength, creating more heavy but accessible songs which had more than a hint of Korn influence – especially in the pounding but groovy guitar work. Also for fans of Staind and Static-X, Cold Sin dropped their self-titled debut EP on Christmas Day via TNZ Records, and as well as 'Letting Go', the pulsating songs 'Chasing Perfection' and 'Numb Sick' show how diverse but consistent this band can be. The closing and acoustic 'Mona' added another aspect, and with dark and emotional themes smothering the whole record, Cold Sin's first effort created a small buzz around the North Carolina area. A second EP is already in the works as Cold Sin set about raising the bar even higher after making such a promising start.

www.facebook.com/ColdSinNC

Crostpaths

Brimming with swagger and verve, UK rapscallions, Crostpaths, are most definitely ones to watch in the next year or so. Rap metal which sounds fresh and revitalised is the order of the day, and the Kent mob announced themselves in 2019 with the infectiously heavy 'Bulldozer' (not a cover of the Machine Head banger). Following it up with the equally impressive 'Pariah' and 'Meridian (Aftermath)'- the three tracks making up the band's debut EP; what Crostpaths has shown in their relatively short existence is their ability to create diverse but heavy music whilst remaining equally catchy and accessible. Unleashing their incredible single 'Rampage' in the summer of 2020 with a chorus that will stick in your head for days, it was the perfect choice of song to lead their latest EP, *Mutated*, which dropped in November 2020 through TNZ Records. The best of British – quite possibly.

www.facebook.com/crostpaths

Darkcell

From the land Down Under, Darkcell formed in Brisbane, Australia in 2012, and with a shock rock image to accompany their apocalyptic industrial metal sound, this quartet are ideal for fans of Marilyn Manson, Rob Zombie and Nine Inch Nails. Having already toured with the likes of Sevendust, Ill Nino and Motograter, Darkcell's big break came in 2016 with their first release via Zombie Shark Records and their fifth overall, *Haunted Reality*. Nightmarish videos were made for 'Preacher' and 'Raise Your Horns (Army of Darkness)', both of which showcase the band's industrial stomp, which is capable of endearing Darkcell to a much larger audience outside of Australia.

www.darkc3ll.com

Death Blooms

Part of Britain's attempt at reviving the nu metal movement, Liverpool's Death Blooms has gathered quite a reputation since their original inception. Announcing themselves with an abrasive debut EP in 2017, the self-titled effort found Death Blooms (not named after the popular Mudvayne song) elect for a visceral and scathing approach. The devastating vocals of Paul Barrow were, and continue to be, delivered with deafening precision, while he also shows off some impressive cleans too. 'Hate:Die' set the quartet's stall out early and they continued their onslaught with the 2019 EP, *You Are Filth*. Going from strength to strength and with hints of fellow Brits Architects, some meaty hardcore elements and more refined melodies seeped in on standout tracks such as the title track and 'Crosses', having been put on the map a little further due to a successful slot on 2018's Download Festival extravaganza. Having recently signed to US indie label, Adventure Cat Records, Death Blooms didn't let 2020 become a total write-off, dropping two stellar new tracks in the forms of 'Life is Pain' and 'Anger' – the second of which might just be the band's best song to date. Both of those songs featured on their 2021 EP, *Fuck Everything*, where five tracks of metallic fury find Death Blooms at their most impressive thus far.

www.facebook.com/dthblms

Ded

A band whose popularity surged through just two single releases, Arizona's Ded is already well on the way to becoming one of the biggest bands of the nu metal resurgence. From the chaotic romps of 'FMFY' and 'Anti-Everything', the latter of which saw Fred Durst direct its music video, to the irresistible selections on the band's debut album, *Mis·an·thrope*, from 2017, Ded's frontman, Joe Cotela, cuts a colossal figure with an extraordinary vocal range of fiery screams, deep and vicious growls and radio-friendly cleans.

Signed to Jordan Schur's Suretone Records and having already shared stages with an excess of rock and metal heavyweights (Korn and Stone Sour to name just two), Ded released three new anthems in 2020 under the titles 'A Mannequin Idol (Mannequin Eyes)', 'Eyes Sewn Shut' and 'Parasite'; ahead of a sophomore album which should drop at some point in 2021 with a barrel load of hype to accompany it.

www.dedband.com

Discrepancies

From St. Louis, Missouri, Discrepancies is another welcome addition to the rap rock scene. Lyrically appealing and largely uplifting, Antonio 'ATG' Metcalf's incredible rapping talents are what separates Discrepancies from the rest of the crowd, and after a self-titled EP in 2014, the quartet's debut full-length was taken on by InVogue Records and released under the title, *The Awakening,* in 2018. Including the pulsating numbers of 'Art of War', 'Not Alone', 'Prevail' and 'Wake Up', Discrepancies showed some of the best and most honest rap rock that we have heard in a very long time; and having returned in 2020 with their next long-player, *The Rise*, tracks such as 'Control' and 'Undertow' confirmed the band is ready to go to the next level.

www.discrepanciesmusic.com

Dropout Kings

Formerly known as Phoenix Down upon their formation in 2016, Adam Ramey's six-piece 'trap metal' band changed their name to Dropout Kings in 2017 and then signed to Napalm Records a year later. Releasing their debut album, *Audiodope*, in the same year, tracks such as 'NVM' and 'Scratch & Claw' propelled the band to a wider audience with Eddie Wellz's impressive rapping and Ramey's highly effective clean and scream vocals. Currently signed to Stay Sick Recordings, Dropout Kings dropped their impressive *GlitchGang* EP in 2020, backing up their distinctive sound with more powerful numbers like the EP's title track and the catchy singalong romp of 'Virus'.

www.dropoutkingsmusic.com

Fire From the Gods

Combining soulful hip-hop vocals with some harsh screams and hardcore ferocity, Fire From the Gods has quickly become one of the hottest bands in the US. The Texan's debut album, *Sleeping with Anchors & Mirrors* saw Eric July on vocals, but it was when AJ Channer took over that the band started earning decent exposure across the US. Honest lyrical content which addressed the state of the world, Fire From the Gods regrouped, signed to Rise Records, and then released the powerful *Narrative* in 2016, which included the pulsating tracks 'Excuse Me' and 'End Transmission'. Bearing some similarities to nu metal legends Sevendust, Fire From the Gods re-released *Narrative* in 2017 and included two new songs produced by Korn's Jonathan Davis, while their latest album, *American Sun*, dropped in 2019 through Eleven Seven Music and received critical acclaim. Don't sleep on this powerful and refreshing band.

www.firefromthegods.com

From Ashes to New

Coming out of Lancaster, Pennsylvania, in late 2013, From Ashes to New let their love and respect of Linkin Park shine through on many a song, catching people's attention with their full-length debut, *Day One,* at the start of 2016. Featuring the same kind of soul-searching rap vocals and catchy choruses that made Linkin Park so popular in their early days, 'Breaking Now', 'Lost and Alone' and 'Through It All' struck a nerve with many from the very first listen, and although the band underwent some line-up changes later on, From Ashes to New seem stronger than ever right now on the back of their 2018 album, *The Future*, and the 2020 stormer, *Panic*.

www.fromashestonew.com

Frontstreet

Based in Lelystad in the Netherlands, Frontstreet fuse effortless rap vocals with deathly and primitive screams on top of some pounding but groove-laden hooks. A debut EP (*Under Pressure)* in 2016 set the Dutch quintet's stall out early before following it up with the sensational debut album, *Reality Check*, in September 2017. Along with the blistering 'Snake', the likes of 'Ghost Town' and the metal ballad, 'Stunning', showed a band confident and capable of stepping outside of their comfort zones. A new track titled 'Don't Cry' followed before 2017 was over, followed by a radio edit of 'Ghost Town', and at the back end of 2020, Frontstreet finally returned with the incredible single, 'F.R.E.E', which featured Dropout Kings frontman, Adam Ramey, and Jynx head honcho, Tommy Roulette.

In Martijn Huijskes, Frontstreet has one of the best rappers in the whole movement, and while they do have a decent following in the US, their next album might be the one to take the five-piece global. Having already supported Crazy Town and Hollywood Undead on the American rockers' visits to the Netherlands, as well as a successful after party show backing up Limp Bizkit in Amsterdam, surely it is only a matter of time before Frontstreet earn the opportunity to venture outside of their homeland and play in front of much bigger audiences.

www.facebook.com/frontstreetband

HeadTrip Trauma

From Creedmoor, North Carolina, HeadTrip Trauma bring back memories of the heavier side of nu metal whilst adding some punishing groove metal elements into their sound. Originally forming in 2014 under the name Injection, a couple of members came and went before HeadTrip Trauma was properly unleashed, and the fearsome foursome are finally starting to forge their own path. Releasing their debut EP in September 2019, the self-titled effort featured the bruising numbers of 'Glassjaw', 'Dead', 'The Haymaker' and the fan favourite stomp, 'Can I Live?'. Having recently released their debut album, *Side Effects*, via TNZ Records, HeadTrip Trauma has gone from strength to strength on the back of new ragers such as 'Nu-Breed', 'No Trust' and the two-minute powerhouse anthem, 'HeadTrip'- confirming that this awesome foursome are definitely worth your ears and attention.

www.facebook.com/HeadTripTraumaOfficial

Heartsick

Lansing, Michigan quartet, Heartsick, formed in 2015, having previously performed under the name Know Lyfe; and in the six years since, they have become one of the most sonically diverse metal bands in America. Their self-titled debut album from 2015 possessed a largely metalcore edge while also throwing in some melodic and atmospheric textures, which would become more prominent on their next record. With 2019's *Sleep Cycles*, Heartsick's stock quickly began to rise. From the instinctive and violent numbers of 'Hate Anthem' and 'Code 105' to the haunting irresistibility of 'Loveletter' and the Deftones-esque 'Shadow', Heartsick's dynamism was on full show for anyone willing to give the band a listen. Also adding hip-hop textures into newer material such as the enthralling 'Thrill of the Hunt', Heartsick is a band begging for nationwide exposure. Offering something different to every other band out there right now, Heartsick look to the here and now to really elevate themselves further afield, and what better way to do it than with their latest EP, *Cinco*.

www.heartsick.us

Infected Rain

A commanding ensemble from Chisinau, Moldova, Infected Rain is a female-fronted band that combines hellacious scream vocals, heavy metallic guitars, and stunning melodic flourishes. The five-piece released their debut album, *Asylum,* at the end of 2011, their sophomore effort, *Embrace Eternity,* in 2014, and a fantastic third record arrived at the start of 2017 in the form of the bruising *86*. In Lena Scissorhands, Infected Rain has a captivating frontman with a weapon of a band behind her, and as well as the songs; go and watch the extremely effective music videos for 'Enslaved by a Dream' and 'Mold', especially.

Very popular amongst metal fans and from a part of Europe that isn't traditionally known for breeding heavyweight metal bands, Infected Rain are overcoming the odds with a terrific and atmospheric sound, as underlined by their Napalm Records distributed 2019 album, *Endorphin*, which included the pulsating 'Symphony of Trust' and 'The Earth Mantra' tracks.

www.infectedrain.com

Jiva Sakti

Certainly, one of the more obscure acts to hit the scene as of late, Oregon's Jiva Sakti, which is loosely translated as meaning 'The Living Force', is a band full of positive energy and cohesive musicianship. Formed in 2018, the band is led by Kris 'Nomad' Keyes, formerly of the bands Blind Justice and Gargantua Soul, and the vivid body paint which enhances his appearance signifies a captivating and entrancing figure. His soulful vocals also incorporate skilful rapping, and Jiva Sakti released their intriguing debut EP, *The Sound of the Universe*, via Imusic/Von Artists at the back end of 2020. Produced by Amerakin Overdose bassist, The Human, and featuring dynamic and soaring melodies amongst the early Noughties-sounding alternative metal, as well as moments of reggae, prog and alternative rock, songs such as 'You Are the Light' and 'World War Me' indicate Jiva Sakti's intentions from the off. This is not a bunch of tree-hugging hippies; this is Jiva Sakti – a band who look to give nu metal a fresh and riveting new aspect with music that is heavy, poignant and hugely inspiring.

www.facebook.com/JivaSaktiBand

Jynx

Forming in 2015, Jynx is a colossal six-headed beast coming out of New York City. Led by the infectious vocal deliveries of Tommy Roulette, Jynx create a fearless mix of brash metalcore with scathing vocal displays, which sometimes move into hip-hop waters. Releasing their debut EP, *Taker*, in 2015, it wasn't really until 2018 and with their second EP, *G.O.A.T.,* that Jynx really started to raise eyebrows. From the crushing title track to the melodic and catchy 'Levitate', the New Yorkers have plenty of ammunition in their lockers as well as incredible skill for creating energetic and unapologetic metal. The 2019 singles 'Clipped' and 'Fails' also went down well with the nu metal community, and what comes next could take the band to the very next level.

www.wearejynx.com

Lethal Injektion

A six-piece from Tucson, Arizona, Lethal Injektion is a band that provide passionate hardcore hip-hop vocals over some highly energetic groove-laden metal. For fans of Papa Roach and Linkin Park, the band has constantly released full-length albums over the last five years, beginning with *Sex Money Power* in 2016, the excellent *Judgement Night* in 2017, *Broken* in 2019, and *Resurgence* in 2020; as well as a whole host of standalone singles. With Jake Ryan providing the effortless rapping and Jonathan Russell undertaking the clean and scream vocals, songs such as 'Blinding Light', 'Memories of You', 'Dead Language' and 'Empire' tell you all you need to know about Lethal Injektion, while a *Remembering Chester Bennington* EP in 2018 saw the band pay homage to Linkin Park's fallen icon with impressive covers of some of the band's most well-known songs.
While Lethal Injektion has struggled to make a name for themselves across America, they still have a dedicated fan base who love and respect what the band does, with cohesiveness and consistency to boot.

www.lethalinjektionmusic.com

Loathe

New British heroes, Loathe, emerged in 2014 with a metalcore and progressive salvo, while also including some Deftones-esque ambience which quickly put the band on people's radars. Following their debut EP, *Prepare Consume Proceed,* in 2015, the Liverpool five-piece unleashed their first full-length, *The Cold Sun*, in 2017. Offering some insight into where the band was heading, 'It's Yours' was the perfect example of what was to come in the future; and when the breakthrough album, *I Let It In and It Took Everything*, catapulted Loathe into the public eye in 2020, the band's ascension truly began. Released via SharpTone Records and many a fan's favourite album of the year, shorter and sharper attacks of rage were mixed with stunning, multi-layered tracks such as 'Aggressive Evolution', 'Two-Way Mirror' and 'New Faces in the Dark'. Helping the band earn a strong following in the US also, Loathe could very well become one of the UK's hottest exports in the years to come.

www.loathesone.com

Loser

Performing murky, grunge-tinged metal and coming out of Detroit, Michigan, Loser is one of the more captivating bands to come out of the nu metal revival. Earning a strong following from their debut self-released album, *I'm Not the Same*, in 2017, Loser's dark and dystopian lyrical content struck raw nerves with many, while the chaotic but entrancing instrumentation revealed the band to be well ahead of their years in terms of talent. 'Dirty Girl' and the sombre, piano-led 'Bleach' were gems, and after signing to Frankie Palmeri of Emmure's label, Redzone Records, Loser released their second opus, *Never Young*, in 2019. Earth-shatteringly heavy but irresistibly catchy, the enormous wall of sounds which were 'Cotton Mouth', 'Pump Fake' and 'Dance on My Grave' found Loser on top form, and when they occasionally throw in those dreamy elements of Deftones, this five-piece really are the cream of the nu metal crop.

www.facebook.com/LoserMI

Mountain Eye

Like their fellow countrymen in Frontstreet, Mountain Eye burst out of the Netherlands in 2019 with their excellent debut album, *Roads Uncharted*. Originally forming in St. Petersburg, Russia in 2017, the alternative metallers crafted their sound ahead of releasing their first material, taking influences of Korn, Linkin Park and Slipknot, to create a sonic barrage of heaviness where the likes of 'Misery', 'Take Control' and 'Verge' bring to mind Chad Gray of Mudvayne in their vocal deliveries. Like with Frontstreet, Mountain Eye has the capabilities of expanding their fan base well outside of the Netherlands, and hopefully, their upcoming second album will do just that.

www.mountaineyeband.com

Neshiima

This Scottish quartet are making sturdy strides after moving away from their earlier tech metal sound in favour of a combination of rock and metal, which is heavily backed up by some feisty electronics and rap vocals. Comprising Liam Hesslewood on vocals, Ross Cloughley on guitar, Craig Rankin on bass and Danny Cameron behind the drum kit, Neshiima released a trilogy of EPs across 2018 and 2019, starting with *Purple* – which includes the standout singalong romp of 'Here Forever'. *Orange* came next and featured the standout song 'Livid', while *Green* rounded off the trilogy in emphatic style, as proven with the lead single, 'Caving In'. Getting some strong support from the likes of *Kerrang!* and *Metal Hammer* in the UK, Neshiima also played the opening evening of the 2019 Download Festival in front of packed crowd; and a cover of the Backstreet Boys pop classic, 'Larger Than Life', received strong praise upon its release in 2020.

www.neshiima.com

NO:IR

Another captivating band taking the UK by storm right now, Bristol's NO:IR produce a genre-bending brand of rap metal which welcomes chaos and despair. Debuting in the summer of 2019 with the single 'Hive', NO:IR put their homeland on notice with some dark and grungey metal which was overseen by Sam Davies' clinical rapping. Backed up by some deathly screams, a monstrous chorus and an effective guitar solo (yes, a guitar solo in nu metal), some strong momentum was earned, which continued with the band's second single,

'Erase:Me', a few months later. Including moments of experimentation while the formula from their first offering remained prominent, 'Erase:Me' was driven with more precision. Another standout chorus and some highly impressive vocals confirmed NO:IR as ones to watch before the nu metalcore treading 'Vanity' was unleashed in May of 2020. A combination of Cane Hill and hip-hop punks Fever 333 best describes the dystopian assault of single number three, and NO:IR has since released 'Placebo', and a stunning debut EP titled *Are We Really Alive?*

Extremely creative and continuously willing to tread new waters, NO:IR is perhaps the most exciting band to come out of the UK metal scene in quite some time, so familiarise yourself with what the quintet has released so far before they unveil what comes next.

www.thebandnoir.com

NoSelf

Originally forming in 2002, Florida four-piece, NoSelf, released two EPs and one full-length album before finally hitting the ground running in April 2017 with the release of *Human Cyborg Relations Episode 1.* The first in a trilogy of album releases which showcased some industrial and alternative metal fused with classic nu metal undertones, 'Casting Stones' mixed raw power with hints of melody and 'Frisco' was a made-for-radio anthem. Signing to Zombie Shark Records in mid-2017, the second and third instalments of the *Human Cyborg Relations* series followed in 2019 and New Year's Day of 2021, respectively. 'Signal Flares', 'ratD4GG3R' and then the new stunners, 'Nexus' and 'Resistance', has seen NoSelf reach their true potential after years of hard work. One of the leading bands of the nu metal revival, NoSelf create modern nu metal better than most.

www.noself.net

Ocean Grove

Melbourne, Australia crazies Ocean Grove formed in 2010 and got their breakthrough with the re-released EP, *Black Label (Sublime Vol.),* through UNFD in 2016. The hugely catchy song, 'Lights On Kind of Lover', was an additional but very welcome track that kept fans content until the excellent debut album, *The Rhapsody Tapes,* followed at the beginning of 2017. Reaching number five on the ARIA Albums chart, the genre-bending music on show was both original and emotive and led by the stirring anthems 'Intimate Alien' and 'Thunderdome', Ocean Grove received worldwide acclaim. Supporting Limp Bizkit on some Australian dates in the first quarter of 2018 put the band further into the public eye, and calling their art 'Odd World Music', Ocean Grove released the summery and catchy *Flip Phone Fantasy* album in 2020, which spawned brilliant tracks such as 'THOUSAND GOLDEN PEOPLE' and 'JUNKIE$'.

www.oddworldwide.com

Paratype

Part of Florida's bustling nu metal scene, Paratype, who have recently changed their name from Stark, are one of the standout acts to emerge over the last couple of years. Mixing old school nu metal vibes with a tasty hard rock/alternative metal formula, the quartet came firing out of the gate in the summer of 2019 with their debut album, *Communion*. From the opening ferocity of 'Tempt' to the excellent lead single choice, 'Trustfall', Paratype showed themselves to be a talented set of musicians who includes in their ranks the effortless and dynamic vocals of Jeremy Hyson. Also on *Communion* featured a spectacular cover of Linkin Park's popular B-side, 'My December', which Paratype put their own hard rock stamp on to offer an alternative to the original piano-driven rendition which Chester Bennington and company brought to fruition.

Recently releasing the explosive newbies, 'Sigma' and 'Break', as well as the potent and fiery 'Jester', when album number two arrives, it will hopefully elevate the Florida four-piece further towards national notoriety.

www.facebook.com/ParatypeMusic

Prison

One of the more abrasive bands to come out over the last few years, Prison is a hardcore band who also fuse some feisty metal into their anarchic sound. The last couple of years has seen the emergence of some nu metal influences seeping through in their music, as shown on the 2019 album, *Still Alive*. Containing deep and heartfelt lyrics looking at mental illness, suicide and abuse, Prison earned an allegiance of fans on the back of such songs as 'Pray for Me' and the Slipknot-esque 'Mental Illness'; and in 2020, the band released two new singles, 'I Don't Want to Be Afraid Anymore' and 'Make Noise', which also featured some rap vocals. Not afraid to tackle such personal themes, Prison may perform fractious and unrelenting music, but it is also extremely appealing to hardcore and metal fans all over the globe.

www.facebook.com/prisonfl

Project Theory

Not exactly a hotbed for nu metal but over in Thessaloniki, Greece, Project Theory have become somewhat of a national treasure. Earning a name for themselves in their homeland by rocking various festival stages and leaving a lasting impression on many a witness of their performances, the quartet signed with US label Sliptrick Records, in 2016, and released their debut album, *Something Between Us*, in the same year. Nu metal mixed with flourishes of metalcore, the album also had a heavy emphasis on rap vocals as emphasised on the standout tracks, 'Final Chapter' and 'Suffer'. Returning in September 2020 with their sophomore album, *Blood & Loyalty*, and providing a more polished sound than its predecessor, it is probably a better representation of the band's nu metal influences. Vocalist, Antreas Boutos, sounds incredibly like Disturbed's David Draiman at times – especially on the album's standout song, 'Until It's Time'; while 'The Way We Follow' is another strong anthem which shows Project Theory to be firmly hitting their stride as of late.

www.facebook.com/projecttheory

REdEFIND

Formed in 2012 by Dustan Snow and Drew Porter, REdEFIND emerged out of Greenville, South Carolina, playing a brand of rap metal that also incorporates metalcore and thrash into their sound. Releasing a debut EP in December 2016 under the title *Raw*, the band appeared to show their love of *WWE* Wrestling with the lead single, 'Suplex City', where a video was also recorded to accompany it. Helping to get their name out to a wider audience, the five-piece supported the likes of Saliva, Hed PE and Mushroomhead in their home state before their excellent sophomore EP *Pros and Cons* announced itself in March 2018. Another wrestling-themed song, 'Tables Turned' was chosen as a single, the fiery 'Whatcha Gonna Do' (didn't Hulk Hogan say that?) confirmed the band to be at their most cohesive, and 'Look Away' brought Korn to mind with a groovy slab of robust metal. Enlisting Jordan Caparell as their new vocalist in time for the 2020 EP, *Let's Party*, REdEFIND's strongest release to date included the mosh pit friendly title track and the sublime rager, 'Step Up'.

www.redefindmusic.com

Relent

A powerful quintet from San Antonio, Texas, Relent delve into their collective pasts to create uplifting rap metal which follows in the footsteps of fellow Christian heroes, P.O.D. Featuring inspiring verses and soaring choruses, Relent have the capabilities of producing relentless metal as good as anything coming out in today's climate, as showcased on their vital 2020 album, *Heart Attack*. 'Rise' opens up on the band's quest for overcoming the odds, while 'LOW' and 'Addicted' include classic nu metal elements good enough to reach all the way across America and back again.
Pressing forward with a new album at some point in 2021, fresh material already released in the form of 'Think You Got It' and 'Last Days' build on Relent's excellent start, as the five-piece continue to raise the bar for themselves and others to follow.

www.relentband.com

Royalty Kult

Launching at the beginning of June 2020, Royalty Kult are already making giant strides in getting their anthemic hard rock out to the masses. Comprising of

Joshua Michael and David Fulford-Brown, the LA duo released their debut album, *Enjoying the End,* in December 2020. Featuring elements of new wave, hard rock and small alternative metal hints, stunning tracks such as 'Stay This Way', 'Bleeding Possibilities' and 'Shadow of a Mountain' are made-for-radio anthems that should bring Royalty Kult further into the public eye. Bad Wolves guitarist, Doc Coyle, guested on the epic closing title track, and while they might not fit into the traditional nu metal category, Michael and Fulford-Brown have shared stages with Jonathan Davis, Taproot, Spineshank and Nothingface over the years; thus, earning vital experience which will help take Royalty Kult further as their name reaches wider audiences.

www.royaltykult.com

Sanity/Switch

Forming in early 2019, Sanity/Switch hail from the Midwest and cite bands such as Coal Chamber, Korn, Deftones and Ded as influences. Using Drop G tuning, Sanity/Switch like to produce raw and intense music which encapsulates a little bit of everything, which made nu metal so impactful the first time around. In the summer of 2020, the quartet unleashed their self-titled debut EP, featuring blistering instrumentation and abrasive vocal displays, as the explosive salvo of 'Venomous' and 'Shattered Glass' firmly attest to. Clocking in at just over twenty-six minutes in length, the EP also features an interesting cover of gothic metal legends, Type O Negative ('Love You to Death'), but it is the original material which rightfully steals the show, and Sanity/Switch is already in the studio working on their second EP with a planned release at some point in 2021.

www.facebook.com/SanitySwitch

Seethe

A project created by Patrick McElravy, who shares his time between 9 Stitch Method and this, Seethe is a one-man Pittsburgh gang delivering earth-shattering industrial metal over some pummeling beats whilst at the same time being thoroughly drenched in electronics.

Constantly striving to hone his craft, Seethe has become a frequent outlet for emotional and deeply personal lyrical themes, relayed with honesty and strength across the June 2020 EP, *Blueprints for Introspection*, the *Abstract Thoughts* album, which followed three months later; and the self-revealing April 2021 concept album, *Departures*. Short and sharp ragers such as 'Lifeless', 'Skin Crawler' and 'Crimson' tell you all you need to know about Seethe, where the music and its content takes you on an uneven journey which ultimately proves fulfilling.

www.seethe1.bandcamp.com

Silentype

Forming in Melbourne, Australia in late 2019, Silentype's creative output has seen two EPs and a couple of singles released in a little over a year, and if you like fractious and unrelenting metal in the style of Mudvayne and Nothingface, then this quartet might just be for you.

Laying their early foundations with *If the Following Symptoms Persist* in April 2020, the Melbourne maniacs went one better at the end of the year with the brutal follow-up, *Year of the Rope*. Like its predecessor, the tight but stripped production (which the band do themselves to avoid any imposing forces on their vision) finds the music sounding raw and abrasive, much like a lot of nu metal releases from back in the day; and the solid slabs of 'Introvert, 'Idiot Flu' and 'Diorama' make for imperative if not slightly unsettling listening. Lyrically inspired by past and current real-life events, as well as tapping into the darker issues in life and the struggle of the artistic mind, Silentype has since dropped the bludgeoning single, 'Blue Dirt', which is just as urgent and enthralling as the rest of their early back catalogue. Silentype may just be the opposite of what their name suggests, however they are still a captivating band who will punish your senses and have a hell of a lot of fun doing it in the process.

www.silentype.bandcamp.com

Sylar

Sylar burst out of Queens, New York, in 2012 and quickly released their debut EP, *Deadbeat*. Placing themselves in the nu-metalcore category, the five-piece then signed to Razor & Tie and put out their first full-length in 2014, titled *To Whom It May Concern*. Soon, the band was on the move again as they inked a deal with Hopeless Records, and nu metal elements were brought in for their 2016 effort, *Help!*, where songs such as 'Soul Addiction', 'Dark Daze' and 'Assume' featured rap vocals, vicious screams, samples and raw but accessible instrumentation. Focusing almost solely on rap rock for the 2018 album, *Seasons,* Sylar produced their best collection of songs to date as the likes of 'All or Nothing', 'Seasons', and 'SHOOK!', which featured P.O.D. Frontman, Sonny Sandoval, saw the Queens mob establish themselves as a band to really watch out for in the years to come.

www.sylarny.com

Tallah

Forming in 2017 and earning some strong exposure due to the fact that Mike Portnoy from Dream Theater's son, Max, was in the band, Tallah exploded out of Pennsylvania and quickly signed to Earache Records. A handful of singles were released in the lead up to their 2020 debut album, *Matriphagy*, and Tallah provided a little bit of everything on a stunning release. A bit of death metal here and some nu metal there, brutal and frenetic chaos much in the vein of early Slipknot saw 'Placenta', 'Cottonmouth' and 'No One Should Read This' earn acclaim from many a peer, while incredible melodies and choruses also confirmed the band to be well ahead of the curve. One of the more sinister and evil-sounding bands to have emerged as of late, Tallah is also one of the most fascinating and talented.

www.tallah.bandcamp.com

Tetrarch

Another new band taken on by the renowned Napalm Records, Atlanta's Tetrarch possess mighty metallic fury with some sublime melodic hooks, as highlighted on their debut release in 2007. *Freak* was both technical and aggressive in its delivery, possessing a mainstream edge with the marauding title track and the fan favourite anthem, 'Pull the Trigger'. Clearly influenced by Korn, one of the quartet's latest singles, 'I'm Not Right' reached 27 on the Mainstream Rock Songs chart in America, as a menacing groove and a huge chorus solidified the track as the standout moment on Tetrarch's powerful debut album, *Unstable*, which dropped at the end of the first quarter in 2021. Get ready for this band to explode.

www.tetrarchmusic.com

Tides of Ire

Helping fly the flag for the UK, Kent's Tides of Ire are a brutal lot who cite Machine Head and Rage Against the Machine amongst their many influences. Packing a groove metal punch with cleaner middle sections, the quintet's debut EP, *The Burning Sea,* was a forceful introduction to a band who hit the ground running. 'December Nights' and 'Repent/Replenish' found Tides of Ire at their most devastating, before they moved into rap metal territory for their 2018 EP, *Deadline*, and the 2019 effort, *Betrayal*. To really see the diversity the band has in their locker, 'Pest' and the stunning epic of 'Sirens' show Tides of Ire to be establishing a sound which they are looking to carry forward, with the intention of becoming one of Britain's premier nu metal-influenced bands upon the release of a new double EP which will be out before the end of 2021.

www.facebook.com/tidesofire

UnityTX

This Dallas, Texas, hardcore and hip-hop quartet include heavy breakdowns, razor-sharp riffs, and an air of grunge in their powerful formula, and over the last year or so UnityTX has finally started to reap the rewards of their efforts. A decent debut EP in 2016 (*The Besides*) saw the band lay down their early foundations, and on the back of the 2017 single, 'Mothasucka', and the 2018 follow-up, 'The Come Up', UnityTX signed to Pure Noise Records in time to release their excellent sophomore EP, *MADBOY*, in September 2019. An ideal crossover band to bring in fans of both rap and metal, the pulsating combo of 'Cross Me' and 'Piece of Mind' embody all that UnityTX is about. There are a lot of rap metal bands out there, but there are none like UnityTX.

www.unitytxroc.com

Waking Tera

North Carolina's Waking Tera have been around since 2010, but it has been a long road that has finally seen the band starting to elevate themselves to wider US audiences. Occasionally dipping into metalcore waters, the band instantly bring Sevendust to mind due to Kalvin Pender's soulful clean vocals, while his mighty screams also put his band into the same discussion as fellow up-and-comers, Fire From the Gods.

After releasing the albums *Envision* in 2012 and *The Jonah Complex* in 2019, the sextet delivered their best offering yet in March 2021 in the form of the EP, *Transition*. The tasty 'Nothing' and 'Edify' see the band's current headspace, while older numbers such as the stirring duo of 'Mirrors' and 'Capture' also deserve frequent rotation.

www.facebook.com/WakingTeraband

Walking Rumor

A fine European addition to the resurgence of nu-metal, Denmark's Walking Rumor joined forces in 2015 and within a year, they had put out their first EP, *The War Within*. Switching between rap rock and then harder, electronic-tinged rock, 'Dedicate to This' and 'Tears Me Apart' show the band's intentions from the off, while the 2020 debut album, *Symbiosis*, showcased a diverse tracklist of songs where the highlights included 'Breaking Point', 'Do or Die' and 'Turn the Tides'. Had Walking Rumor been born in America, they would have undoubtedly been placed on a bigger stage by now, and while they may be restricted to Scandinavia for the time being, it doesn't deter from the fact that this band creates excellent music which deserves to be mentioned along with the best of the new crop of nu metal-related bands.

www.walkingrumor.com

9 Stitch Method

Based in Pittsburgh, Pennsylvania, 9 Stitch Method is an alternative metal duo who originally started out in 2016 as an online project between Patrick McElravy and Joshua Colich. Before long, 9SM was playing shows through the utilisation of backing tracks as they ventured throughout the Tri State area, and an early buzz around the duo earned them opening slots for well-established acts such as Hinder, and nu metal veterans, Soil. Releasing their debut album, *Jaywalking Somnambulist*, in 2019, 9SM showcased their brash and chaotic brand of metal, which sometimes ventures into deathcore territory. However, a reliance on hints of melody is also a welcome addition on standout tracks such as 'Black Sheep' and 'Sleep'. Not wanting to sit still for too long, 9SM released a new EP, *Zero Somatic Part 1*, in the summer of 2020 via Brutal Business Entertainment, containing more tasty metal onslaughts where 'Ether' and 'Obsolence' find the band gaining in both confidence and songwriting craft.

www.facebook.com/9stitchmethod

Zonezero

Forming in 2017 and making steady waves early on, Zonezero launched themselves out of Columbus, Ohio, with their 2020 EP, *Strychnine Dream*. For fans of Chevelle, Deftones and Spineshank, you only need listen to the sucker-punch anthems of 'Losing Grip' and 'All in Your Head' to find a band with cohesiveness beyond their young years. Creating atmospheric metal with a feisty but artistic crunch- as the latest singles, 'Misdirected' and 'Virus' confidently underline, there is a bright future ahead for Zonezero, who are set to blast off and never look back. They've also recorded a rather impressive cover of 'Be Quiet and Drive (Far Away)' by Deftones for good measure, if you need any further reason to check out this exciting up-and-coming band.

www.zonezero.bandcamp.com

Long Live Nu Metal

Regardless of the negativity surrounding the nu metal movement, its impact on heavy music cannot be denied. Bringing mainstream exposure back to hard rock and heavy metal was something which may have proved unpopular with 'metal heads' who much preferred their beloved music to remain underground, but I doubt you will find one band from that era who aren't thankful for what nu metal did for their careers in terms of notoriety, record sales and huge tours playing to thousands of adoring fans.

Of course, with its successes came its downsides, most notably the hungry sharks known as major record labels who saw the opportunity to make a profit off bands who created music for the love of doing so. For every band that were turned into global megastars, five (or maybe even ten) were given the wrong end of the stick, having their dreams dashed by a lack of support and promotion in getting their art out to a wider audience. And, when their albums inevitably bombed through no real fault of their own, these bands were thrown onto the scrapheap, fading into the obscurity from which they came only a year or two beforehand.

The power of nu metal's passionate fan base allows such bands to have a belated moment in the spotlight in the present day, thanks in great part to social media which, had it been readily available at the turn of the new millennium, would have been an integral tool in helping spread their name further afield.

As some musicians interviewed in this book touched upon, the nu metal movement was the last great era for the music industry, when record sales were at an all-time high and record deals were worth a lot of money. When illegal downloading really took off in 2002, every band and record label suffered, as did fans who still craved physical copies of their favourite artist's music. Witnessing first-hand the closures of many record stores here in the UK, it was sad to see but not entirely surprising, so imagine bands and labels' despair at the hundreds of thousands and even millions of pounds and dollars which were lost due to internet piracy – a crime which largely went unpunished. The music industry never really recovered, and while most of the majors are still active today, money made and the value of record deals certainly aren't what they once were.

On the plus side, every one of us who was old enough to experience that era was given an overdose of nu metal from magazines, TV and radio, taking it all in and absorbing it, yet still we were left begging for more. Today, the likes of Korn, Limp Bizkit, Slipknot and System of a Down still headline festivals all around the world – their legacies still being written whether their lofty positions are somewhat based on nostalgia or because of such incredibly consistent careers. I believe it is for the latter reason.

The modern revival will never reach the heights of what came before it, that is obvious, but all these bands coming through make it, in many ways, just as exciting as the first wave. They won't sell millions of records, they won't headline arena tours, and most won't even be able to quit their day jobs, but what we are seeing is the same appetite, dedication and talent to try and propel themselves to the best level possible. I believe they have a strong chance of succeeding with their goals, even if success today is measured very differently from what it was two decades ago.

This book is as definitive as it can be, but there is still plenty more to discover for yourselves on the wonderful world of the internet, because after all – nu metal will forever be the gift which keeps on giving.

Matt Karpe

On Track series

Tori Amos – Lisa Torem 978-1-78952-142-9
Asia – Peter Braidis 978-1-78952-099-6
Barclay James Harvest – Keith and Monica Domone 978-1-78952-067-5
The Beatles – Andrew Wild 978-1-78952-009-5
The Beatles Solo 1969-1980 – Andrew Wild 978-1-78952-030-9
Blue Oyster Cult – Jacob Holm-Lupo 978-1-78952-007-1
Marc Bolan and T.Rex – Peter Gallagher 978-1-78952-124-5
Kate Bush – Bill Thomas 978-1-78952-097-2
Camel – Hamish Kuzminski 978-1-78952-040-8
Caravan – Andy Boot 978-1-78952-127-6
Eric Clapton Solo – Andrew Wild 978-1-78952-141-2
The Clash – Nick Assirati 978-1-78952-077-4
Crosby, Stills and Nash – Andrew Wild 978-1-78952-039-2
The Damned – Morgan Brown 978-1-78952-136-8
Deep Purple and Rainbow 1968-79 – Steve Pilkington 978-1-78952-002-6
Dire Straits – Andrew Wild 978-1-78952-044-6
The Doors – Tony Thompson 978-1-78952-137-5
Dream Theater – Jordan Blum 978-1-78952-050-7
Elvis Costello and The Attractions – Georg Purvis 978-1-78952-129-0
Emerson Lake and Palmer – Mike Goode 978-1-78952-000-2
Fairport Convention – Kevan Furbank 978-1-78952-051-4
Peter Gabriel – Graeme Scarfe 978-1-78952-138-2
Genesis – Stuart MacFarlane 978-1-78952-005-7
Gentle Giant – Gary Steel 978-1-78952-058-3
Gong – Kevan Furbank 978-1-78952-082-8
Hawkwind – Duncan Harris 978-1-78952-052-1
Roy Harper – Opher Goodwin 978-1-78952-130-6
Iron Maiden – Steve Pilkington 978-1-78952-061-3
Jethro Tull – Jordan Blum 978-1-78952-016-3
Elton John in the 1970s – Peter Kearns 978-1-78952-034-7
Gong – Kevan Furbank 978-1-78952-082-8
The Incredible String Band – Tim Moon 978-1-78952-107-8
Iron Maiden – Steve Pilkington 978-1-78952-061-3
Judas Priest – John Tucker 978-1-78952-018-7
Kansas – Kevin Cummings 978-1-78952-057-6
Level 42 – Matt Philips 978-1-78952-102-3
Aimee Mann – Jez Rowden 978-1-78952-036-1
Joni Mitchell – Peter Kearns 978-1-78952-081-1
The Moody Blues – Geoffrey Feakes 978-1-78952-042-2
Mike Oldfield – Ryan Yard 978-1-78952-060-6
Tom Petty – Richard James 978-1-78952-128-3
Queen – Andrew Wild 978-1-78952-003-3
Renaissance – David Detmer 978-1-78952-062-0
The Rolling Stones 1963-80 – Steve Pilkington 978-1-78952-017-0
Steely Dan – Jez Rowden 978-1-78952-043-9
Steve Hackett – Geoffrey Feakes 978-1-78952-098-9
Thin Lizzy – Graeme Stroud 978-1-78952-064-4
Toto – Jacob Holm-Lupo 978-1-78952-019-4

U2 – Eoghan Lyng 978-1-78952-078-1
UFO – Richard James 978-1-78952-073-6
The Who – Geoffrey Feakes 978-1-78952-076-7
Roy Wood and the Move – James R Turner 978-1-78952-008-8
Van Der Graaf Generator – Dan Coffey 978-1-78952-031-6
Yes – Stephen Lambe 978-1-78952-001-9
Frank Zappa 1966 to 1979 – Eric Benac 978-1-78952-033-0
10CC – Peter Kearns 978-1-78952-054-5

Decades Series

Alice Cooper in the 1970s – Chris Sutton 978-1-78952-104-7
Curved Air in the 1970s – Laura Shenton 978-1-78952-069-9
Fleetwood Mac in the 1970s – Andrew Wild 978-1-78952-105-4
Focus in the 1970s – Stephen Lambe 978-1-78952-079-8
Marillion in the 1980s – Nathaniel Webb 978-1-78952-065-1
Pink Floyd In The 1970s – Georg Purvis 978-1-78952-072-9
The Sweet in the 1970s – Darren Johnson 978-1-78952-139-9
Uriah Heep in the 1970s – Steve Pilkington 978-1-78952-103-0

On Screen series

Carry On… – Stephen Lambe 978-1-78952-004-0
David Cronenberg – Patrick Chapman 978-1-78952-071-2
Doctor Who: The David Tennant Years – Jamie Hailstone 978-1-78952-066-8
Monty Python – Steve Pilkington 978-1-78952-047-7
Seinfeld Seasons 1 to 5 – Stephen Lambe 978-1-78952-012-5

Other Books

Babysitting A Band On The Rocks – G.D. Praetorius 978-1-78952-106-1
Derek Taylor: For Your Radioactive Children – Andrew Darlington 978-1-78952-038-5
Iggy and The Stooges On Stage 1967-1974 – Per Nilsen 978-1-78952-101-6
Jon Anderson and the Warriors – the road to Yes – David Watkinson 978-1-78952-059-0
Nu Metal: A Definitive Guide – Matt Karpe 978-1-78952-063-7
Tommy Bolin: In and Out of Deep Purple – Laura Shenton 978-1-78952-070-5
Maximum Darkness – Deke Leonard 978-1-78952-048-4
Maybe I Should've Stayed In Bed – Deke Leonard 978-1-78952-053-8
The Twang Dynasty – Deke Leonard 978-1-78952-049-1

and many more to come!

Would you like to write for Sonicbond Publishing?

We are mainly a music publisher, but we also occasionally publish in other genres including film and television. At Sonicbond Publishing we are always on the look-out for authors, particularly for our two main series, On Track and Decades.

Mixing fact with in depth analysis, the On Track series examines the entire recorded work of a particular musical artist or group. All genres are considered from easy listening and jazz to 60s soul to 90s pop, via rock and metal.

The Decades series singles out a particular decade in an artist or group's history and focuses on that decade in more detail than may be allowed in the On Track series.

While professional writing experience would, of course, be an advantage, the most important qualification is to have real enthusiasm and knowledge of your subject. First-time authors are welcomed, but the ability to write well in English is essential.

Sonicbond Publishing has distribution throughout Europe and North America, and all our books are also published in E-book form. Authors will be paid a royalty based on sales of their book. Further details about our books are available from www.sonicbondpublishing.com. To contact us, complete the contact form there or email info@sonicbondpublishing.co.uk